A Single Garment

A Single Garment

*Creating Intentionally Diverse Schools
That Benefit All Children*

GENEVIEVE SIEGEL-HAWLEY

Harvard Education Press
Cambridge, Massachusetts

Paperback ISBN 978-1-68253-434-2
Library Edition ISBN 978-1-68253-435-9

Library of Congress Cataloging-in-Publication Data

Names: Siegel-Hawley, Genevieve, author.
Title: A single garment : creating intentionally diverse schools that benefit all children / Genevieve Siegel-Hawley.
Description: Cambridge, Massachusetts : Harvard Education Press, 2020. | Includes bibliographical references and index. | Summary: "Drawing on a wide range of sources, as well as her own experience as a parent, former student and teacher in Richmond, Siegel-Hawley provides a richly layered account of four area schools each committed to building successful diverse school communities as a foundation for a just, democratic society — "the single garment" evoked by Martin Luther King, Jr"— Provided by publisher.
Identifiers: LCCN 2019035483 | ISBN 9781682534342 (paperback) | ISBN 9781682534359 (library edition)
Subjects: LCSH: Multicultural education—Virginia—Richmond. | Culturally relevant pedagogy—Virginia—Richmond. | Community and school—Virginia—Richmond. | School environment—Virginia—Richmond. | Education and democracy—Virginia—Richmond.
Classification: LCC LC1099.4.V6 S54 2020 | DDC 370.11709755/23—dc23
LC record available at https://lccn.loc.gov/2019035483

Published by Harvard Education Press,
an imprint of the Harvard Education Publishing Group

Harvard Education Press
8 Story Street
Cambridge, MA 02138

Cover Design: Endpaper Studio
Cover Photo: Rawpixel.com/Shutterstock.com

The typefaces used in this book are Legacy Serif ITC and Futura.

To Eleanora Rose and Myles Delfin
and their once and future peers

I am cognizant of the interrelatedness of all communities . . .
Injustice anywhere is a threat to justice everywhere. We are
caught in an inescapable network of mutuality, tied in a single
garment of destiny. Whatever affects one directly, affects all
indirectly.

—Dr. Martin Luther King Jr.
A Letter from Birmingham Jail, 1963

Contents

Preface

This project began with an old-fashioned letter to my daughter, written in borrowed moments just before the 2016 election. I'd been asked to speak at an annual series of lectures on the state of metropolitan Richmond, Virginia. My topic was education. The event was hosted by St. Paul's Church, a faith community established in 1845 whose initial intertwinement with the Confederacy later gave way to a ministry focused on social justice and racial reconciliation.

In my search for the most effective way to communicate about the critical importance of school integration—effectiveness measured, in my mind, by changes both in individual behavior and in broader policy—I'd landed on the idea of reading to the gathered crowd a letter to my daughter, Posey. She'd just started preschool. It would be about what our family wanted for her education, and what we'd inherited from our history here in Richmond.

Ta-Nehisi Coates's *Between the World and Me* had been published the year before, written as a letter to his teenage son, and I was in the middle of revisiting James Baldwin's *The Fire Next Time*, which contains a letter to his nephew, as I sat down to write. As further inspiration, Nikole Hannah-Jones had recently authored a topical article for the *New York Times Magazine* called, "Choosing a School for My Daughter in a Segregated City." What, I wondered, would a letter sound like from my perspective? That of a white parent trying to map out an equity-minded approach to her kid's schooling along a path littered with historical and contemporary inequality? (It should go without saying that my efforts fall woefully short of Coates's, Baldwin's, or Hannah-Jones's work.)

The letter, which opens this book, details the many ways in which deliberate segregation by race continues to shape educational opportunity in Richmond—and in the country writ large. But the notes of hope contained within it were the catalyst for an intensive research study. At St. Paul's, I'd spoken of two local schools purposefully working to nurture diversity in the midst of wide and deep systems of segregation. I wanted to know more about how and why these efforts had come about. What could families, educators, policy makers, and scholars interested in racial justice and the benefits of integration learn from them? Were there other local examples? And were they working?

To answer these questions, among others, from 2017 to 2019 I worked as a researcher deeply immersed in those two racially and economically integrating schools, along with two others, in Richmond. I interviewed over seventy diverse stakeholders, observed classrooms, and attended orientations, field trips, awards ceremonies, and teacher professional development days.

I want to be clear about my involvement with the four schools explored in this book: the Sprout School at the Children's Museum, Ecoff Elementary School, Binford Middle School, and CodeRVA Regional High School. I selected them for their intentional work around racial and economic school integration, which in many ways is paying off. I also chose the schools for the rich variation in grade level and urban, suburban, and regional locale they provided. In most cases, I had a sense of their variation and intentionality from personal experience. My daughter, Posey, has gone to preschool at Sprout since it opened its doors. I'd encountered the principal of Ecoff Elementary several times at community events, in part because of his knowledge of local school desegregation history. I went to Binford Middle as a child, and the current principal was an early student of mine at Virginia Commonwealth University. I've served as a member of the advisory board for CodeRVA Regional High School (though I did not attend meetings during active fieldwork). In short, my life as a researcher, teacher, student, and mother had been bound up for some time in the lives of these schools.

There are strengths and weaknesses to these myriad levels of involvement, of course. On the one hand, prior relationships with school leaders meant access and established trust—crucial assets for any intensive qualitative study, especially one centered on race. But on the other hand, they raise questions about dual or multiple roles and potential objectivity. I dealt with these tensions partly by making it clear which hat I was wearing when (e.g., my mom hat at a Sprout family event versus my researcher hat). To protect participants in the research process, I changed or masked the names of most interviewees, with the exception of public-facing figures like community, district, or school leaders. In terms of objectivity, I benefited from the superior research assistance of Virginia Palencia, who helped transcribe and reflect upon interviews and site visits. She entered graduate school as a newcomer to the Richmond area, with no prior contacts at the four schools. We shaped our notes and thoughts on the schools independently before reviewing them together. Her outside perspective acted as either validation or invalidation of my more involved one. As a further safeguard, leaders affiliated with all four schools read through relevant chapters and offered feedback and commentary.

Make no mistake, though. This book is written by someone who believes intensely in the value of school integration, a perspective shaped by numerous personal and professional experiences with it. Yet those same experiences have also taught me how hard and continuously we have to work to achieve integration in a tremendously segregated society, which is why you'll encounter stories of struggle alongside stories of success as you read.

I wouldn't have a story to tell at all without the leadership associated with our four Richmond area schools. A most heartfelt thanks goes to this group, whose openness and commitment to the research project remained unwavering. Many others supported the work as it evolved. A special note of gratitude to my editor Nancy Walser, whose wise guidance and gentle guard against my tendency to spin an overly long tale made this book much stronger. Research leave and support provided by Virginia Commonwealth University gave me the time and resources needed to complete the project. In addition to Virginia Palencia, three student assistants, Najia Lindh, Sarah Haden, and Ash Taylor-Beierl, gave me very helpful assistance with editing and source documentation. Ash also read the entire draft, making critical suggestions and asking clarifying questions throughout. Erica Frankenberg, Tom Shields, Yvonne Brandon, and Kim Bridges offered invaluable feedback along the way. Educators, students, and advocates affiliated with the National Coalition on School Diversity delivered inspiration at the outset; any proceeds from the book are dedicated to them. And, as always, my (growing) family provided sustaining love and ridiculousness on the days when I wondered if this book would ever get finished.

It did, so let's get started.

A Letter to My Daughter
Schools and the Single Garment

October 28, 2016

Sweet Posey,

First, "what's in a name?" as Shakespeare once wrote. Your full name is Eleanora Rose, a dash of whimsy to flavor your namesake, Eleanor Roosevelt. You are named for one of your mother and father's heroes, a woman who fought doggedly for human and civil rights throughout her long career in public service. Note that your nickname, Posey, didn't arise from anything other than yet another maternal flight of whimsy.

I sit down to write you this letter as someone who has committed a career to trying to understand the societal structures that divide and unite us along lines of difference. As families and policy makers continue to wrestle with enduring issues of race, inequality, and schools, I want to lay out a vision of what your father and I aspire to when it comes to your education. These aspirations are rooted in our belief in the inter-relatedness of humanity and the evils of segregation, described in Dr. Martin Luther King Jr.'s *Letter from a Birmingham Jail*. "Injustice anywhere is a threat to justice everywhere," he wrote. "We are caught in an inescapable network of mutuality, tied in a single garment of destiny." And also: "Segregation distorts the soul and damages the personality. It gives the segregator a false sense of superiority and the segregated a false sense of inferiority." To fully understand how Dr. King's words ground our hopes for your education though, Posey-girl, you must first understand your heritage.

You were born in the spring of 2014, about six months before white students became a minority in our nation's schools—and about four months before young Michael Brown, who bore the same name as one of my students at John Marshall High School, was shot and killed by a police officer in Ferguson, Missouri. His death set off a national reckoning with race and the criminal justice system long overdue and viscerally renewed with each videotape of an unarmed black man killed by an officer of the law.

As a searing episode of *This American Life* reminded us, Michael Brown's death was also an indictment against our still profoundly segregated society—and the schools that reflect it. One of his mother's most wrenching statements soon after he was killed was this: "You took my son away from me. You know how hard it was for me to get him to stay in school and graduate? You know how many black men graduate?" Virtually all of our nation's dropout factories—high schools where fewer than 50 percent of students graduate—are concentrated in racially and economically isolated school systems. Like roughly two of every five black and Latinx students in this country, Michael attended an intensely segregated and struggling school, cut off by school district boundary lines from broader opportunities available in the St. Louis metro area. Michael made it through those educational hurdles only to have his life taken from him just after graduating.

Michael Brown didn't have a say about the circumstances into which he was born, Posey, any more than you had a say in yours.

You were born to a mother whose middle name belongs to a viciously cruel slaveholding family in Chesapeake—one of our forebearers. You were born into a state that, in 1819, made the gathering of slaves or free blacks at schools unlawful assembly subject to corporal punishment. Almost half a century later, when the first public schools for freed men and women were established during Reconstruction, the white-dominated Virginia statehouse, fearful of empowering black citizenry, starved the new institutions of much-needed funding. These first schools were absolutely sites of emancipatory education and resistance, Posey, and don't you forget it, but they were also separate and unequal by design. In 1902, our state became the first in the nation to enshrine into law public school segregation.

Another half century later, in 1951, black high school students in Prince Edward County, Virginia, led a ten-day strike demanding facilities equal to those afforded white students. The disparities between the buildings serving black and white students in Prince Edward were glaringly apparent. The school for black students, Robert R. Moton High, was overcrowded, built of wood instead of brick, warmed by stoves rather than steam or hot water heat, and lacked indoor bathrooms.

Civil rights lawyers filed a suit on behalf of those courageous students, which eventually become one of the five cases consolidated into the landmark *Brown v. Board of Education* litigation. It was the only one among the five instigated by student activists, the leader of whom is immortalized in a statue I will take you downtown to see. *Brown* went beyond the students' initial demand for equitable facilities, striking at the heart of racial inequality by seeking to overturn the "separate but equal" doctrine itself. Yet once again, our state of Virginia led the way backward, rising up to meet *Brown* with the campaign of Massive Resistance to school desegregation.

Posey, you were born in Virginia's capitol, Richmond, which was also the capitol of the Confederacy. The view from the hospital windows where you came into the world looks out to the warehouses that stored tobacco picked by slaves and to the river that carried human chattel to and from the second-largest slave trading center in the country. Our city fought fiercely to preserve slavery, the engine of its economic might—and a stain on its moral consciousness.

On the way to the hospital, I rode past the incongruously named Martin Luther King Middle School. It struggles mightily, under still separate and unequal circumstances, to serve children from most of Richmond City's public housing projects, intentionally isolated together behind the barricades of our federal interstates and in close proximity to the city jail. Martin Luther King Middle is what the UCLA Civil Rights Project calls an apartheid school—less than 1 percent white—and 94 percent low income.

Posey, how can this still be? What of our segregated souls and our intertwined fates? Our single garment?

In the early 1970s, something crucial slipped out of Richmond's and our nation's grasp. This was back when your grandfather was scooting around the Fan wearing a motorcycle helmet with the fist of Black Power emblazoned upon the back, catching alluring glimpses of your grandmother in the Strawberry Street Laundromat. It was also when the African American plaintiffs in our local, long-running school desegregation case, *Bradley v. Richmond*, returned to federal court with a request backed by the city school board. Nearly two decades after *Brown* was handed down, plaintiffs wanted a workable, metropolitan remedy for injustice.

The board unveiled a city-county school desegregation proposal involving schools in the city of Richmond and Henrico and Chesterfield counties. At the time, Richmond schools were about 70 percent black, and Henrico and Chesterfield schools were over 90 percent white. Judge Robert Merhige of the US Eastern District Court of Virginia supported the proposal. His rationale can be summed up with this statement: "The proof here overwhelmingly establishes that school division lines between Richmond and the counties here coincide with no natural obstacles to speak of and do in fact work to confine blacks on a consistent, wholesale basis within the city, where they reside in segregated neighborhoods."

Just six months later, the US Court of Appeals for the Fourth Circuit reversed Judge Merhige's decision. The ruling came with the additional influence of a number of national organizations interested in the possible impact of the Richmond case, which was destined for the Supreme Court. The National Education Association, the Congress of Racial Equality, and the American Civil Liberties Union filed briefs in support of consolidation. On the other side, the US Justice Department, with the approval of President Nixon, supported the Virginia State Board of Education and the counties of Henrico and Chesterfield in the appeal against the merger. The *Bradley* case presented the first test of a politically reconfigured Supreme Court's position on metropolitan consolidation, an issue with sweeping implications for the future of school desegregation in a rapidly suburbanizing society.

On May 21, 1973, a split 4–4 vote (Justice Lewis Powell removed himself from the deliberations, stating a personal conflict as former chairman of the Richmond City School Board) upheld the appellate court's reversal of metropolitan consolidation. The Supreme Court's decision meant that court-ordered desegregation was limited to the city of Richmond. Posey, the same 5–4 majority on the Supreme Court that has overseen sweeping reversals of civil rights victories across all spheres of society, very much including education, held from before I was born and persists into your childhood. A different court, with a different understanding of the ongoing impact of our racial history, may hold the key to a different set of civil rights possibilities as you grow older.

When our regional school systems failed to come together back in the 1970s, we paved the way for an accelerated process of white and middle-class flight not seen in other Southern communities that *did* consolidate. When it became clear to Richmond's white families that moving just over the city-suburban boundary line would allow them to avoid a massive shift in the social order, many chose to exit. Still others sought to steer clear of desegregation by enrolling their sons and daughters in private schools.

But, Posey, I can't underscore this enough: these choices do not mean that desegregation efforts are futile. An objective look at trends in our divided metropolitan community compared to less divided ones elsewhere shows that the broader and more comprehensive a school desegregation plan, the more stable and meaningful it is. Not only are city-suburban school desegregation plans linked to widespread and lasting school desegregation, they are also linked to much faster declines in housing segregation. We just didn't go far enough.

So, Posey, that is the legacy of school segregation and inequality that you inherit. It is directly related to the fact that nearly half of all of Richmond's black students still go to intensely and doubly segregated schools—by both race and poverty. Our region's growing Latinx student population is rapidly facing similar circumstances.

For too long, we have pretended as if this is the natural order of things, as though it is utterly disconnected from our history. As though school segregation doesn't flow from decades upon decades of discrimination in our housing markets; as though touting the sanctity of neighborhood schools doesn't usually mean sanctifying segregated schools. As though an educational policy paradigm that stigmatizes and punishes highly segregated schools working hard to serve our most disadvantaged children can improve deeply rooted societal inequalities. As though there was and is nothing we can actually do about it when, in fact, we have many examples of successful school desegregation policy.

Our family has pledged not to ignore our history, Posey—and to actively and intentionally fight against it. This is the only way that we as individuals can begin to break the cycle of segregation and live up to the principles articulated by Dr. King. Much broader shifts in policy and action are required, too, which will take the mobilization of entire communities.

Posey, you just started your new preschool, Sprout, located in one of your favorite spots, the Children's Museum. It's a pathbreaking partnership between the YWCA and the Children's Museum, one that allows the school to seek out diverse students, even as so many other daycare and preschool options remain segregated. Sprout offers sliding-scale tuition, with partial and full scholarships for two-thirds of the families made possible by donations from individuals, corporations, and private foundations.

But, I have a confession that I want to make to you in the spirit of honesty—and to acknowledge the anxieties that many advantaged families feel when they consider a truly diverse school. You see, few if any want to feel as if they aren't putting their child in a position to imitate their own success—or to surpass it. On one of the first afternoons that we were driving away from Sprout, I wrestled with the thought that your new friends didn't know as many words as you did, something that's borne out in many research studies. All young kids have the very same capacity to soak up language like a sponge, but kids from lower-income families tend to be exposed to fewer words. Yet Posey, with the advantage of years of reading the piles of research on the benefits of school diversity, here's what I came to pretty quickly.

You aren't going to lose your words. You're going to learn new and different ones. And you're going to share your own words. Most importantly, Eleanora Rose, you're going to learn how to communicate—and stand together—with communities other than your own. The Sprout

School is mutuality hard at work during one of the most important periods in child development. It is also one antidote to the bias that infects us at a very early age—the same bias that contributed to Michael Brown's death. (Speaking of bias, dear reader, if I had waited a few more afternoons to write this letter, I would have realized that most children of few words in my daughter's classroom were just shy.)

When it comes to your elementary school education, Posey, we will go where we are assigned, wherever that may be for Byrd Park residents in a few years. Our intentional choice of a racially and economically diverse neighborhood nearly a decade ago also linked us to an elementary school that deviated little from Richmond Public School's overall white enrollment.

As a child, though, I benefited from the city's open enrollment policy, loading into a carpool of white students from Church Hill each morning and riding across the city to Fox, where your grandfather knew the principal. Open enrollment was put into place alongside a neighborhood school policy in the 1970s, part of an effort to stem white and middle-class flight from Richmond Public Schools. Back during the early stages of the Great Recession, what transportation was offered for open enrollment students was cut, even though so many of our Richmond families have one or no cars at home. Also, as your grandfather's relationship with the principal suggests, navigating open enrollment remains something that the families with the most information and political power are best equipped to do.

Both of those policies, neighborhood schools and open enrollment without transportation, together have created a perfect storm of school segregation in a deeply and persistently segregated city.

What was true in the 1970s is still true today, Posey. We will not comprehensively solve the school segregation crisis in our city—or any city—without cooperating across school district boundary lines. But here in Richmond, we could do a lot better than two elementary schools that are 60 percent to 90 percent white in a system that is roughly 10 percent white.

For your secondary education, Posey, permit me to lay out a dream of Dr. King's single garment realized. What if, building on the many available specialty programs, our major area school districts worked together to offer a system of school choices guided by student interest and firmly grounded in a commitment to equity and diversity? What if every area secondary school specialized in some sort of academic theme or programming—and what if every family had to choose? For this to work, for choice to actually be fairly available to all families with secondary students in the region, we would have to offer transportation and we would have to accept students on the basis of their interest in the school, not the school's interest in them. (A side note here, Posey. We like to pretend that test performance is an objective indicator of a student's ability, but it's not. It's a reflection of opportunities and privileges spread out unequally over many generations.) This whole system would require broad outreach and communication so that families understood the process, and it would also require diversity goals. Stable diversity doesn't happen without intentionality, and goals are the first way to communicate your intention and hold you accountable for it.

Choice systems like this have existed in metropolitan school districts like Louisville, Kentucky; and Raleigh and Charlotte, North Carolina. And we have a fledgling, very small-scale experiment of it here in the Richmond area, in the form of CodeRVA, a new regional school committed to innovation, workforce development, and equity. It's a start, Posey, and we've got a few years before you get to secondary school to grow it into something bigger.

For the time being, we also need to work within our separate area school districts. As new generations choose to reinvest in our city, and as working- and middle-class black, Latinx, and Asian families settle in our suburbs, we should be working for and celebrating intentional diversity within our racially and economically changing schools. Families and leaders need to set anxieties aside and push for students to be treated equally within these schools, to come into frequent contact with one another, to work together cooperatively toward shared goals, and to be guided by strong leaders who believe in and model the value of diverse and equitable schools.

The basic problem with school integration, Posey, is a lack of collective will for it—a failure to see how our fates are bound up in one another and how segregation continues to damage all of us. There's an economic case to be made for integration, to be sure. If we allow our rising racial majority to languish in still separate and highly unequal schools, our economy will suffer mightily. But this is a moral issue too, perhaps *the* moral issue of our—and your—increasingly fragmented time.

I'll borrow another quote often attributed to Dr. King to conclude. "The arc of the moral universe is long," he said, "but it bends toward justice." I believe that to be true, Eleanora Rose, but I sure do wish it would bend a little faster sometimes. It's your father's and my hope that you and your new Sprout friends, and all of the other new friends you'll meet along the way in your education, will grasp hold of that arc with a firm grip, guiding it down toward more justice, more mutuality—and less division. We'll be right here pushing on it with you.

Introduction

On a late October day in 2016, not too long before I read aloud my letter to Posey in Richmond, more than one hundred educational stakeholders from across the country converged in a large, well-lit room at the US Department of Education to talk about creating and sustaining diverse, equitable schools through voluntary integration. I was there as an education researcher, graduate of racially diverse K–12 schools, former teacher in apartheid schools, and member of the National Coalition on School Diversity, a cosponsor of the event. Everyone was seated together at oversized round tables; mine was filled with school leaders from several large Virginia and Maryland districts. It was just weeks before the election.

During an afternoon question-and-answer session, former US Secretary of Education John King described school integration as the only educational reform that could heal the divisions laid bare by the Trump and Clinton presidential campaigns. He was reiterating and expanding upon remarks he'd been making throughout his brief tenure as the top school official in the country, statements that lifted up the power of diverse schools to develop the bonds necessary for fruitful workforce and civic participation.[1]

Secretary King's statements were rooted in interdisciplinary research that showcases the significant cognitive, social, emotional, and civic benefits related to diverse schools. In these settings, particularly when well designed, students of all backgrounds experience a robust exchange of ideas, experiences, and viewpoints. This builds critical,

flexible thinking and creative problem solving.[2] Early contact with
other groups in racially diverse schools can also cultivate friendships
across racial, ethnic, and cultural lines—meaningful relationships that
help combat bias and stereotyping.[3] As King reminded us, in a society
heading toward rule by a plurality of racial groups, rather than domi-
nation by a single majority, diverse schools promote crucial skills for
the twenty-first-century workforce and for a cohesive, well-functioning
democracy.[4]

From that October meeting in Washington, DC, a modest but
symbolically significant $12 million federal grant grew wings. It was
called Opening Doors, Expanding Opportunities, to be awarded to up
to twenty districts, or consortia of districts, interested in planning to
increase diversity in their schools. Funds would support community
engagement, data analysis, the development of diversity goals, and pi-
loting activities in districts that qualified for school improvement grant
funding.[5] As of January 2017, at least twenty-six districts had indicated
they would apply.[6]

Both the convening and the grant would come to represent the remarkable culmination—for now—of a federal executive branch push to
highlight the importance of diversity in public schools. Remarkable because it had been decades since the federal government had explicitly
acknowledged the creation and sustenance of integrated schools as a
policy goal. Culmination because shortly after its announcement, the
incoming Trump administration swiftly discontinued the grant on the
grounds that it was not a smart use of taxpayer dollars—though the department spokesperson was careful to say it did not reflect the administration's commitment to school diversity.[7]

The lack of sustained federal attention has not been because K–12
integration was widely achieved in the wake of the landmark 1954
Brown decision outlawing separate but equal schooling. Far from it. In
fact, on the sixty-sixth anniversary of *Brown*, the Government Accountability Office, at the request of two top Democratic congressmen, released a detailed national analysis of contemporary school segregation
and its consequences.[8] The findings were stark and damning. Between
2000 and 2013, the number of students attending schools in which

more than 75 percent of students were low income and black or Latinx more than doubled to 8.4 million.[9] Racial and economic polarization also was evident: 16 percent of all public schools in the United States served high concentrations of racial minorities and students in poverty, while another 16 percent served low concentrations.[10] These figures mattered because they are closely related to educational opportunities. Schools with high percentages of students of color and students in poverty were much less likely to offer advanced math or science classes and AP courses. They further were characterized by high rates of exclusionary discipline.

Crucially, the release of the report itself, along with several proffered remedies, offered additional affirmation of growing federal interest, this time from the legislative branch, in acknowledging and tackling school segregation after so many years of neglect. Action on both the executive and legislative fronts during the later years of the Obama administration was spurred by heightened media attention and renewed advocacy around school segregation.

The Trump administration's subsequent retrenchment is not the first time opposing forces have halted forward progress on desegregation at the federal level. Indeed, concerted federal implementation of *Brown*'s integration mandate ended almost as swiftly as it began. After more than a decade of Southern intransigence, the threat of losing funds in the wake of executive enforcement of the Civil Rights Act of 1964, coupled with desegregation guidelines and tools outlined by the Supreme Court in 1968 and 1971, respectively, yielded notable declines in segregation for black and white students in the de jure South.[11] But before that same progress could reach the de facto segregated North and West, a politically transformed Supreme Court dealt a crushing blow to the future of metropolitan school desegregation.[12]

The Right Time and Place to Revisit Integration

It's fitting that a look at contemporary school integration efforts—the subject of this book—examines what is happening in Richmond, Virginia, a city and state where pivotal battles over desegregation took place and where demographic shifts are creating new opportunities for diversity within and among districts. The schools profiled in this book, as well as others across the United States that I will point out along the way, stand as important examples of bottom-up workarounds to a long history of legal, political, and social pressure to maintain school segregation.

Progress in Richmond, like the rest of the country, has been halting and slow. It was white leaders in Virginia who led the South during the late fifties and throughout the sixties in fighting *Brown v. Board of Education* viciously and effectively. Alongside damaging rhetoric and overt attacks splashed across editorial pages, Virginia delayed desegregation with tactics like public school closures, private school vouchers for white families, and a state-operated pupil placement board, which allowed just a handful of black students to integrate white schools in Richmond and elsewhere in the state.[13] By the late sixties and early seventies, as federal courts considered school desegregation remedies for Richmond—and countless other central city systems across the nation—government-backed residential segregation posed immense logistical challenges to integration between the largely black urban and predominately white suburban school districts.[14]

In 1971, correctly anticipating the landmark *Swann v. Charlotte-Mecklenburg* ruling permitting the use of busing to sever the link between residential and school segregation, federal district court Judge Robert Merhige ordered cross-town transportation in the city of Richmond.[15] For the first time since *Brown*, all Richmond city students, black and white, were subject to the requirements of a desegregation order. Six months later, plaintiffs, now joined by the Richmond school board, returned to court requesting the merger of Richmond, Henrico, and Chesterfield schools to expand desegregation beyond Richmond's predominately black school enrollment.[16] Judge Merhige agreed with the plaintiffs, ordering the city-suburban consolidation on January 10, 1972.

But it was not to be.

As I wrote to Posey, a year later, in a 4–4 tie, the Supreme Court let stand an appellate decision overturning the Richmond-Henrico-Chesterfield merger. And one year after that, in 1974, the Supreme

Court issued a nationally binding decision in *Milliken v. Bradley*. The 5–4 ruling similarly engaged the issue of desegregating schools across the city-suburban boundary line, this time in the Detroit area, but breaking the tie that split the court in the Richmond case meant the decision applied to metro areas around the country. *Milliken* erected a national wall between city and suburban schools, effectively prohibiting meaningful and stable school desegregation from taking hold in most communities.

During my twelve years as a white student in Richmond's city schools, the overall white enrollment in the system hovered around 10 percent. And it still does. Persistent segregation today, in Richmond and elsewhere, highlights the lack of political will to voluntarily do what the courts backed away from ordering—and what the Opening Doors, Expanding Opportunities grant was trying to incentivize: help communities overcome balkanized metropolitan spaces to ensure that children have access to equal educational opportunity. The ongoing struggle to do so highlights the need to revisit the principle of Martin Luther King Jr.'s "single garment" and what we want our public schools to do for our kids and our society.

Public schools play an utterly essential role in stitching that garment together. Attended by roughly nine out of ten students in the United States, public education is the communal institution that many of us encounter first, and for the most sustained period of time. In an age of standards, accountability, and market-based choice reforms, it is easy to forget that we designed public schools to serve both the advancement of individual students *and* society as a whole. As the unanimous decision in *Brown* declared:

> Today, education is . . . required in the performance of our most basic public responsibilities, even service in the armed forces. It is the very foundation of good citizenship. Today it is a principal instrument in awakening the child to cultural values, in preparing him for later professional training, and in helping him to adjust normally to his environment. In these days, it is doubtful that any

child may reasonably be expected to succeed in life if he is denied the opportunity of an education. Such an opportunity, where the state has undertaken to provide it, is a right which must be made available to all on equal terms.[17]

Milliken's retreat from the vision of public education outlined by *Brown*—along with the comprehensive school desegregation that vision required—unraveled much of our single garment.

Today's "Patchwork" Communities and Local Support for Integration

Yet in metro areas around the country, a "patchwork metropolis" has emerged, as young, affluent, and largely white professionals flock to some city neighborhoods and as racial diversity and poverty mushroom in the suburbs.[18] In terms of sheer numbers, more people in poverty now live in the suburbs than in the cities. Some of the growth can be explained by migration from cities to suburbs, but it can also be understood as aftershocks from the Great Recession, with families struggling to maintain a toehold in the middle class. Racial and economic divisions remain extremely intense, hence the patchwork, but taken together, these changes may represent a window of opportunity for the 80 percent of Americans—and their children—who reside in metropolitan communities. [19]

Against the backdrop of our patchwork metros, mutuality in the form of school integration represents a path forward. Too few studies in recent years have called attention to what's working when it comes to fostering school integration. Yet, as demographic change renders schools across metropolitan communities temporarily diverse, helping practitioners and policy makers understand how to intentionally harness and stabilize that diversity becomes increasingly urgent. And while federal executive branch leadership on school integration has receded, at least temporarily, there is much that states and metros can do to further opportunities for diverse and equitable schooling.

The Richmond area offers up a Southern example of a community that left its city-suburban boundary lines intact—like the vast majority of metros nationwide. Yet Richmond's contemporary city, suburban, and exurban communities are shifting, subject to what scholar Amy Stuart Wells calls "metropolitan migrations."[20] As prior distinctions and divisions blur, and as the Richmond community continues to wrestle with the intertwined legacies of slavery and Jim Crow segregation, a new generation of local stakeholders is purposefully supporting diverse schools.

About This Book

This book will explore the leadership, policies, and practices surrounding efforts to promote twenty-first-century school integration. It does so through the lens of four Richmond area schools committed to the work of mutuality through racial and economic integration. The four schools encompass preprimary, elementary, middle, and high school, and range from urban to suburban to regional. All reflect intentionality around bringing diverse groups of students together to benefit children and communities. Integration doesn't happen by accident; it takes strong leadership and carefully designed policies and practices to bring it to fruition. School fieldwork and roughly fifteen in-depth, semistructured interviews with stakeholders at each school, including past and present leadership, faculty, families, and students, are layered onto an exploration of segregation in a metropolitan milieu.

A Single Garment brings an interdisciplinary understanding of old and new research related to the legal, political, policy, social psychology, and sociological issues surrounding school integration. It merges questions around external integration considerations like student assignment policy, housing policy, diversity goals for students and teachers, outreach and marketing, and transportation with internal integration ones like how students are assigned to classrooms and how families are engaged, who gets access to what curricula and which teachers, how often students experience cooperative activities, and how racial tensions are arbitrated and discipline meted out. Generally, school stakeholders were asked to reflect on the opportunities and challenges created by diverse schools. By exploring both the internal and external dynamics of school integration, it's possible to see what it would take to reproduce various successes in certain schools across broader systems of schooling.

A word about terminology. In a nod to our contemporary lexicon, I'll often use the phrase "diverse schools," or "diverse and equitable schools," to describe school integration. But I also use the word "integration" with intention—and with an eye toward our troubled history of school desegregation. Dr. King famously outlined the difference between desegregation and integration in his 1962 speech "The Ethical Demands of Integration." He spoke of desegregation as "eliminative and negative," a short-term goal of removing "legal and social prohibitions" to racial contact and equality. Integration, in King's mind, was more long term, involving "the welcomed participation of Negroes in the total range of human activities" or "genuine intergroup, interpersonal doing."[21] Put differently: the removal of barriers to racial desegregation, accompanied by proactive strategies to achieve numerical diversity in schools, is a precondition for integration—but it is only the beginning of the work needed to dismantle the "otherness" that segregation helped create. Many of the external, or outward-facing, policies and strategies employed by the four schools studied move them closer to the goal of numerical diversity. Once attained, internal, or inward-facing, leadership, practices, and structures help prod them along the continuum of school integration toward what Berkeley professor john powell calls "true integration."[22]

Importantly, *A Single Garment* engages school integration across diverse circumstances. Through the analysis of the four schools, readers will understand how our urban, suburban, and metropolitan contexts have shifted over the past several decades and what those shifts mean for diverse and equitable schooling. As such, the reader will come to see that these four schools operate within broader systems of metropolitan inequality. A unique feature of this book is that it doesn't consider leadership in isolation from policy, or system-level issues like student assignment as separate from within-school ones like tracking. The work of weaving together the single garment, in other words, involves both external and internal school integration—and our four schools are working hard to address both dimensions. I draw details from my own experiences as a white student, parent, and professor into the book at times to further illustrate how some of these dynamics play out. It's my hope that the scope of the book renders it pertinent to a broad audience of students, parents, teachers, leaders, and policy makers concerned with advancing equal educational opportunity in the twenty-first century.

The basic argument is this: to move forward together as a multiracial, functioning, and fair democratic society, we must see public schools as central to weaving together our single garment. More than ever, this means collectively creating and maintaining a commitment to diverse, inclusive schools—and seeing them as institutions that benefit all children in deeply important ways. It means understanding how individual choices help create systems of equity or inequity and how those choices are shaped by systems. It means working to support and connect all kids as they walk through the main door of the building together, and also as they walk through classroom doors together. Relatedly, it means understanding that the work of meaningful school integration is continuous and complex.

A Single Garment proceeds as follows. The first chapter presents relevant research and theory surrounding mutuality in the form of school integration. It engages literature from multiple disciplines and sectors to answer a central question: why does school integration matter? This material lays the groundwork for understanding the choices and priorities of the four schools presented in subsequent chapters.

Chapters 2 through 5 serve as portraits of Sprout, Ecoff, Binford, and CodeRVA's efforts to foster integration amid segregated systems. Note that each of the four school-related chapters unfolds in the same basic order: a discussion of the dynamics of school segregation in preschool, urban, suburban, or regional contexts; an exploration of the origins stories related to the four schools; and finally, an analysis of the external and internal integration work at each site.

We'll see how leaders navigated complex and sometimes opposing demands to create a socioeconomically diverse preschool at Sprout—and later how the faculty drew on its own racial diversity to create better experiences for students. We'll examine how housing policy influences school policy at suburban Ecoff, where a racially and economically diverse enrollment hinges on empathic, inclusive leadership and an attendance boundary that encircles—at least for the moment—a wide variety of neighborhoods and families. Within Ecoff, an emphasis on social and emotional learning (SEL) offers regular opportunities to learn and dialogue about the single garment. We'll then take a look at Binford Middle's rapid growth and rising diversity, guided by a leader strongly committed to its new arts integration focus and to serving a group of students reflective of the city. We'll also peek into its past, examining a trajectory that included my own middle school experiences there in the early 1990s. And finally, with CodeRVA, we'll zoom out to capture the ongoing importance of metropolitan efforts to integrate students. An emphasis on high-demand, innovative programming, workforce development, and equity brought together a powerful coalition, led by area superintendents, that culminated in the opening of the Richmond area's first regional magnet school.

The final chapter in *A Single Garment* looks across the four cases to synthesize key themes related to the leadership, policies, and practices that support intentionally diverse schools. This chapter underscores the ways in which internal and external integration are interwoven and discusses how to systematically extend school-based accomplishments. The book's core contention—that mutuality in the form of school integration must become a national goal—is revisited, along with the role of local, state, and federal policy makers in advancing that goal.

As recent and distant history indicates, with political will, progress can be swift. In the end, I hope readers will more clearly understand each child's success in the way I've come to understand my daughter's: as bound up in another's success, and as rooted in the forward movement of a healthy, democratic society.

CHAPTER 1

Why School Integration?

I F RESEARCH FINDINGS ALONE were enough to make the case for more intentional integration, we would have fewer segregated schools in America. As battles for and against desegregation have proceeded over the past decades, the evidence in favor of diverse schools—as well as popular support for them—has increased. But much of this research, especially related to the academic benefits of integration, remains largely unknown. Any case in favor of integration should therefore begin with an overview of the strong and compelling research pointing to myriad benefits for privileged and nonprivileged students alike, not to mention for the health of our democratic society as a whole.

We grasp some of the advantages associated with school integration intuitively. In my interviews with stakeholders associated with the Sprout, Ecoff, Binford, and CodeRVA schools, the benefits of enrolling in diverse schools came up repeatedly. An African American school teacher who'd attended racially and ethnically diverse schools growing up said she gained "[f]riends. Lifelong friends. And culture. My children call people aunt and uncle that don't look anything like them, because they're my dearest and closest friends." A white parent of a student of color explained, "Children who are around people who don't look like them become less racist. I think we as a society could use a little less racism." Other families spoke of how important it was for kids to be exposed to the "real world" and to experience life "outside a bubble." One of my former teachers in Richmond Public Schools, who sent his own white children through the system, said he thought their educational experiences and friendships shaped their interest in becoming civil servants.

What seemed clear from these and many other responses was that stakeholders felt that contact across lines of difference nurtured openness, expanded friendships and horizons, and solidified commitment to civic institutions. Those sentiments will be backed up by the research explored in this chapter. What's missing here, though, is a sense that racially and economically diverse schools can help all students thrive academically. Which is also true. Lacking a full understanding of school integration's cognitive benefits makes the political case for integration more difficult to make than it should be.

Generally speaking, public support for the idea of school integration has climbed since the *Brown* decision. By 2007, virtually all Americans agreed that black and white children should attend the same schools.[1] But more recent polling data from 2017 highlighted the same disconnect that emerged from my Richmond area interviews. It suggested that, while families of all races overwhelmingly valued racially diverse learning environments, they may not be fully aware of their many positive academic attributes.[2] Seventy percent of respondents would prefer that their child went to a racially diverse school, but only about 50 percent thought that diversity was important for learning.[3]

This chapter shows that whether or not a child's school is integrated matters for a number of critical, connected reasons. First, school integration does promote stronger learning, along with the skills needed for a thriving, modern workforce. Second, it reduces prejudice and opens up access to the multifaceted information and opportunities that flow through social worlds. These two outcomes relate to a third: school integration strengthens citizenship for our multiracial democracy. Finally, integration creates more equitable access to key educational resources like high-quality, engaging curricula; strong, diverse teachers; and funding. So when it comes to the material and human resources that matter most for schools, diverse schools fare better than racially segregated, high-poverty ones.

Integrating Schools Promotes Stronger Learning and Skills for a Thriving Workforce

Research shows that diverse schools and classrooms set the stage for stronger learning outcomes across all student groups. These outcomes include but go beyond test scores. Students with different ways of seeing and thinking about the world, based on differing experiences moving through it, add depth, creativity, and nuance to schoolwork that homogeneous settings simply can't produce. Diverse spaces nurture critical thinking, collaboration, and communication—all elements required for a twenty-first-century education and life beyond it.

Katherine Phillips, a social psychology professor at Columbia's business school, likens participation in diverse groups to "going to the gym for your mind." A series of studies she coauthored finds participants prepare more intensively for work in heterogeneous groups, partly in anticipation that consensus might be more difficult to reach. During work sessions with diverse groups, members consider multiple points of view on an issue, often simultaneously.[4] Positions are explained more carefully, and conflicts force participants to grapple with new ideas. One "murder mystery" study stays with me, in which Phillips and her coauthors divided college students into racially heterogeneous and homogenous groups. Each team received common information, while each individual group member received a set of clues to which only he or she was privy. Teams then had to work together to solve the mystery. The racially diverse groups performed significantly better on the task than the racially similar teams, largely because the diverse teams worked harder to elicit information from individual members, not falling prey to the idea that everyone had the same data and perspectives.[5]

Similarly, Scott Page, a researcher at the University of Michigan, uses careful mathematical models to reveal a "diversity bonus" for diverse teams working together on difficult problems. Creative solutions are readier when team members bring heterogeneous perspectives and expertise to an issue.[6] His models apply specifically to higher education and industry, though confirming evidence flows from multiple disciplines, including sociology, psychology, economics, and demography.[7]

Higher education has grasped the potential embedded in diversity since the early days of the country's founding. In a presidential farewell speech, George Washington envisioned a national public university so that "young men from different parts of the United States would be assembled together, & would by degrees discover that there was not just cause for those jealousies and prejudices which one part of the Union had imbibed against another part."[8] Further emphasis on educational diversity came with approach of the Civil War. The Harvard president at the time urged universities to consider enrolling students from different regions of the country "to remove prejudice by bringing them into friendly relations."[9] Following the war, a subsequent Harvard president sought diversity in admissions to foster "the wholesome influence that comes from observation of and contact with people different than ourselves."[10]

Research bears out the value of higher education's long-standing emphasis on diversity. Studies from the post-secondary sphere show that exposure to diverse classmates tends to trigger something called "cognitive disequilibrium," or the disconnect between prior beliefs and new information. Higher-order thinking and stronger integrative complexity of information are the result.[11]

Higher education law and literature additionally point to the link between student body diversity and the legitimacy of our institutions. In *Sweatt v. Painter*, one of the lawsuits preceding *Brown*, the Supreme Court ruled against segregated law schools, saying a law school "cannot be effective in isolation from the individuals and institutions with which the law interacts."[12] This line of thinking extends across many other sectors, including government, education, and business. In our diversifying society, if universities do not admit and graduate more students of color, institutions and workplaces that require postsecondary education for employment increasingly will be out of step with the populations they serve.

While preK–12 schools often have been slower to understand diversity's fundamental importance to learning and development, many of the same tenets hold true.[13] As the conduit to the worlds of higher learning and work, any critical-thinking, cross-cultural, or problem-solving skills that haven't been developed during earlier education must be remediated later. This is already the case. In universities, students of color suffer "racial battle fatigue" around the repeated need to educate white peers struggling to meaningfully interact across racial lines for the first time.[14] In the workforce, in one year alone, Google spent $150 million on diversity and bias training initiatives. Intel estimated spending $60 million a year for its five-year diversity plan.[15]

To be clear, the bonuses derived from diversity don't accrue automatically. It takes hard work for a diverse team (or school, or classroom) to cleave together and thrive. Cross-racial trust is a fundamental ingredient and, in a society grappling with the past and present effects of deep-seated discrimination, hard won.

In addition to better preparing students for learning, living, and working in a multiracial society, diverse schools hold the advantage of positive peer effects. These are the varying outcomes linked to students' friendships and social relationships within their cohorts. Effects begin early. As one prominent early childhood academic put it, "Young children learn with and from their peers in the highly social context of preschool and lower-skilled children appear to benefit cognitively from sharing classrooms with higher skilled peers."[16] For instance, preschool research indicates that language formation, fluency, and expressiveness are closely linked to language-rich classrooms and peers.[17] Verbal exchanges among classroom participants are important, along with how questions are formulated and the ease with which ideas are rephrased or extended through language. The benefits of language-rich classrooms flow more strongly to preschoolers who may not experience the same verbal opportunities outside of school.[18] One large-scale 2017 study found, for instance, that low-income students enrolled in preschools with more economic diversity showed substantially more growth in test scores than their peers in preschools targeted solely toward low-income families.[19]

Later on, peers matter because they can positively influence views on school and class attendance, completion of assignments, and college enrollment.[20] Peers also may have a negative impact; one study showed that knowing a close friend or acquaintance who dropped out increased the chances of someone else in their peer group doing the same.[21] Peer makeup further shapes how adults interact with students, influencing teacher expectations as well as instruction and family involvement.[22]

All students receive academic benefits in racially and economically diverse schools, though, as we saw with preschoolers, the benefits accumulate more dramatically for historically disadvantaged groups.[23] In diverse schools, low-income black or Latinx students report higher academic achievement across multiple academic subjects, including math, science, language, and reading, than their peers in more segregated settings.[24] At the same time, historically advantaged students who are both white and higher income tend to score well on tests regardless of peer composition. This may relate in part to the numerous resources—strong parental education, tutoring, after-school and summer extracurricular activities—surrounding them outside of school.[25]

Here are some numbers to back up these assertions. A recent federal analysis of the racial achievement gap found that achievement—measured by test performance on the National Assessment of Educational Progress (NAEP), otherwise known as the Nation's Report Card—was lowest for black and white students in schools with the highest concentrations of black students. However, after controlling for socioeconomic status, achievement differences between schools with high and low concentrations of black students disappeared for white students. These findings specifically applied to white students attending racially isolated black schools, though multiple past studies of student outcomes in desegregated schools also indicated no declines and some gains in white achievement.[26]

Crucially, researchers have revealed that the racial achievement gap closed most rapidly and significantly during the desegregation era, according to NAEP data.[27] Across all age cohorts and subjects, black versus white achievement on the NAEP shows a narrowing gap between 1973 and 1990. Likewise, a state-level analysis of NAEP test scores found that states with the lowest school segregation also reported the narrowest achievement gap.[28] International evidence from the thirty-six countries that constitute the Organisation for Economic Cooperation and Development (OECD) underscores a related, though distinct,

point: when socioeconomically disadvantaged students attend socioeconomically advantaged schools, they score the equivalent of one-and-
a-half years more of schooling than similarly situated peers attending
socioeconomically disadvantaged schools.[29]

Although it can be difficult to disentangle the benefits of racial diversity from economic diversity, in part because researchers have tended
to either emphasize both or home in on racial diversity, we do know
that school racial diversity is linked to higher academic achievement as
well as improved attitudinal and democratic outcomes. When it comes
to economic diversity, multiple studies have concluded that the socioeconomic composition of a school matters more for achievement than
an individual student's socioeconomic standing entering school.[30] Similarly, an analysis of millions of student test scores revealed that racial
disparities in student exposure to school poverty are a central explanation for the achievement gap.[31]

Peer effects research—an important but limited way of understanding the myriad benefits of diversity—has often relied on narrowly defined outcomes for students, typically achievement on standardized
tests. Though accountability policies ensure that test scores remain the
currency of the day, the discussion of diversity's educational benefits
must be extended. Most standardized tests simply aren't designed to
measure significant learning outcomes linked to diversity—things like
heightened creativity, the ability to see and relate to multiple points of
view, and comfort working across lines of difference to solve complex
problems. Increasingly, though, these are qualities that colleges and em-
ployers value.[32]

In addition to being overly focused on test results, peer effects research tends to overlook the many assets students of color carry into
educational settings, characteristics that are important to consider
when building a case for the way integration benefits all students. In
an influential paper published in 2005, Tara Yosso explored how Latinx
students experienced higher education and synthesized their assets
into various forms of cultural wealth. These included high and hope-
ful future aspirations, perseverance, grit, resistance to social inequality,
adept linguistic communication and storytelling, strong familial and

communal ties, and the ability to comfortably traverse different social contexts.[33] Other research has pointed to the strengths of nondominant groups when it comes to collaboration, metaphoric thinking, and systems thinking related to science.[34]

At the same time, the cultural wealth that dominant students bring to diverse settings remains important. Sonia Nieto, an education researcher at UMass Amherst, writes,

> The weight of cultural capital can't be ignored. To do so would be both naïve and romantic because it would deny the reality that power, knowledge and resources are located in the norms of dominant cultures and languages. To imply that working class students and students from dominated groups need not learn the cultural norms of the dominant group is effectively to disempower the students who are most academically vulnerable.[35]

Fundamentally, exposure to and exchange of these different assets are valuable for all students.

Diverse schools and classrooms lend themselves to contact with peers of differing racial and economic backgrounds. From that contact flows another realm of advantages linked to school diversity. These social advantages, which include reductions in prejudice and stereotyping, are more critical than ever in a rapidly diversifying society still balkanized along racial and ethnic lines.

Integrating Schools Reduces Prejudice and Binds Together Disparate Social Worlds

In schools, simply bringing students from different backgrounds together—regardless of conditions within the building—can alleviate prejudice. Indeed, multiple studies confirm that school desegregation reduces prejudice and cultivates better relationships between groups.[36] It's even more effective than living in a diverse neighborhood for developing positive attitudes toward out-groups. This is partly because, unlike more happenstance encounters in neighborhoods, school desegregation creates structured opportunities for cross-racial interactions and true interracial friendships. Friendship is the most meaningful arena when it comes to attitudinal change; deeply knowing an individual from a different group makes you more likely to extend favorable treatment to the entire group.[37]

Conversely, racial separation creates harm. Prejudice arises out of the human desire to understand ourselves as part of a group. It revolves around questions like "Who am I?" and "Where do I belong?" People are wired to define themselves as part of an in-group or an out-group (or an "us" versus a "them"). In detrimental conditions like segregation, individuals in power are easily convinced of their own group's superiority and work to exclude others from key resources and opportunities.[38]

The social-psychological damages of racial separation formed a central rationale for the 1954 *Brown* decision. Citing studies from the field of psychology, the justices declared, "To separate them [black students] from others of similar age and qualifications solely because of their race generates a feeling of inferiority as to their status in the community that may affect their hearts and minds in a way unlikely ever to be undone."[39]

We know that color consciousness and associated prejudices begin at a very young age under regimes of segregation. Kenneth and Mamie Clark, a pair of young, married, African American social psychologists renowned for their cutting-edge research on the relationship between segregation and self-esteem in young black children, produced much of the social science evidence informing the justices' decision in *Brown*. One set of experiments involved child preferences for baby dolls identical except for their skin color. Gathering groups of black children aged three to seven, the Clarks would ask questions about the racial identity of the dolls and which ones "looked bad" or were a "nice color."[40] Most of the black children—even the youngest—preferred the white dolls. A related Clark study drew connections between school segregation and color consciousness, finding that black children in racially isolated schools were more aware of their race than black children in more diverse schools.[41]

Experiments conducted by different researchers during the same time period confirmed and extended these results for both black and white children. One showed that an overwhelming majority of white children (89 percent) preferred white dolls, along with a significant majority (57 percent) of black children. This particular study also tested racial associations with housing and poverty; majorities of both races were more likely to provide the brown dolls with worn clothing and housing in an apartment unit instead of a brick single-family home.[42]

More recent research on young children suggests that racial bias begins developing between the ages of three and five.[43] Toddlers first notice differences in skin color around eighteen months. About a year later, they start to categorize people in the same way they categorize objects as being similar or different. Some scholars call this the "preprejudice stage" when racial differences are observed but no meaning is attached to them.[44] But preschoolers quickly begin to take verbal and nonverbal cues from adults and peers in their often separate worlds, as well as from books, TV, and movies. They tune in to racialized messages about who's in charge of groups and institutions (including schools), who's favored and disfavored, and who's got access to which resources.

An expert in racial identity development, Dr. Sandra Chapman, explains that she loves the Dr. Seuss book *Sneetches*, in which the Star-Belly Sneetches feel superior to the Plain-Belly Sneetches. She says, "It's a perfect example of the fact that adults are informing young children and they can either affirm their experiences—they have stars, they feel so privileged, they're so important and validated and affirmed—or, wait I'm not so sure maybe there's something missing in who we are? And that information can also get translated to children as well."[45] This is also when personal and group identities begin to take shape. Between the ages of four and six, children start assuming a preference for same-race friends when observing others.[46] By kindergarten, kids display racial awareness and can link race to social status.[47]

What all of these studies clearly indicate is that racial separation and the unequal footing it creates insidiously shapes children's perceptions of themselves and others very early. Dr. Martin Luther King Jr. perhaps put it best: "[S]egregation distorts the soul and damages the personality. It gives the segregator a false sense of superiority and the segregated a false sense of inferiority."[48]

The perceptions of individuals, children or otherwise, are informed by systems. Systems of segregation operate through stigma and status inequality. Segregation marks groups as inferior and thus not worthy of equal access to an array of educational, social, economic, or political benefits.[49] Physical separation fosters social separation—and this is where prejudice finds fertile soil.

Integration, on the other hand, creates conditions that can redefine group contours. As Elizabeth Anderson, professor of philosophy at the University of Michigan, put it in her book *The Imperative of Integration*, "By expanding the boundaries of 'us' to include members of different social groups, integration turns in-group favoritism from an obstacle to a tool of interracial concord."[50] So if anxiety and fear fester with separation, empathy, care, and trust grow with contact.

There's a single, crucial theory threading through the research on interactions between different groups. It was presented in a carefully researched book called *The Nature of Prejudice* in 1954, the same year, coincidentally, that the Supreme Court handed down *Brown*. The hallmark of a strong theory is whether or not it holds across different groups and situations and through time. This one does.[51] It's called the intergroup contact theory, developed by Harvard social psychologist Gordon Allport, who used the early desegregation of housing projects, police departments, and the merchant marines to hypothesize four conditions under which exposure to different groups—racial, ethnic, religious, or otherwise—reduces prejudice.[52] These conditions are important not only for integrating school social worlds, but also for facilitating the belongingness and engagement foundational to academic achievement.[53]

The first of Allport's four conditions is equal status across the different groups. That is, when groups come into contact, they should do so on equal footing. The second and third conditions involve actions to reduce intergroup conflict and promote cooperation toward shared goals. The final condition, underlining the importance of leadership, is normative support for cross-group contact from leaders, laws, or customs. Allport also theorized that these four optimal contact conditions were interconnected, working together to reduce prejudice.

More than six decades later, hundreds of national and international studies have tested Allport's conditions. Research consistently shows significantly higher reduction of prejudice when contact between different groups is structured to meet Allport's conditions.[54] It also finds, as Allport suspected, interlocking relationships among the four conditions. Of the four, institutional support has the most impact when it comes to reducing prejudice.[55] Contemporary studies have uncovered additional elements related to positive contact across groups. Because anxiety is so central to feelings of dislike, deemphasizing the salience of group identities like race or religion helps ease intergroup contact.[56] One way to accomplish this is to create superordinate identities.[57] In schools, these might take the form of cooperative group, classroom, or team identities.

Notably, research shows that simply exposing to one another groups previously kept apart reduces prejudice.[58] A meta-analysis of results from over five hundred studies found that, even when Allport's conditions aren't fully met, greater contact reduces prejudice.[59] "Familiarity breeds liking" has been the basic conclusion of many research experiments, highlighting the relationship between exposure and affection across a range of groups and settings.[60] Evidence also uncovers the potential for a more generalized liking for other out-groups after exposure to a single one.[61]

Ultimately, contact alone helps reduce the anxiety that lies at the heart of prejudice. When coming into contact with another group for the first time, people worry about how they should act, how they'll be viewed, and whether or not they'll be found wanting.[62] Repeated contact lowers the stakes and chips away at the unease.

During a period of intense worry around school safety, it's also important to understand that research links diverse schools to stronger student mental health. More racial/ethnic diversity among students cultivates more complex social identities—in other words, students are better able to answer the "Who am I?" question in multidimensional ways.[63] Students of all races in diverse, multiethnic middle schools subsequently report feeling safer, less victimized, and less lonely.[64] This is especially true in schools with numerous racial/ethnic groups approaching relative parity in size.[65] School diversity also relates to less bullying and improved power sharing among peers.[66]

When students experience school desegregation early on, it increases the likelihood they will seek out desegregated spaces—in the form of postsecondary options, workplaces, and neighborhoods—over their life course.[67] This creates opportunities for perpetuation across generations. Choosing a diverse neighborhood because of your own exposure to diversity means your child will likely enroll in diverse schools linked to that neighborhood.[68]

Truly, the stakes surrounding greater social integration today couldn't be higher. The lack thereof represents a fundamental explanation for our growing inequality. This is because social networks, understood as our webs of family, friends, and acquaintances, shape access to opportunity across many related dimensions. Said differently, there's truth to the old adage, "It's not what you know, it's who you know." When our social circles are segregated, so too is the valuable information about schooling, neighborhoods, and employment contained within them.[69]

And in the swiftly diversifying United States, social circles remain extremely separate indeed. Whites report the most segregated networks: a 2016 survey found that the average white American's social circle was 91 percent white and just 1 percent black. Fully three out of four whites report no people of color in their social networks.[70]

Unequal rationing of opportunity is nurtured by the myopia formed in separate social worlds.[71] If we surround ourselves only with people of similar backgrounds and perspectives, how can we embrace different lived experiences? And if we can't understand our increasingly divergent realities, how will we muster the political will to tackle the democratic costs of inequality?

Integrating Schools Strengthens Citizenship for Our Multiracial Democracy

Public schools serve many purposes. Among the most central is preparation for life as a citizen in a democratic society.[72] Schools teach students the history of our participatory democracy. They illuminate the gap between how democracies function in reality and how they function in the ideal. From there, students learn how to make informed decisions in service of democracy's continuation.[73]

This assumes, of course, that civics education remains a priority. School integration matters here. Students in diverse, multiracial schools (serving three to four racial/ethnic groups) are more likely than students in segregated, high-poverty schools to report opportunities to learn civic and political knowledge and skills, according to a Chicago survey of nearly fifty thousand students.[74] Surveys of diverse schools in a number of districts around the country also show that students of all backgrounds feel positively toward civic engagement.[75] Civic learning opportunities in diverse schools can offset lower civic participation in families and neighborhoods. But schools have to directly focus on citizenship outcomes, not just assume they will occur as a by-product of being in a classroom community. And teaching method counts too; instruction that includes opportunities for service learning, discussion of current events, and regular engagement with controversial topics like race prompts the best civic outcomes.[76]

As our democratic society becomes more multiracial and more unequal, school integration represents a key antidote to tribalism in our politics as well as a crucial avenue to greater social cohesion.[77] A socially cohesive society is one that embraces the needs and views of all groups within it, one that helps its citizens understand the single garment, or the idea that their individual prosperity is dependent upon cooperation with a larger community.[78]

How does school integration foster cohesion in a diverse democracy? As Roz Mickelson and Mokubung Nkomo point out in a highly detailed review of research, the answer to that question brings together many of the academic and social outcomes flowing from school integration. Diverse schools and classrooms give students practice navigating difference. They build perspective-taking and problem-solving skills in all groups. Discussions about democracy and its shortcomings tend to be richer, more complex, and more empathic among diverse peers. Diverse schools are linked to higher educational and occupational attainment for historically marginalized students, which reduces inequality and allows for more even participation in the political process.[79] They establish an early basis for citizens to interact on equal terms, helping students understand the crucial difference between generosity toward those in need and giving everyone what they need to succeed.[80] Without equal status contact among different groups, it's possible to do the former, much harder to do the latter.

Ultimately, diverse schools can produce citizens and leaders who viscerally understand the struggles of groups beyond their own. Graduates have learned to see, understand, and respond to the needs of others.[81] They have practice constructing shared points of view. They feel more accountable to and connected with a broad, rather than narrow, community of us.[82] As two stakeholders wrote in their push for more equitable access to the competitive magnet schools in Montgomery County, Maryland, "We know that a more diverse student body would be indispensable to fostering a generation of compassionate, socially responsible learners and thinkers."[83] Specifically addressing preparation for the high-status careers sought by many of the magnet students, the authors went on to say in a 2016 editorial for the *Washington Post*:

> While many magnet students see cutting-edge medical research internships as a great way to advance health care, few are aware of the barriers in translating and delivering these measures to the marginalized communities in Montgomery County. As many of our peers have expressed aspirations to become the next generation's leaders in politics and science, to truly understand their mission and calling, it is critical that they stand alongside communities outside their own. Likewise, students who hail from a disadvantaged community and have an authentic appreciation of its challenges would be helpful in brainstorming solutions.[84]

In addition to arguments for a healthier society, these magnet stakeholders make the case for school integration more broadly. They remind us that access to a Montgomery County magnet school, and the social networks attached to it, links students to cutting-edge medical

internships. The academic benefits that flow from diverse schools—
heightened critical thinking and problem solving—are also on display.
And finally, they argue for more equitable access to county magnet
schools because of the high-quality curriculum contained within.

Integrating Schools Encourages Equitable Access to High-Quality, Engaging Curricula

School integration is related to the presence of more challenging curricula. In 2016, the federal report from the Government Accountability
Office (GAO) found that, compared to more diverse settings, schools
serving high shares (75 percent or more) of black, Latinx, and low-
income students offered far fewer advanced math and science courses at
the middle and high school levels.[85] For instance, just under 50 percent
of high-poverty black and Latinx schools provided seventh-grade Algebra I, compared to 79 percent of low-poverty black and Latinx schools
and 65 percent of diverse schools. Though the discrepancies narrowed
somewhat when it came to eighth-grade algebra, they persisted—deny-
ing many middle school students in segregated high-poverty black and
Latinx schools the opportunity to gain a foothold in challenging math
classes. High-poverty black and Latinx schools were also much less
likely to offer high school Advanced Placement (AP) classes (which gar-
ner students college credit if they perform well on the assessment) or
calculus and physics than other types of school settings.[86]

The only exception to pervasive curriculum disparities was in the
realm of gifted and talented classes. A slightly higher percentage of
high-poverty black and Latinx schools (59 percent) offered gifted and
talented coursework than low-poverty black and Latinx schools (55 percent). This may reflect a drift toward segregation *within* high-poverty
black and Latinx schools, as families vie for access to limited resources
like gifted and talented programs.

Indeed, segregation within schools has consistently undermined—
but not erased—the benefits of desegregation.[87] Sometimes referred to
as second-generation segregation, or tracking, the racially identifiable
sorting of students into separate classrooms cordons off access to more

complex curricula. Lowest-track classes suffer the most; in some diverse schools, these learning spaces look much like instruction in segregated, high-poverty settings. [88] School integration efforts, as this book will show, thus involve tackling educational inequalities within the school as well as beyond it.

The stakes attached to unequal access to a challenging curriculum are high. These courses better prepare students for participation in civic society and postsecondary pursuits, boost chances of college admission by padding grade point averages (GPAs), and, in the case of successful AP test performance, shave off the cost of higher education. Perhaps more fundamentally, advanced courses lend themselves to more rigorous instruction and deep student engagement.

A dramatic narrowing of the curriculum in schools and classrooms serving historically marginalized students is a significant by-product of the standards and accountability movement. Teaching carefully tailored to content assessed by annual testing permeates high-poverty schools and classrooms. Some argue that this is appropriate; students must start with the basic skills before progressing to more complex and challenging material.[89] Others worry, though, that steady doses of "drill and kill" instruction geared toward rote memorization foster stress and detachment from school.

Take an example from a widely recognized teacher working in a racially segregated, high-poverty Hartford, Connecticut, school under the federal accountability law passed in 2001, known as No Child Left Behind (NCLB). As reported in Susan Eaton's powerful book about school desegregation efforts in Connecticut, before NCLB, the Hartford teacher had designed a captivating unit on monarch butterflies. It involved an intensive search and retrieval mission for eggs scattered on neighborhood milkweed plants. Students watched as the eggs hatched and carefully tended caterpillar jars over the summer, sending their teacher postcards about metamorphosis. In the fall, they set the butterflies free. Eaton wrote, "Even the few [third-grade] students whose anti-school defenses were already erected lowered their drawbridges for this lesson."[90] Yet as district pressure to perform well on the Connecticut

Mastery Tests ratcheted up, lessons once animated by children's budding interests and rich with expeditionary learning were squeezed out
by formulaic writing drills and intensive test preparation.

Intensive test preparation in racially segregated, high-poverty
schools can be fueled by a desire to show that the racial or economic
makeup of students doesn't have to determine performance. Roman-
ticized by iconic movies like *Stand and Deliver* or *Lean on Me*, turning in
strong, schoolwide scores on testing becomes a rallying cry for students
and staff alike. In a policy environment that so heavily sanctions—and
pillories—underperforming schools, those attitudes reflect some measure of self-preservation. But all of it rests on the assumption that tests
accurately and solely reflect school-related inputs like strong teaching.
So many interrelated nonschool factors—family socioeconomic status
(SES), neighborhood context, early-years care and instruction, to name a
few—also influence those scores.[91] Perversely, schools serving high shares
of students from historically marginalized communities have the most
to overcome and often the fewest resources with which to do so.

On the other side of the coin, schools and classrooms serving white
and/or affluent students have viewed state-mandated standardized tests
as a floor, not a ceiling, for performance. This offers more freedom for
creative exploration in classrooms and more time to bring material to
life. A survey of school leaders in the aftermath of NCLB found that just
one in five principals in low-minority schools reported reduced time for
the arts, compared to one in three principals in high-minority schools.[92]
Suburban districts were also less likely than urban ones to decrease instructional time for subjects other than math or language arts.

With the advent of the more rigorous Common Core State Standards, however, even the most privileged schools began to zero in on
content and test preparation. Massachusetts was the only state where
about half of tested students previously had reached proficiency under
the higher Common Core bar; in almost every other state, the vast majority were set up to fail.[93] In New York, after about 70 percent of students flunked the new Common Core aligned tests, a wave of protests
took the form of the "opt out" movement. Roughly one in five New York

students did not take a required standardized test by 2015. And more affluent districts reported higher percentages of students opting out.[94]

This aspect of the backlash against the Common Core raises an interesting question: if our nation's most advantaged families do not think heavy emphasis on test preparation is in the best interests of their kids and schools, why should it be considered good policy for anyone else?

Integrating Schools Improves Equitable Access to Strong, Diverse Teachers

Strong teachers are among the most influential factors within a school when it comes to student performance.[95] The ingredients that go into strong teaching include some combination of experience, subject-matter expertise, rigor and quality of training, adept verbal communication, and warmth.[96] So we know that good teachers are crucial to student success and what kinds of characteristics define them. But we also know that, despite their fundamental importance to student opportunity, quality teachers are perhaps the most unevenly distributed resource in the educational landscape.

In schools, experienced, high-quality teachers are differentially sorted across classrooms, with the strongest instructors often teaching in the least challenging classrooms.[97] These same patterns emerge on a much broader scale within and across school systems.[98] Teachers in struggling, segregated schools get paid the least, miss the most days of work, and turn over most frequently.[99] Punitive accountability and assessment systems, already indicted for stifling creative and challenging curricula, additionally harm teacher hiring and retention efforts in schools serving high concentrations of students in poverty. Once these schools are branded an accountability failure, it's much more difficult for them to recruit and hold strong teachers with plentiful options for employment in less stressful environments.[100] Conversely, more racially and economically diverse schools tend to attract stronger teachers.[101]

During a time of growing racial mismatch between faculties and students, it's critically important to understand that diverse schools are more likely to report diverse faculties than segregated schools.[102]

Intensely segregated white schools (where black and Latinx students made up 10 percent or less of the enrollment) reported in 2006 that 96 percent of the teachers were white, on average. In intensely segregated nonwhite schools (where white students made up 10 percent or less of the enrollment), white teachers accounted for just 38 percent of the faculty. The mutually reinforcing nature of teacher and student segregation is long-standing, as the courts recognized in a number of early desegregation orders.[103]

An example from the Charlotte-Mecklenburg schools brings the teacher-student segregation dynamics to life. In 2001, a federal district judge declared Charlotte-Mecklenburg schools free from court oversight of desegregation despite broad public opposition.[104] A policy that prioritized choice and neighborhood-based student assignment swiftly resegregated students.[105] Economist Kirabo Jackson at Northwestern University used the student assignment policy shift to assess whether or not teachers also resegregated. He found that schools enrolling higher shares of black students after desegregation ended saw a decline in high-quality teachers (defined by years of experience and performance on certification tests). High-quality white *and* black teachers were more likely to leave schools with significant proportions of black students, though the teachers that remained were disproportionately black.[106]

The segregation and resegregation of teachers is damaging. Racially diverse faculties can help model effective cross-racial teamwork and interactions.[107] They create stronger teams in general, because diversity brings new perspectives and insight to complex challenges.[108] They send the message that teachers and leaders can and should come from any racial background. They can reach students with a diverse array of perspectives, needs, and learning styles because they themselves are diverse.[109] Teachers of color on diverse faculties may additionally offer support systems for families and students of color in the school, have higher expectations and produce higher achievement of students of color, and can be more likely to recommend students of color for gifted and talented courses than white teachers. [110] (At the same time, recent evidence suggests that high levels of student diversity in classrooms can help mediate some of the negative impacts associated with student-teacher racial mismatch.[111])

Despite their myriad benefits, racially diverse faculties are all too rare. Many black teachers in the South lost their jobs during the early days of court-ordered desegregation.[112] One study, based on data from 781 Southern school districts between 1964 and 1972, estimated that desegregation led to a 31.8 percent reduction in black teacher employment.[113] Teacher credentials became more salient during this era, a discrimination tactic that effectively thinned the ranks of African American faculty.[114] Past discrimination maps onto contemporary struggles to recruit and retain teachers of color. College enrollment rates and certification and credentialing requirements remain a barrier, as does the diminished status of the teaching profession, the low pay, and the funneling of teachers of color into segregated schools struggling with accountability sanctions.[115]

Integrating Schools Improves Educational Outcomes by Equalizing Funding

Three decades before the resegregation that made Kirabo Jackson's research on student-teacher segregation dynamics possible, Charlotte stood poised to implement one of the nation's farthest-reaching city-suburban school desegregation plans. Within the city, West Charlotte High, a segregated black school, prepared to open its doors to both white and black students for the first time. When they opened, the school boasted new paved parking lots, two tennis courts, and a completely overhauled interior.[116] A West Charlotte student who graduated one year before the desegregation-related upgrades said, "It took integration to get the parking lots paved. Those gravel parking lots had been out there for years, and we had asked and asked for paved parking lots . . . and then I come back when I'm in college, we're one of the model schools and everything's paved, the office is immaculate. And I'm like, what a difference a day makes."[117]

With desegregation, then, came a swift effort to equalize grossly disparate material resources in Charlotte. Those disparities rigidly and intentionally defined segregated education despite the Supreme Court's 1896 "separate but equal" doctrine. Fully funding a dual system of public schools for children living in the same geographic area was expensive, even if white political will had existed to do so. The result: when public schools for black children were provided at all, they were characterized by highly disparate funding. In the Deep South, states typically spent five to six times as much on white students, ranging from $31 to $37 per white student compared to $5 to $7 per black student.[118]

Even when northern philanthropic associations stepped in to fill the void in public financing for black education in the South, black communities had to provide matching dollars. They did, often at great expense. In Alabama, the Rosenwald Fund helped pay for the construction of nearly 350 schools during the early 1900s. Of the total $905,545 spent building the schools, rural black communities, comprised largely of impoverished tenant farmers, raised close to $350,000 with a mixture of public and private efforts. The Rosenwald Fund contributed about $200,000. White taxpayers offered $68,000; black taxpayers roughly $292,000.[119] Black citizens thus bore the significant financial brunt of a system of public school segregation designed to blunt access to the same opportunities afforded white citizens.

With all of this in mind, early legal strategies to dismantle government-sponsored segregation focused on forcing states to equalize spending on white and black schools, reasoning that the outlay would be prohibitively expensive.[120] After a series of victorious lawsuits demanding truly equal facilities for black and white students in higher education, NAACP lawyers turned to the K–12 arena. Would they continue a case-by-case strategy of litigating starkly unequal facilities? Or would they strike at segregation itself? Despite serious internal misgivings, in 1950 Thurgood Marshall helped convince the NAACP's leadership that a direct attack on segregation should guide the organization's legal strategy for elementary and secondary public education.[121] This battle culminated in the five cases that made up the unanimous 1954 *Brown v. Board of Education* decision outlawing state-sponsored segregation.

The "linked fates" theory of school desegregation held that equalization of educational resources would occur once the fortunes of white students were bound up with students of color.[122] In other words, sending black and white students to the same schools would increase the likelihood of more equal educational investment (fiscal and otherwise) across all schools.[123] Desegregation was and continues to be at least partially about resource equalization.

If facility upgrades like those at West Charlotte High represented one dimension of equalization by virtue of school desegregation, reduced pupil to teacher ratios and higher per-pupil expenditures represented others. These resources mattered. One sophisticated study pointed to smaller class sizes and higher per-pupil spending as potential causal mechanisms for an array of long-term benefits for black graduates of desegregated schools.[124] Using large-scale data sets containing information on the life trajectories of black children born between 1945 and 1970, Rucker Johnson, professor of economics at UC Berkeley, concluded that experiencing school desegregation meant increased educational and occupational attainment, attendance at better colleges, higher earnings, and better health outcomes. It also reduced the likelihood of incarceration.[125] Multiple other studies confirm these findings.[126] Moreover, desegregation had an intergenerational effect. Having a black parent who attended desegregated schools was linked to higher achievement and attainment for the next generation.[127] That bears repeating: higher educational attainment linked to school desegregation persisted across generations of black families, underscoring both the importance of desegregation for social mobility and the role parent education plays in reproducing outcomes for children, grandchildren, and beyond.

So, to recap, the benefits of school integration begin early, extend across the life cycle, and reach down through generations. They are multifaceted, connected to gains in learning, achievement, attainment, mobility, prejudice reduction, civic engagement, and democracy. Some of these gains flow from the resources associated with school integration, others from contact with diverse teachers and peers. And benefits accrue most strongly to all students when leaders support and structure frequent contact in ways that promote equal status, cooperation, and shared goals.

We've been accumulating this evidence for decades now, but it has been subsumed beneath a policy regime that favored trying to make separate equal. For leaders and stakeholders involved in contemporary school integration, familiarity with the research base is critical to creating schools that work well for all students—and for building support for more systemic change. As such, this first chapter stands alone as a summary of what we know about segregation, desegregation, and integration, but it also lays critical groundwork for understanding integration efforts at each of the four Richmond area schools. Let's turn to the first of the four, the Sprout School at the Richmond Children's Museum.

CHAPTER 2

The Sprout School

Seeding the Promise of Brown *Through Intentionally Diverse, Early-Years Education*

The classroom for older students at the Sprout School in the Children's Museum of Richmond hums with movement and purpose. Small tables and chairs hug the edges of the room, leaving an open space for circle time and play in front of a set of large bookshelves. A door toward the back of the classroom opens to a secret passageway into the museum. Huge blocks, art supplies, and books featuring a diverse cast of characters are room staples; other toys and activities rotate in and out. Student work papers the room.

Sprout teachers develop a sense of the single garment among their diverse students in a very literal way through something called the string game. My daughter, Posey, and her classmates sit together in a circle while the teachers unwind a huge ball of yarn. Each child and adult in the circle gets to hold a piece. They talk about what it means to be part of a community, saying things like, "You forgive each other!" or "I want to see love in our community and share it" or "We need to help everybody and be nice and work like family." They also talk about what it feels like when friends are kind or hurtful. To illustrate the latter, a teacher will simply cut the string. When someone harms another member of the community, the lesson goes, everyone suffers. The severed thread slices through individual and communal ties, and repairing the breach requires attention to all.

The string game is just one of the many ways this unique preschool has taken on the multidimensional challenge of intentional integration. Leveraging partnerships across the city, the Sprout School—currently with seven classrooms across two locations—combines diversity goals for admission and robust outreach with a rigorous student-centered curriculum to build cross-racial relationships among our youngest citizens and their families. It's a small program, but a powerful example of the way forward for integrating preschool learning environments.

Dynamics of a Segregated Preschool System

The best available national data indicate that about 40 percent of preschool children attend intensely segregated public schools (settings in which 90 percent or more of students are either white or nonwhite). Preschool students are more racially segregated, on average, than their heavily segregated K–12 counterparts.[1]

The Sprout School isn't included in the federal or state statistics on preschool enrollment. We collect very little comprehensive data about US childcare providers, making it difficult to precisely track the scope of segregation and opportunity for our youngest children. Our nonsystemic data collection adheres closely to the nonsystemic provision of early-years care.[2] A lack of public commitment means that a good deal of childcare for infants up to four-year-olds happens in the private or nonprofit sectors, or through informal group home care. This is what experts call a "mixed economy," with providers and families navigating a complex web of public services, transfers, and benefits alongside market-based dealings and private familial and communal arrangements.[3] A patchwork system leaves families with highly differentiated levels of quality, affordability, and availability when it comes to childcare.[4] Across the income spectrum, the typical family spends about a quarter of their annual income on childcare, rising to more than half for single parents.[5] Variable purchasing power at either end of the spectrum too often equates to variable quality—though low-income children benefit most from high-quality programs. These early gaps in opportunity become a serious contributor to later gaps in school achievement.[6]

Breakthroughs in neuroscience, among other fields, point unequivocally to the importance of child development in the earliest years.[7] Partly as a result, ensuring equitable access to high-quality preschool has become a central, bipartisan thrust in education policy circles. Access to racially and economically diverse preschool remains at the outer edges of the debate, however. This must change. For all students, real cognitive, social, and emotional assets emerge from exposure to diverse classrooms at an early age.[8]

Origins of a Diverse Preschool

The vision for Sprout, when I first read about it in the local newspaper, was to create an intentionally mixed-income preschool where one-third of families would pay full tuition, one-third would pay partial tuition, and one-third would receive full subsidies. The Reggio-inspired school aimed to serve children aged two and a half to five and would represent a public-private partnership between the YWCA, Richmond Public Schools' Head Start, the Virginia Preschool Initiative (VPI), and the Children's Museum.[9] The Children's Museum location was poised to open in the fall of 2016, just in time for Posey to join the youngest class. I forwarded the article to my husband with a string of exclamation points and one tiny question mark as preamble. They had me at intentional diversity. Posey adored the Children's Museum. I didn't know what "Reggio-inspired" meant but figured it couldn't hurt. Here was evidence of a new direction for early-years care in the city, based partly on a hunch that parents would see intentional integration as a benefit to their children and their community. It drew me in on both personal and professional levels.

Just why did that particular vision for the school emerge? In a heavily segregated preschool sector, what prompted the emphasis on mixed-income families, along with the progressive curriculum and the Children's Museum partnership? And how might others learn from the Sprout experience? Interviews across the organization's leadership team point to a handful of key ingredients: a mission-driven belief in the power of integration, financial necessity, new leadership with experience managing multiple preschool funding streams, the needs and desires of families, and strong partnerships that yielded a new location, rebranding, and high-quality programming.

YWCA's Mission Drives Provision of Integrated Early-Years Education

The Richmond YWCA has been providing childcare for the city since 1891, a service central to its core mission of "empowering women." The second crucial piece of that mission is "eliminating racism."[10] There's some institutional memory around the Richmond YWCA being at the forefront of the early struggle for racial integration in the South. The director of the Sprout School, Kathleen Eastman, notes that you can see the emphasis on eliminating racism if you "look back at historical stuff on what the YWCA did, like getting a nasty letter from the attorney general because we let black and white women socialize together in the early '60s." Even earlier, in 1930, the Richmond YWCA helped extend the work of the Southern Commission on Interracial Cooperation—an attempt to oppose the most violent outgrowths of Jim Crow, like lynching, without directly confronting segregation.[11]

Fast forward to the present and you can see the seeds for Sprout sown in that early history. The chief executive officer, Linda Tissiere, tied the commitment to integrated education to "[o]ur roots around social justice and the elimination of racism. If you're ever going to be able to help children grow up with the core value of justice for all," she continued, "it has to start when kids are young. They have to be exposed to people that are different than them. Being able to start teaching children when they're two, three, four, and five years old, we believe, is how we're going to change and break that cycle of racism we have." There's truth to this, as we've seen from the research. The earlier and the more equal status the cross-racial contact, the more easily bias can be staved off.

The YWCA's mission made the provision of quality, integrated childcare a natural extension of the organization's work. But something else was behind the launch of the mixed-income preschool model—something that had posed an existential threat to the Richmond YWCA's capacity to provide early-years education at all. It was hemorrhaging money.

Mixed-Income Model Was a Financial Necessity

In 2012, when Tissiere became the new CEO of the Richmond YWCA, her board asked her to begin phasing out the existing preschool program. Enrollment had dwindled to about forty students and the financial cost to the organization was substantial. Feeling as if—back to the mission again—the "empowerment of women can't happen if we aren't taking care of children," Tissiere asked for a year to learn more about the preschool and to try to find a way to rescue it.

Tissiere conducted a "listening tour" when she first began leading the YWCA. Her many prior professional experiences—public radio journalism, community and public relations, middle school Spanish teacher, corporate philanthropy—didn't lend themselves to an immediate or intimate understanding of the challenges confronting the YWCA's preschool. So she visited with stakeholders, internal and external. She met with every staff person. She attended meetings and trainings for the organization's different programs. She read all she could. And she came away understanding that (1) the educational and developmental need for preschool was greater than ever, and (2) the YWCA preschool needed to diversify its funding streams, comprised solely of federal Head Start money and endowment funds, in order to serve more kids.[12]

The basic issue with the former financial model, according to the YWCA's leadership team, was that it cost more to educate children all year and for a full day than the per-student reimbursement from Head Start. Every time the team crunched the numbers, it came up with the same result—to serve a student full day/full year, which was what working families needed, it cost about $10,000. Head Start reimbursed $5,000 per student solely for regular public school hours and only for ten months. Even with the YWCA's established fund-raising potential, trying to close that yearly gap was draining resources away from an already overstretched organization. The preschool was one part of the YWCA's operation; there were many other programs to consider as well.

After learning and listening as much as she could, Tissiere and the rest of the leadership team at the YWCA decided the only way to remain solvent was to offer preschool to both full-pay and subsidized families based on income and need. The team thought that if at least a third of the families were paying full tuition, with another third paying at least some of the cost to educate a full-day child, it would have a narrower gap and could more easily raise the money to cover it.[13]

Along with the hiring of a new chief development officer, Rupa Murthy, in 2015, two other events helped catalyze the one-third full-pay, one-third partial-pay, and one-third no-pay funding model for the YWCA preschools. One was the entrance of a new preschool director with experience leading mixed-income centers. The other was the completion of an evidence-based effort to understand what Richmonders wanted when it came to early-years care.

New Leadership with Experience in Mixed-Income Preschools

Kathleen Eastman speaks quickly and directly, words somersaulting over each other to make their points. As a white woman from a middle-class background, she's warmly curious about other perspectives and traditions, saying, "[They] are what makes life interesting and beautiful and fun." Eastman came to the Richmond YWCA with experience leading intentionally diverse preschools in Boston and Rochester, having overcome various bureaucratic hurdles to educating young students from different racial/ethnic backgrounds and income levels together. Most significantly, she'd figured out a way to bring Head Start and non–Head Start students into the same schools and classrooms through "braiding."[14]

In the suburbs of Boston, Eastman decided to try braiding the Head Start and non–Head Start students together for the first time. "Braiding," she explains, "is when you have kids in the same classroom from different funding sources. When you braid it, they work together but they can all be separated back out . . . in order to show how your class [funding] allocations work." According to the development director, the downtown Sprout location is the only preschool in Richmond currently braiding Head Start kids into classrooms with non–Head Start students.

Over the years, Eastman had heard about proposals to administer Head Start differently through a sliding-scale fee. That made sense to her because "if every child went to Head Start and you just paid according to your means, there'd be no stigma to it." Eastman also noted the political potency of expanding the group benefiting from preschool, saying "it would certainly be funded till the end of time."[15] Her lived experiences had given her an understanding both of how segregation works to stigmatize groups and institutions and of how linking the fates of different groups can yield powerful political and social gains.[16]

Eastman's prior experience with braiding didn't hurt when it came to making the case for doing so at Sprout. Neither did the organization's long-standing relationship with Richmond Public Schools' Head Start program. Still, there have been limits. Braiding is currently happening only at the downtown YWCA preschool. Expanding to the second site at the Children's Museum would mean more classrooms for federal officials to monitor at a separate location—not an insurmountable obstacle, but one just the same.

Surveying Family Needs and Wants

To bring more families on board generally, and to add a diverse range of full- and partial-pay families specifically, the YWCA needed to understand what the Richmond community wanted when it came to early-years care. So in 2015, the organization hired both a consultant and a well-known community facilitator to gain and act upon qualitative knowledge regarding the community's early education needs.

A close reading of the documents generated by this process offers insight into what diverse stakeholders value in early-years care. Highlights from in-depth interviews with twenty area families representing a range of racial/ethnic and socioeconomic backgrounds included a set of technical considerations like cleanliness of facility, parking, and affordability, alongside more normative considerations like knowledgeable staff, strong communication, and loving caregivers for infants.[17] Beyond infant care, variations in values emerged. Some families of older children in the sample wanted strong academic and social skills preparation, lots of structure and consistency, and clear expectations and rules. Others emphasized opportunities for critical thinking, play-based and experiential exploration of the world, and a child-centered curriculum. These preferences didn't cut cleanly across racial/ethnic lines, though lower-income families in the sample were somewhat more likely to emphasize skills and order.[18]

Nearly all of the families interviewed, regardless of race/ethnicity, said they wanted their children educated in an environment that "looks like the real world" in terms of diversity. At the same time, families from a range of income levels expressed concern about preschool settings with "too many" children from any one socioeconomic strata. Without providing actual numbers, families said they were looking for true income diversity.

The report also walked the YWCA through the family decision-making process for early-years care. As in K–12 education, information flowing through social networks plays an outsized role in where families end up.[19] Recommendations from trusted institutions like pediatricians' offices, online research, and/or personal knowledge of an institution also factored into early-years care decisions.

Once the report was complete, YWCA and community leadership spent an early April day in facilitated conversation. The purpose was to move the research into action with an extended brainstorming and planning session. The closing paragraphs from the write-up generated by the day's conversation emphasized local hunger for affordable, diverse preschools:

> There appears to be strong interest among parents from a variety of backgrounds for care beyond the small, expensive, niche programs within the city that currently are perceived to offer the highest quality programs. Young, city-dwelling families ("Millennials") appear to be interested in remaining within the City of Richmond and are seeking quality childcare and educational opportunities for their children that mirror their values of community and diversity.[20]

To build what the community wanted, major, interrelated takeaways from the day included developing key partnerships, rebranding the YWCA's childcare offerings to positively influence word-of-mouth exchanges, and adopting the Reggio Emilia curriculum.

Building Preschool Diversity Through Partnerships

Partnerships enabled the YWCA to accomplish many of the goals emerging from its research-based brainstorming. These partnerships, which included the Children's Museum, Head Start, the state-funded VPI, a local advertising firm, and an elite private school, often stemmed from preexisting relationships. And they were vital, given the lack of public funding to support the development of diverse preschools, along with the piecemeal nature of early-years care.

The partnership that yielded a new YWCA preschool location at the Children's Museum percolated for several years, strengthened by Tissiere's relationship building. A leadership change at the Children's Museum delayed collaboration, but progress finally came when a new executive director for the museum was hired. With previously cultivated trust between the two executives, both organizations agreed to move forward.[21] They shared missions aimed in part at children and viewed the partnership as mutually beneficial.[22]

Around the same time, an offer of pro bono branding assistance came from a member of the YWCA's board who worked at a well-known local advertising firm. With the new mixed-income model, new location, and curriculum, Tissiere said, "[W]e recognized that we needed to call this preschool something different than the Child Development Center at the YWCA." Research on school integration suggests that she was right. The YWCA had to unravel the stigma associated with its segregated downtown preschool if it wanted to appeal to a broader range of families. After looking at results from the market research and brainstorming session, the partnering advertising firm offered some recommendations. The YWCA piloted those initial names with informal focus groups and ultimately settled on the Sprout School. Two new preschool classrooms at the Children's Museum became the Sprout School at the Children's Museum and the five downtown YWCA classrooms became the Sprout School at the YWCA.

Another relationship emerged. This time it was with an area private school specializing in the Reggio Emilia approach. After reading about Sprout in the local newspaper, Mary Driebe, a teacher at the

Sabot School, went to her director and said, "Why are we not involved in this?" Sabot subsequently offered some sessions geared at training YWCA teachers in the Reggio method. And Driebe went on to become the Reggio consultant for the YWCA. Reggio was a final, fundamental piece related to the redesign of the YWCA's preschool offerings.

Building Preschool Diversity Through High-Quality Programming

The YWCA's interest in Reggio, a child-centered curriculum, dated back "many, many moons," according to Tissiere. Familiarity with the approach, combined with the fact that Reggio worked well overlaid on the Head Start and VPI curricular standards, made it a natural fit. Its play- and inquiry-based approach was also the preferred choice of the Children's Museum, following in the footsteps of a similar preschool-museum partnership in Portland, Oregon. Given the push to draw in full-pay families, it didn't hurt that two high-status, well-known local preschool centers also utilized the Reggio approach. And finally, although some families had preferred a more traditional emphasis on skills building, the qualitative research with local stakeholders had turned up considerable interest in progressive preschool models.

Turning again to the importance of changing the narrative of the school, Tissiere told me, "Everyone perceives us as a Head Start center with a Head Start curriculum, so we need to look at what kind of curriculum is out there that is considered best practice that would be attractive to non–Head Start families and that aligned very well with the creative curriculum that we were [already] doing." The Reggio approach, in other words, would become part of Sprout's revamped identity even as it also became a crucial opportunity for rethinking teaching and learning.

These various elements—mission alignment, financial necessity, leadership with experience navigating diverse preschools, surveys of community needs, strategic partnerships, and a focus on high-quality programming—all contributed to a new Richmond preschool focused on income diversity in the midst of a broader landscape of preschool segregation. Let's now turn to how Sprout navigated the first hurdle of integration—successfully getting a diverse group of kids into the same school together.

Sprout and External Integration

External factors related to integration in preschool (and other grade-levels) include things like strong outreach, innovative curricula, faculty diversity, easy-to-access locations, and student diversity goals.[23] Fundamentally, families have to know about a preschool choice before they can make it. The uneven nature of early-years education means that, unlike public K–12 schools, there's no centralized assignment of children to any one preschool location. All families are making choices across splintered sectors of care. The Sprout School and its leadership and staff took these factors into account to make its integrated model viable.

Varied, Extensive Marketing and Outreach

Communicating information about the new Sprout location at the Children's Museum to as wide a group of families as possible had to be the initial priority. The director, Eastman, was convinced that appealing locations, strong programming in the form of Reggio, and a new name would yield success. She instinctively understood what we've learned from K–12 magnet schools: draw matters when it comes to attracting a diverse group of families.[24] Eastman told me, "[T]he cachet, the Children's Museum, would bring in families like yourself, but it wouldn't stop there . . . it would spread and the Sprout name would allow us to bring in full pay children downtown, at other locations—and that's happened."

I should note here that when I first began the research for this chapter, I didn't fully realize there *were* multiple Sprout preschool locations. I thought the downtown YWCA was a separate entity. It's not though; the programmatic overhauls discussed in these pages slowly have been aimed at both locations. As Eastman's quote reveals, the idea was to fully establish the new mixed-income and curricular model at the Children's Museum location first, and then to begin infusing it into the downtown Sprout. I focus mainly on Sprout at the Children's Museum because it offers an example of full implementation. Still, I don't ignore what's happening at the downtown Sprout, as it's very much a part of the larger vision for the YWCA's new preschool model.

In fact, Eastman's hunch was correct: the cachet of the Children's Museum drew a range of families. The central branch of the museum is located in the heart of the city, near the local ballpark, a science museum, and the Redskins' training camp. It's easily accessible via public transit. Through its "Access for All" fund, the Children's Museum offers free annual memberships to local families making less than $35,000 a year, along with "summer service days" with free admission for emergency medical technicians, firefighters, police officers, military members, and veterans. Murthy, describing a series of open houses before the Sprout School at the museum location opened, said, "Because [the Children's Museum] is a trusted organization with families, we get families from everywhere, all walks. It's a really cool feeling to have an open house there and see how many families are looking for a diverse preschool. So I think the Children's Museum has . . . gotten new people in the door [of Sprout]."

Later, once children were enrolled, class time in the museum became a walking advertisement for Sprout. On any given day, you might find a group of about twenty-five racially and economically diverse preschoolers, including my daughter, outfitted in beige Sprout School T-shirts, busily constructing projects in a large art space, serving each other food in the pretend diner, or playing in little wooden houses outside. Ms. Janelle, one of the teachers, says that when families in the museum ask about the school, she tells them, "This is a great opportunity. Your child will learn so much and it's a great, diverse school."

The museum wasn't the only form of outreach, of course. Because the YWCA serves Head Start and VPI families and students, the organization benefits from the outreach and networks those programs have established. As Murthy said, "Head Start has been a huge amplifier of our mission because they're recruiting in neighborhoods that we may not be in." Serving children younger than the traditional three- or four-year-old Head Start/Early Head Start students has also helped. Murthy calls the new eighteen-month-old toddler room added by the YWCA to its downtown location "the farm team" for the older Sprout programming. Another point of entry: survivors of domestic violence who seek help through the YWCA have access to scholarship spots in the Sprout program. During weekly counseling sessions, their children are free to participate in school activities.

Beyond the open houses and the word-of-mouth exchanges facilitated by the Children's Museum, Head Start, and VPI, early publicity
helped disseminate information about the new Sprout location. At least
one teacher and two families I spoke with heard a Sprout-related interview Murthy and Eastman did on public radio. Driebe, the Reggio consultant, and I read about it in the newspaper. There's an ongoing social
media campaign on Facebook and a team of people who fan out into area
rec centers to drop off fliers (though not, as of yet, in multiple languages,
representing a barrier to access for families who don't speak English as
a first language). An easy-to-read website communicates key information about the program and application and enrollment procedures. It
includes emails and phone numbers for more personal contact and offers information about waiving application fees as needed. The Sprout
School sets up tables at different community events, too. And the YW-
CA's leadership team had so many different ties into the community that
it was easy to ask local officials and elected leaders to get the word out.

Sprout's extensive and varied outreach efforts appear to be working.
My husband and I first met Eastman in August 2016, about two weeks
before the two Sprout classrooms at the Children's Museum opened.
She was giving us a tour, explaining the Reggio approach and how the
museum would facilitate experiential learning. Her response to my
question about the value of racial and economic diversity in preschool
was spot on and heartfelt. When she finished, we said, "Sign us up."

We weren't the only ones. The intentional income diversity, the museum, the location, and the curriculum offered a range of potentially
appealing organizational aspects. Interviews with current families at
Sprout at the Children's Museum illustrate how those various components, along with word of mouth and outreach, worked together to create
the first two classes of diverse students. They also highlight the perpetuating nature of school desegregation—nearly all of the interviewees had
experience with diverse school settings in their own childhoods.[25]

For instance, one mother, who is white, grew up attending public magnet schools across the South. She valued diversity for her own
daughter, April, because, she said, "I don't think it benefits you to only

be around people who agree with you or have your exact experience . . . [Diversity] just makes your life a little fuller and . . . gives you a greater sense of empathy when you see how people live differently."

April's mom learned about Sprout at the Children's Museum after picking up some information at a museum table. She already knew about the YWCA's preschool program because she had referred families to it as part of her role with a local school system. April's mom was seeking a diverse daycare facility, but wanted "actual diversity" because her daughter had been the only white kid in her former preschool. She heard a ringing endorsement of Sprout from a friend who already sent her child there. To top it off, the creative, child-centered curriculum appealed to her: "I wanted her to still have fun and play and go at her own pace and not just sit and learn ABCs." This last statement dovetailed with other families seeking more progressive early-years instruction.

The African American mom of another one of Posey's peers, Jasmine, heard about Sprout from her cousin. She did some research, applied, called, and attended an open house. The fact that tuition was based on income was important because "as hard as you work, even with a college degree, they're not paying you enough." This mother didn't want to live beyond her means and was familiar with the YWCA because she'd worked for it as a teenager. The intentional diversity struck a note with her, partly because she went to diverse schools herself. "That was the way I was raised, and I'd prefer my child to be in that environment," she said, adding, "otherwise they won't be comfortable in the real world. I want her to know how to interact with different cultures, different people from different walks of life. Different religions. Everything."

Shiloh's mother, who is Jewish and emigrated to the United States with refugee status as a child, said that her early experiences grappling with anti-Semitism in her former country led her to seek out diversity for her children. She liked that Sprout was a school "where lots of different kids from different backgrounds could attend"; she loved that it was in a museum and was intrigued by the curriculum. "I read up on it," she told me, "and I just really liked the Reggio Emilia method of education. I thought it would fit Shiloh's curiosity and personality." She'd heard about Sprout through a YWCA fund-raiser and also knew another family (ours) who'd chosen it for their child. Her children had left the previous daycare we had attended together partly for religious reasons but also because "most of the students were Caucasian and most of the teachers were African American. We wanted something more," she explained, "where Shiloh was exposed to different types of kids and different types of teachers and didn't see those roles as how the world is."

Racially Diverse Faculty Attract Racially Diverse Students— and Vice Versa

Shiloh's mom was onto something—the racial makeup of teachers *is* a key part of attracting a diverse group of families through the schoolhouse door. Remember that faculty desegregation became a critical component of the legal desegregation process after *Brown*.[26] Recall, too, that school diversity and faculty diversity are interrelated; a more diverse student body is linked to a more diverse faculty.[27] (Faculty diversity is also an important internal integration issue; I'll talk more about how this plays out at Sprout in the section below.)

Sprout at the Children's Museum employs a racially diverse teaching staff, 50 percent white and 50 percent black, with very little turnover. Organizational leadership feels strongly that staff diversity contributes to the strength and health of the YWCA. CEO Tissiere openly acknowledges that her white, middle-class background doesn't always align with the people served by the organization, saying, "I need to rely on others to help me understand where are clients are coming from, where our families are coming from. What does that look like, how does that feel, and how can we best help them?"

Tissiere went on to say that she wouldn't be able to make sound decisions without soliciting careful input from a diverse group of organizational leaders, staff, and stakeholders. Research suggests that she's right, finding that more diverse groups consistently come up with better ways of understanding and solving problems.[28] Eastman and Murthy felt similarly, extending that basic idea to the importance of hiring diverse new staff members. They both said that the YWCA is very conscious of building diverse leadership and faculty. Murthy explains why: "You know the leadership in our schools, the lead teachers, it's all very intentional, it's part of who we are so we try really hard to hire African American teachers so that our African American students can, you know, see themselves in the teachers they love and they learn from."

Sprout at the Children's Museum's diverse group of teachers learned about it through many of the same information channels and came for many of the same reasons as the diverse set of families. One teacher heard about the new museum school, the intentional diversity, and the Reggio approach on the radio. Another one worked at the downtown location and wanted to be a part of the Reggio launch at the museum. Still others knew the YWCA as an organization or heard about the new preschool from former colleagues. These formal and informal exchanges—through diverse networks rather than segregated ones—grew the staff quickly.

It helped that the pay was comparatively good, too, which was important to the YWCA as it worked to fulfill the "empowering women" aspect of its mission. Though many early childcare organizations are committed to disrupting intergenerational poverty for their students, the pay (averaging $10 per hour) in these centers often leaves workers below the poverty line themselves. Childcare is the second-lowest-paid occupation in the country, impacting a workforce that is majority female and far more racially and ethnically diverse than the K–12 teacher one.[29] By preschool, teacher wages improve marginally (averaging $14 per hour).[30] Because the pay remains so low, childcare workers seeking higher education don't always see a financial benefit. Though a degree raises hourly wages, it doesn't always increase them enough to pay for itself. This can lead workers to seek employment elsewhere.

Sprout works to pay teachers as much as possible, up to $14 per hour. Perhaps relatedly, the majority of Sprout at the Children's Museum teachers have either started or completed postsecondary education. Eastman said, "We try to bring [pay] up to the standard of living but it's hard. This is a profession and I think it's going to be hard until we actually agree as a country to support early childhood. As long as you're asking parents, who are at the beginning of their careers, to pay for part of it, it's impossible." She trailed off, in an uncharacteristic loss for words.

Committing to Diversity Goals

At various points in the development of Sprout, Tissiere, Murthy, and Eastman paused to imagine what it might mean for their mixed-income model if the school were ever to face overwhelming interest from full-pay families. They were more worried—needlessly it turns out—about a lack of interest. No matter what happened, they hoped to adhere to the mixed-income commitments—one-third full pay, one-third partial, and one-third fully subsidized. These were the income diversity goals tied closely into the YWCA's mission. The goals became guideposts as the leadership navigated rising interest in the Sprout School programs and in the Sprout at the Children's Museum in particular.

Sprout is now oversubscribed, and Eastman operates a dual waiting list, one for families who qualify for subsidies and one for families who don't. This helps her ensure that economic diversity goals are met, though she admits it can still be challenging at times. For one, sibling preferences—important for family stability, convenience, and satisfaction—can slowly unbalance a school. And the financial necessity of the mixed-income model is an additional pressure on the diversity goals; an overload of interest from affluent families is good for school resources on the one hand, but bad for the diversity at the core of its mission on the other. The organization mostly has weathered these challenges over the past several years, but it requires constant vigilance and commitment.

External integration efforts have allowed Sprout at the Children's Museum to approximate its income diversity goals from the first year of inception. Strong outreach, positive exchanges of information about the school through heterogeneous social networks, appealing locations and programming, an easy-to-navigate enrollment process, and a stable and diverse teaching staff yielded an economically and racially diverse enrollment. In 2017, 37 percent of Sprout at the Children's Museum families earned incomes that amounted to more than $75,000 a year for a family of four, which translated to 300 percent or more of the federal poverty level.[31] Twenty-two percent earned incomes at or below the federal poverty level, which in 2017 was $24,600 for a family of four.[32] The remaining 40 percent earned incomes between 100 percent and 300 percent of the federal poverty level.[33]

In terms of racial diversity, about 60 percent of the students at the Children's Museum location identified as black, 37 percent as white, and 3 percent as other race in 2017. The lack of Latinx students at this location is noteworthy, given rapid increases in the Latinx enrollment in the region's K–12 schools. National numbers indicate that Latinx students are least likely to enroll in preschool, however, and Sprout has not yet begun publishing its marketing and outreach materials in multiple languages.[34] The Latinx community is also geographically concentrated and isolated south of the James River, relatively far from the Sprout schools' more central location.

Economic diversity was closely but not wholly linked to racial diversity at Sprout at the Children's Museum. In a city that, like so many others, struggles with the deeply entangled legacies of racial segregation and intergenerational poverty, about 80 percent of black families served by Sprout at the Children's Museum were below or close to the federal poverty line. At the same time, 20 percent were in the highest income bracket for the school. The imperfect correlation between race and poverty is important for two reasons. First, it helps prevent students, families, and teachers at the school from reflexively categorizing poverty and race together. Second, in a society hurtling toward a system of courts that refuses to recognize the ongoing salience of race, socioeconomic status may be held up as a substitute.[35] These data, though based on one school, at least point to the pitfalls of using poverty as proxy for race in school desegregation efforts or affirmative action programs.[36]

When it comes to Sprout at the Children's Museum, we've seen evidence of successful external integration. In other words, there's racial and economic diversity at the school, a precondition for the work of internal integration. But it's just a first layer. Internal integration, including curriculum, relationships, resources, and structures, helps Sprout's leadership and faculty nurture all of its diverse students.

Sprout and Internal Integration

On a row of high shelves in the Forest Room sits a photograph of Marcus. He's nearly four, squinting into the sun a little bit, smiling, about to say something to whoever is taking his picture. Underneath is a pencil sketch of himself based on the photo. A word-for-word narrative of his explanation of the picture is typed out beside it: "I look like my daddy. I like the color blue. I'm going to look like my daddy but he's going to work . . . If I know I'm going to school I'm part of a community." Beside him is Ashlee, who's five, with soft brown pigtails and luminescent light brown skin: "I draw my hand, arms, and legs and body and head, hair, my eyes are a hole. I draw everything about me. I like my hair the way it is!" Shiloh is next, her picture displaying a petite four-year-old with pale skin and very long, wavy brown hair: "This is my lips, eyes and nose and my red face because I have a red face. I like my braids like Moana's mommy . . . I'm just dying to be five!"

The self-portrait activity is quintessential Reggio: a blend of discovery, creativity, and community. From it, we catch glimpses of emergent identities for the children, race still at the periphery, surfacing occasionally when it comes to crayon colors. Affirmation of these budding identities, racial and otherwise, is developmentally important, leading the Sprout teachers to build a whole unit around "Who am I?" There's something innately positive about the activity itself—the taking of the portrait, the encouragement to draw yourself, the unedited documentation of your thoughts as you're drawing, the proud display of everyone's work afterward.

Addressing Race at Sprout at the Children's Museum

Integrated preschool classrooms that bring white children together with children of color offer opportunities for conversations about race beginning at a young age and unfolding naturally. As a parent and researcher, I was curious about how the staff reacted and guided these conversations.

Teachers in the Forest Room classroom at the Children's Museum (children are sorted by age; this room serves kids ages three and a half to five) noted that drawing is an activity where race regularly surfaces in class conversation. This was especially true for the older students in the room. One teacher described a close, cross-racial friendship between two five-year-old girls. Isla was doing a portrait of her friend and grew frustrated because she couldn't find just the right shade to capture Ashlee's skin. In another case, two children casually engaged in drawing-table conversation about the differences between their skin colors.

"There was one incident where a child may have asked of the color of another child's skin or pointed it out," one of Posey's teachers told me.

"How'd you respond?" I asked.

"Well, we kind of did not have to," she said, thinking back to the moment. "One of the children who was white was coloring and pointed out their skin color: 'I have white skin.' Another child was coloring and said they had brown skin. And they just went back and forth just discussing the color of skin and eventually it just died down. Until they say 'why [is there a difference]?,' we basically have not talked about it, not purposefully. Until then, let us not go too far with them, wait for them to come to us."

Her response was very much in keeping with a Reggio orientation—the teacher observing the interaction, pausing to see where the kids would take it and weighing options from there. And it's not unaligned with what developmental psychologists have recommended when it comes to talking with children aged three to five about race.[37]

The teacher continued, though, pointing to some ways the school could more directly address race and difference within the Reggio framework. She told me: "So, it might look like a provocation [something that sparks interest or thinking]. Okay, for example—'I have a dream.' We may put something on the table. Like maybe a Martin Luther King book that we have read the day before. The provocation would be, 'What's your dream?' And the [kids] can sit there and write out or draw what their dream is. And that comes from the book."

She gives the teachers room to grow here, too, saying, "[W]e're still learning as we go."[38] The idea is a balance between child-led exploration of areas of interest and adult-guided instruction on matters fundamentally important to cognitive and social development.

In the younger Sprout at the Children's Museum classroom—children ages two and a half to three and a half—observations and conversations about racial differences emerge with less regularity. They're usually talking about "the color of their shirts and pants," one of the teachers in the older classroom observed with a smile. The younger students in this age group are just beginning to grapple with categorizing things as alike and dissimilar, a practice gently encouraged by teachers in the room.

Teachers and families connected to the younger Sky classroom did converge upon a single, powerful story when asked whether and how race surfaced. It's an anecdote that turns on its head the findings from Kenneth and Mamie Clark's famous 1940s-era doll experiments, in which a majority of black and white child participants preferred white dolls and assigned them positive characteristics.[39] Seventy-plus years later, Sprout staff and families reported that one of the white students desperately wanted the same skin color as her black teacher and peers. Ms. Janelle explained, "Lila wanted to be the same complexion as me. She wanted to be brown like me. Her mom said she almost broke down in tears, saying that she just loves me and loves her friends and just wants to be brown." After hearing this story from Lila's mom, Ms. Janelle, her serene assuredness on full display, pulled aside the little girl and said, "You don't have to be the same color as me. You are my special friend and it's okay to be different, we can still be special friends. So it's okay if you want to be brown, but you don't have to be because you are special in your own way and own skin."

Ms. Janelle's response, as appropriate and sensitive as it was, grew more from instinct than training. An area for growth emerging from my initial set of Sprout interviews centered on the need for more direct training on working with diverse kids and families. As one teacher said, "We've never had any formal discussions or professional development. I feel like maybe we should." Though a faculty member had some exposure to material about teaching across cultures in a community college course, she was the exception, not the rule. Follow-up conversations revealed that a well-regarded training session for all YWCA staff had taken place, run by an outside consultant and revolving around personal identity. Further practice for the faculty may make it easier to more intentionally introduce race and justice into the curriculum and into interactions with families.

Trusting Relationships Among Racially Diverse Faculty

Regular interactions among the small, diverse faculty, formal and informal, have solidified a close-knit teaching community at Sprout at the Children's Museum. To a person, the teachers describe trusting relationships among the staff. Said one African American faculty member, "We work so well with one another even though we are all different in our ethnic backgrounds." For her, the Sprout relationships contrasted sharply with her previous preschool, where leadership seemed to treat staff differently based on race or ethnicity. Other Sprout at the Children's Museum teachers talked about being a family and how supportive the team was during times of struggle or crisis.

Caring relationships among teachers served as a built-in resource for dialogue about how to handle difference in the classroom. Faculty brought various strengths and perspectives to those conversations—and to their teaching more generally. For instance, the interracial staff of Sprout at the Children's Museum debriefed about some of the drawing episodes during their training break. Ms. Brittany, a black faculty member, described the benefits linked to staff diversity: "We are different in our backgrounds so that we learn from each other and it's easy to teach the children. Also if I don't know the answer to something [related to race or difference,] I can ask and it's fine because we all learn from each other." One of the white teachers volunteered, "Yeah, we totally support each other. I always feel like we make jokes." She illustrated this with a tale of being asked to fix the hair of one of her black students, the results of which prompted her to find Ms. Brittany to say, "Um, I really messed up Jacqueline's hair, can you help it?" And Ms. Brittany laughed and showed her how to do it. These teacher relationships help model and normalize positive cross-racial interactions for the students.[40]

Leadership Supportive of Contact Across Lines of Difference

School and teacher leadership that supports contact across lines of difference is crucial to successful internal integration. Eastman spoke fervently about the importance of recognizing and reveling in difference, while at the same time drawing attention to the things that universally connect us. Positive leadership around diversity is critical to both facilitating positive intergroup contact and creating a work environment filled with purpose and meaning.[41] She smiled and said, "When my daughter was little, she was in an integrated program, because I worked in integrated programs, so she went to my programs. And she said, 'You know, mommy, there are a little bit brown people, there are brown people and there are yellow people.' And to me, it was like, kids recognize differences, they recognize them very early and you need to help them understand which differences are important and which differences aren't."

So when kids first begin to notice racial or cultural differences, she honors their observations, while also making a point of helping them understand shared similarities. Eastman communicates the same messages to parents and teachers, too. Sometimes she does an exercise where she asks participants to brainstorm about what's different and what's the same between varying cultures. "The things that are the same [across cultures] are the things that matter," she explained. "You know, family, we take care of our children, we want to be successful . . . [T]he things that didn't matter are just kind of these surface things, of how we did that." Ultimately, she wants her school community to know that "[w]hat matters between human beings is respect and working together and trying to bring everybody up. And that, you know, it's not a competitive thing. You don't have to—somebody doesn't have to fail for you to win. We can all work together."

In contrast to national numbers indicating that white students are the most racially isolated, a majority of white Sprout leaders and faculty describe exposure to racial diversity in schools growing up—and point to it as an important component of why they wanted to teach in a diverse setting.[42] This bolsters the idea that desegregation is perpetuating, so that early experiences with racial diversity lead people to seek it out later in life.[43] With few exceptions, white leaders and teachers at the school seemed comfortable talking about race, including their own whiteness and related privilege. The black Sprout faculty were less likely to experience exposure across racial lines as students themselves but welcomed it in their current setting. One of the black teachers put it this way: "Everybody needs to be open to grow. That's what diversity brings—a new way of thinking."

Building an Intentional, Caring Preschool Community

At Sprout, there's plenty of room in the Reggio curriculum for paying attention to community.[44] Circle time serves as a primary space for doing so. At least once a day, the kids and the teachers gather on the rug in the shape of something that more or less resembles a circle. They read books, play games (like the string game described at the beginning of the chapter), and share art, among other activities, all of which gives the teachers a chance to "read experiences in the classroom and what they're interested in." A regular game involves going around the circle and sharing how you're feeling. Sometimes the teachers transcribe the conversation and read it back to the kids; other times they'll pass out a mirror so the kids can see their faces when they talk about different emotions. The power in the game, according to the faculty, revolves around listening and being heard. "Maybe there isn't a right or good answer [to the feelings]," explained one of the teachers. "That's a good thing to learn at a young age . . . but you also know that your peers and teachers are listening to you." Families also referenced the feelings game in their interviews. Shiloh's mom said, "Coming from a therapist background, I think [the game] is amazing because kids are able to identify feelings . . . [S]tarting them at an early age just increases their emotional spectrum in the future."

Mealtimes further showcase the emphasis on community. All of the students at Sprout at the Children's Museum, from age two and a half to five, sit in mixed-race groups around the two classrooms for lunch. They sing together, hands in their laps, waiting for the food to arrive at the table. It's served on large plates, and the kids have learned to pass it around, serve themselves, and share the portions. One of the Forest Room teachers, whose quiet presence radiates empathy when she talks about her students, told me that you can hear lots of "'Can you pass this,' or 'I'm so hungry, get it on my plate,' or 'Next time I won't pour so much milk' . . . [T]he kids think about the food on their plates, their friend's plates and how much is left." Meals, too, are a time when you can observe the development of more expressive language in action.[45] One teacher told me: "I know Aaron will say something and the other kids will be like 'Wow, what does that mean? What are you talking about?' And he'll say back, 'Oh, it means this.' It's really funny to hear them talk about stuff at lunch, they are definitely sharing language too."

Sometimes those language exchanges lead to conflict. Eastman talked about several middle-class families at her socioeconomically integrated center in Rochester who decided to leave, saying to her, "I'm out, that kid is swearing all the time, I'm out." She thinks integration gets harder for families of school-age kids who want to avoid peers who may have been "exposed to more and hurt more and done more." When I asked her how she handles those conversations with unhappy families, she looked at me and replied, "How do you?" But she went on to explain that she asks specifically what families are seeing at home that's raising concerns and then spends time empathizing. And she also tells families, "You need to talk to your child about what the teachers are doing. The teachers are here to keep everybody safe, they're here to help because, you know, he's going to see these things throughout his life. Things are going to happen that, you know, disturb the equilibrium."

Relationships Between Family and School

Working to establish the conditions for intergroup contact among families linked to a school is nearly always overlooked as a component of school-community engagement. There are so many other competing demands on educators. But families provide a good deal of the leadership that's key to positive contact across racial lines.[46]

At Sprout at the Children's Museum, frequent contact between families of different means and races does occur. In addition to the daily drop-offs and pickups, families are welcome on the field trips and are regularly invited to various classroom celebrations. Still, aside from engaging with the students, there's little opportunity in these moments for adults to get to know one another in a structured way.

When I can, I venture out to meet Posey's class and its associated families on field trips. Posey loves the rides with her friends in the YWCA's big orange-and-white van. One brisk day, after walking about a quarter mile from our house, I find Posey and her classmates disembarking from the van into a small parking lot. A handful of parents and grandparents are there to meet them for a visit to one of Byrd Park's three lakes. Today, the lakes are enjoyed for what they add to the scenery and sometimes for fishing. In the not-so-distant past, they were whites-only public swimming areas—shuttered when desegregation threatened to open the water to physical contact between blacks and whites.

Several generations later, Posey's racially diverse classmates meander along the path surrounding the lakes, teachers and families interspersed among them, scouting for fish, geese, and turtles. The lead teacher, who resembles a tall, graceful willow tree in the landscape behind her, finds a good spot for the class to gather. The children play Duck, Duck, Goose in the thin spring sunshine, Aiden's grandmother gamely chasing one of the kids around the circle. The children take turns tagging each other, cheering on both the chaser and the runner, giggling, scooting in beside one another in search of safety. There's fluid interracial contact among the children (here's Marcus looking at a goose and saying, "I like his eye!" and here's Posey cackling next to him, "I like his booty!"), along with evidence of teachers seeking to bolster struggling-in-the-moment children (here's Ms. Stephanie hugging Daniella close and saying, "Let's observe and draw these geese together").

The family members in attendance smile quietly at one another and focus on the children. I think about how a little more structure to our conversations and interactions might help us overcome some of the walls erected by adulthood and systemic racial separation. But I also see the challenges and distractions for families of this age group, too, as Jackie's dad warns her away from the edge of the water and Posey dissolves over the prospect of tacos for lunch (and my eminent departure). With children present, adult icebreakers would need to be built into or around the students' activities—short, simple, with the possibility of familiarity developing over time.

Walking back to the van, one of the teachers provides gentle discipline for a wayward blonde straggler. Holding onto his hand, Ms. Laura calmly lays out a consequence that flows from the behavior: "Tucker, you're sticking with me because you ran off and it scared me."[47] Tucker complies, trotting along beside her toward the parking lot.

Equal Status for Students at Sprout at the Children's Museum

A couple months later, I'm on the playground with the older students at Sprout at the Children's Museum, observing group dynamics during what's probably the least regulated part of the day. Posey, Shiloh, and Marcus are ducking in and out of a little play house, laughing and chasing. Two pairs of five-year-olds, one male, one female, both interracial, are playing at either end of the yard. A white student who's been struggling to maintain constructive relationships with her peers during morning activities is off by herself. I see one of the teachers quietly approach and initiate a conversation. Suddenly the teacher exclaims, "Guys, come over, Violet found a spider! It's alive!" In the frenzied rush to see Violet's discovery, her status increases and she assumes a proprietary air over the spider. "Don't kill it," she instructs her classmates.

This kind of teacher-student interaction, defined by close observation and a gentle intervention into kids' worlds to elevate or repair social status, was readily in evidence throughout my various observations. It's part of Reggio's—and preschool's—general emphasis on community and relationships. It's also a critical component of the conditions for positive intergroup contact and, relatedly, for internal integration.[48]

Equal status among students comes into play during instruction, too. Children enter the program at different starting points and move along the continuum of learning at different paces, especially given the age range in each classroom. In response, teachers work to "generate different experiences and scenarios." They offer the example of writing names to sign into the classrooms (mimicking the adult requirement to sign students into school). Some of the students carefully work on the first letter and then "scribble a bit." But instructors view that writing just the same as those who can write out their first and second name.

They don't call attention to the differences but do allow students to trace and teach each other their names. There's a concerted effort to encourage collaboration and to look to other children for help. "At different times, different kids get to be the expert or the mentor," said one teacher. During a focus group session, the staff shared that the new parents reported that their kids loved Sprout because "instead of giving us the answers, [the teachers] help us help each other."[49]

When questioned about whether they worked to promote equal status among their charges, teachers affiliated with both classrooms reflexively responded with a variation on "of course." One of the Forest Room faculty said, "I try my best to share my love with all of them, to spend personal time with them, to teach them all the same things or something different if they want. That's a real value." And in the Sky Room, "I treat these kids like they're my own children. When people ask me how many kids I got, I tell them all the time, fourteen. My class count." Though bias, unconscious or conscious, seeps into classrooms in many different forms, a good starting point for equity and diversity work is the principle these Sprout at the Children's Museum teachers articulated: what would schools look like if every kid was my kid?[50]

Strong Outcomes for a Promising Preschool Integration Model

We see many different aspects of internal integration at work in Sprout at the Children's Museum. Community and collaboration define relationships across lines of difference between students, teachers, families, and leaders. Trust helps hold many of those relationships together during moments of confusion or conflict. There's time for developing children's interests, imagination, and empathy within a framework of equal status contact. Areas of growth also emerge—integration is continuous work—around teacher-led antibias curricula and teacher training for diverse classrooms.

Overall, though, like the external integration outcomes for Sprout at the Children's Museum, internal ones are strong. All children are going to kindergarten "writing their first name and most can also write their last name. They know the vast majority of their letters, at least upper case, and basic math skills like counting, patterning and sorting," reported the director, based on individual assessments. Family surveys and interviews yielded high levels of satisfaction, and observations and interviews highlighted leaders' and faculty's commitment to diversity, growth, and improvement, alongside a strong sense of purpose. Equal status interactions and opportunities for collaboration among faculty and students abounded.

It's May of 2018 and rain soaks the families scrambling up the grand front entrance to the downtown YWCA. Gift bags for the students are piled in the hall, and music is thumping out of the gym. Many of the kids are in their Sunday finest, girls in dresses, tights, and Mary Janes; boys in miniature suits. This is the annual Sprout School dance, a chance for both locations to come together and celebrate. It's a racially diverse crowd, about 70 percent black and 30 percent white. The Sprout at the Children's Museum kids are mixing together freely, a younger group that includes Posey dodging through clumps of families in a game of chase, and an older one showing off dance moves. Teachers are serving food and drinks from behind a long table. Kathleen Eastman is there, periodically breaking into the Running Man dance and trying to entice families onto the dance floor. I see Linda Tissiere standing at the edge of the crowded room smiling, taking in the evidence of the past several years' work.

I'm terrible at remembering to take pictures, but my husband isn't. One that he captured stays with me when I think about Sprout at the Children's Museum. Four young girls, two white, two black, stand in a close circle with their arms wrapped tightly around each other. They're all laughing, delighting in the moment. Posey is among them, raising her eyebrows as if to say, "Isn't this wonderful?" Yes, Posey, it is.

CHAPTER 3

Ecoff Elementary School

Using Attendance Zones, Leadership, and
Curricula to Support Suburban Integration

I TURN OFF THE WINDING, two-lane road into Ecoff Elementary School's entrance early one morning in 2018, the June heat ascending but not yet oppressive. A line of cars is snaking through the parking lot, families and students idling patiently until the front doors open. I've come to interview the principal at Ecoff, where intentional integration efforts are in full bloom.

Ecoff's students walk into an environment rich with symbolic affirmations of diversity. Brick lines the walls of the front hall for the first eight feet or so, but above it is a sweeping mural of grass and blue sky. Nestled in the grass is the word "Hello," written and translated in multiple languages—I see Spanish, Hebrew, Korean, Vietnamese, French, and Chinese at first glance. A few steps more, and Ecoff's motto, "Everyone empowers everyone," an age-appropriate reminder of how the single garment works, anchors a bulletin board. Along the halls, dream catchers, the school's symbol, hang at various intervals. Ecoff's leadership worked to shift the school mascot from an American Indian to the dream catcher as part of an effort to be more culturally sensitive. In a region continually grappling with Confederate shadows and its treatment of American Indians, asserting new, more inclusive symbols, images, and frameworks is a first step to healing the wounds of the past.[1]

Drawing from an attendance zone located in one of the most diverse swaths of Chesterfield County, Ecoff's student body is a microcosm of the multiracial student demographics across the sixty-plus schools that constitute the Chesterfield County Public Schools (CCPS) system, which in turn is a microcosm of Virginia.[2] In 2015, white students made up roughly 50 percent of the enrollment at Ecoff, similar to trends in the county, state, and nation. Black students accounted for 32 percent, and Latinx students about 11 percent. Ten years previously, white students made up 72 percent of Ecoff's enrollment; black students, 19 percent; and Latinx students, 5 percent. Districtwide, the student poverty rate has grown 80 percent since 2004, faster than in any other major school system in the Richmond area.[3] But racial and economic shifts have been unevenly concentrated in certain parts of Chesterfield's school system.[4] And the swift pace of change has created intense pressure to confront growing educational inequities in a county that, during my childhood, reported the highest number of Ku Klux Klan organizations in the state.

This chapter is about leaders rising to meet the challenges and opportunities posed by changing demographics in Ecoff and Chesterfield. It explores how Ecoff thrives as a diverse elementary school with the help of responsive leadership and programming that taps into current interests around social-emotional learning. Elementary school is another critical juncture for integration. Gains associated with diverse schools are strongest over long periods of exposure, and children's understanding of race and identity unfolds rapidly during this period.

Dynamics of a Resegregating Suburban System

In Chesterfield County, racial and economic change has been clustered in the east, where Ecoff sits, and just over the city of Richmond's southern boundary.[5] Carrie Coyner, a school board representative for this section of Chesterfield, said, "It's very diverse with wealthy neighborhoods but also with the absolute lowest income in Chesterfield County in the same place." There are golf courses and mobile home parks, quaint clusters of shops in the town of Chester and a run-down commercial strip called the Jefferson Davis corridor.

The Jefferson Davis corridor grew as part of Route 1, a former artery for the entire East Coast. When Interstate 95 was constructed as a bigger, faster replacement for Route 1 in the 1950s, disinvestment spiraled. In hopes of staunching the flow of resources and people, the county relaxed development rules along the corridor. Coyner reported that developers built poor-quality housing soon after, and any kind of business willing to set up shop in the area did so. The northern section of the Jeff Davis corridor wasn't governed by the same rules as other parts of the county.[6] "That mistake of the past," Coyner said, "is what has led to it being such a concentrated area for our lowest income families. A lack of treating them like everybody else."[7]

Coyner, both a school board member and a real estate lawyer in the county, has raised concerns about growing racial and economic inequities between east and west Chesterfield that, in the long run, threaten to chip away at Ecoff's diversity.[8] She worries about the concentration of new schools and high-quality housing built in the west since the late 1990s, especially in areas without needed infrastructure like sewers and lights. "My fear for my older [eastern] community," she said. "is that we're allowing [people to leave] by what we are developing in other places. [It will make it easier] for people to choose to not live together."

Nationwide, a gradual outmigration of black families from cities to their inner suburban rings, coupled with Latinx immigration directly into suburbs, has blurred the once-distinct boundary between city and suburb. The Fair Housing Act of 1968 opened up access, on paper, to the suburbs for some families of color.[9] In the early 2000s, predatory mortgage lending practices made suburban homeownership possible for people in the near middle class, though they also became most vulnerable to financial crisis.[10] Displacement from gentrification, while not hugely significant, also has played a role.[11]

Yet, as Chesterfield illustrates, suburbia's growing diversity is often unevenly concentrated. Persistent housing discrimination, racial disparities in wealth, exclusionary zoning, segregated social networks and experiences, and schooling choices all conspire to keep families of color and families with fewer means locked out of higher opportunity suburban areas. This happens in several ways. One is that realtors often show families of color homes in already resegregating neighborhoods, based in part on assumptions about client preferences.[12] Another is mortgage discrimination. A black family making $157,000 a year is less likely to qualify for a prime loan than a white family making $40,000.[13] A third reason is that available affordable housing in suburbia (in and of itself a battle) tends to be located in lower-opportunity areas that lack access to the strongest schools.[14] A fourth is that developers and suburban politicians maintain segregation through zoning and land-use policies.[15] Suburban areas and schools associated with large, single-family houses on big lots are usually accessible only to families with means. Since US wealth is so unequally concentrated in the hands of whites—in no small part because families of color were excluded from the first explosion of suburban ownership and wealth expansion post-WWII—exclusionary zoning keeps many families of color out of high-opportunity segments of suburbia. [16] Finally, social networks and experiences influence perceptions of schools and inform suburban housing decisions. Prospective homebuyers often have large "blind spots." These holes in their mental image of an area help preemptively close the door on unfamiliar communities.[17] National research shows that families with children are unevenly clustering more within suburbs now than ever before, in large part because advantaged families are seeking access to the most advantaged suburban schools.[18]

In Chesterfield, Laura Lafayette, who grew up in the county and who's now the chief executive officer for the Richmond Association of Realtors and executive director of the Partnership for Housing Affordability, shares Coyner's worry about growing divisions:

> They haven't meant to, but they've driven disinvestment from one area of the county [to the east] by the concentrated investment in the other [to the west]. And then these brand new shiny schools are perceived as good schools, so of course that spurs residential growth, but it also spurs an increase in cost of housing. You have to have certain resources to be able to access those schools if we're going to have attendance zones that are clustered around the school as opposed to attendance zones that are intentionally diverse.

These comments underscore the close relationship between suburban school and housing segregation, something Coyner and Lafayette have sought to bring forward into the local consciousness—and an issue that's often ignored altogether. A spate of highly sought after new housing developments in one part of Chesterfield means an uptick in student enrollment, putting pressure on the system to build new schools. Developers willing to proffer land to the county incentivized officials to select school sites in exclusive new communities. And if student assignment is driven solely by where you live, as it largely is in Chesterfield, residential segregation in the neighborhoods surrounding a school is reflected in its attendance zone and, subsequently, its enrollment.

In Chesterfield and around the country, the politics surrounding attendance zones often create adjacent areas with markedly different student populations.[19] Several subdivisions and neighborhoods, for instance, are divided between the two other elementary schools that lie in close proximity to Ecoff but whose student body is considerably whiter.[20] Coyner initiated a small-scale rezoning effort confined to the eastern part of Chesterfield, which included Ecoff, in 2018. It was an opportunity to address overcrowding, socioeconomic imbalance, and irregularly drawn lines that had created islands of neighborhoods sent to one school, split off from adjacent communities that were sent to another.[21]

Redrawing attendance boundaries to reassign students often ignites battles over which neighborhoods gain access to which schools. Simplistic accountability ratings that punish schools of concentrated poverty and racial segregation exacerbate perceptions and politics, since high scores correlate with whiter, wealthier student populations.[22] Conversations about homes and schools have been digitized by real estate apps like Zillow or school apps like Great Schools. Within seconds, prospective home buyers can access interconnected information about housing prices, attendance zones, test scores, and student racial and economic diversity. Affluent families who have researched this information and bought pricey homes linked to schools with high test scores and lower student body diversity tend to be most resistant to changes proposed in attendance boundaries.[23]

Given that the politics involved in changing attendance boundaries tend to be thorny, I asked Coyner what she thought led to eventual adoption of the rezoning in 2018. Numerous information sessions—held at all impacted schools—helped, she thought, along with the use of multiple rationales for reassigning students. More socioeconomic balance was one of those rationales, but not the only one. There also was plenty of communication, which included Coyner talking about the value of healthy, integrated schools, something she modeled by sending her children to diverse schools in the area she represents.

Origins of a Diverse Suburban Elementary School

Virtually all of the students who attend Ecoff are zoned for the school and live in surrounding neighborhoods. Said differently, the school's diverse enrollment reflects the diversity of the communities encircled by its attendance boundary. I knew this, which is why I asked Coyner to give me a driving tour of the zone. Coyner's roots are in Chesterfield, and with her open, genuine manner and commitment to living out her values, she's been able to bridge large political gulfs in the community she represents.[24] A fellow school board member from the western part of the county described Coyner this way:

> What she's done along the Jeff Davis corridor for some of those communities, working in partnership with the faith base, and the YMCA . . . has been some really great work. And that community is very diverse, but there's this really deeply embedded rural white population. It's very conservative, and she's been able to confront [anxiety over recent demographic change] in a manner that is at least, maybe not totally accepting, but they're not coming out in a way that you know, to boycott what's happening in public education. So I think that's a skill.

We met at Coyner's office on a steamy August day in 2018. She works right next to the eighteenth-century courthouse and present-day county government offices at the heart of Chesterfield's civic life. The outer edges of Ecoff's attendance boundaries were just a minute or two away by car.

Coyner narrated the ride easily, pointing out landmarks from her childhood and from her community involvement today. Ecoff's zone includes the village of Chester, the original epicenter of what had been a largely rural community. Coyner remembers coming to the Chester post office or the pharmacy and taking dance classes in an eighties-era strip mall built to blend in with the village. The largely white population that surrounded the Chester of yesteryear has aged in place, and a new mixed-use development has cropped up partly to serve it. It's a cheery community, with summer-themed flags flying and grass freshly mown, anchored by several bustling businesses and a spacious new public library. A mix of apartment units and smaller single-family homes with easy first-floor entries define the residences. Cars fly by on a busy road nearby; there's no public transit in the Ecoff zone.

The zone contains one large church—the pastor sends his son to Ecoff and is a fixture at the school—and the Cultural Center of India. We drive through a mix of pleasant houses and apartments, many ranch-style or Victorian-style homes dating back to the early eighties or nineties and a smattering of others constructed more recently. Some parts of the zone feel more rural than suburban, including the land right around the school. There's still a good deal of undeveloped space, prompting Coyner and others to push for reinvestment in this eastern slice of Chesterfield. Open land means little chance of current residents being displaced, while proximity to county government and major roads and interstates makes it ideal for both residential and commercial development. Plus, Ecoff's external integration efforts have been working so far, making the neighborhood attractive to a range of families. Visible and welcoming leadership, an emphasis on social and emotional learning, carefully cultivated home-school connections, and a diversifying faculty put the school in demand, according to staff and other locals.[25] The pastor of the church we drove past noted, "I've got at least four families that moved to the area after they kind of heard about the school and the church and wanted to be a part of it." Ecoff's principal agreed, saying he has had families who used information gleaned from the school's brochure "as a determining factor in where they buy their house."

Still, according to Coyner, feeder patterns that funnel Ecoff's students into several middle and high schools are barriers to enticing housing developers to the Ecoff attendance zone. As we drive through one of the few new subdivisions consisting of spacious single-family homes rather than duplexes or apartments, Coyner tells me that the developer erroneously thought the land was zoned for a proximate middle and high school with comparatively higher test scores and fewer students of color. When the parcel turned out to be linked to different schools, the developer lost $1,000 per lot. This corresponded with depressed demand, because middle- to upper-middle-class families were less likely to seek houses attached to what test scores indicated were lower-performing schools—performance that's closely linked to concentrations of poverty and the disparate opportunities that students confront in and out of school.[26] Increasing school segregation, in other words, tracks closely with disinvestment, as developers seek higher profits elsewhere. School attendance zones are shaping new patterns of residential segregation as well as old.[27]

Lower middle and high school test scores relative to schools in the western part of Chesterfield also have impacted some of the older ranch home communities within the Ecoff attendance boundary. Owners looking to move struggled with resale values, particularly during and after the Great Recession. The assessment for single-family homes in the Ecoff zone, on average, is $223,527, but the average sale price is about $50,000 less than the assessed value. The reverse is true for Chesterfield County as a whole, where the average sale price is roughly $60,000 more than the assessed value.[28] Many homeowners in the Ecoff zone thus decided it made more financial sense to rent instead of sell. Those rents tend to be relatively inexpensive, opening up access to Ecoff for families of more limited means. Several aging apartment complexes, as well as landlords willing to accept housing choice vouchers, provide additional affordable housing options. The Ecoff attendance zone has more than double the share of multifamily units (36 percent) than Chesterfield as a whole (14 percent), as well as more renters (27 percent) than the county as a whole (23 percent).[29] These various factors contrib-

ute to a more diverse array of housing in Ecoff's zone than in Chesterfield, which contributes to more student diversity at the school.

One worries, though, about further acceleration in Ecoff's attendance zone diversity. If more inclusive development doesn't take root
across eastern *and* western Chesterfield, Ecoff eventually will resegre-
gate.[30] More affluent families will take advantage of new housing tailored to them in other parts of suburbia, leaving a concentration of
lower-income housing in the Ecoff zone. As Coyner noted during our
wide-ranging conversation, it would be much easier to balance growth
and development across the county if all Chesterfield's schools were
diverse and excellent. Her sentiment highlights a fundamental reality
about the school-housing relationship—without integration goals and
efforts across both the school and housing sectors, good work in one
can be undermined by issues in another.

Ecoff and External Integration

External integration at Ecoff—the elements that go into creating and
maintaining a diverse suburban elementary school—is a balance of responsive, empathic leadership; strong programming; and concerted efforts to attend to the varied needs and concerns of families who live in
an attendance zone that, at least for now, encircles a diverse population.

Responsive Leadership and Programming That Celebrate Ecoff's Growing Diversity

Dr. Joshua Cole is intense, driven, friendly, and sensitive, with brown
hair and square black eyeglasses. He comes from a family who modeled inclusivity in a white, mostly working-class Michigan town. Cole
sought out leadership roles and exposure to more racial/ethnic diversity in college, becoming a resident assistant and volunteering in the
multicultural center and diversity office. He was one of a handful of
white men doing similar work at Central Michigan University. An array of early teaching experiences further shaped Cole's interest in racial
and social justice, ranging from rural Michigan to Australia to Detroit
Public Schools.

Wanting to reach more students, Cole began working toward a principalship. He received his PhD at Virginia Commonwealth University along the way, writing a dissertation about school desegregation in Richmond Public Schools after the system was released from court oversight.[31] He said that the interviews linked to the project helped him "learn a lot about history of Virginia and our nation, really. It drove me to make practical change in terms of the injustices that exist."

When we spoke in 2018, Cole had been the principal at Ecoff Elementary for seven years. In that time, he'd seen the student demographics change dramatically. Cole rattled off the numbers matter of factly: during his tenure, the share of students qualifying for free and reduced lunch increased 20 percentage points to about half of the student population, and the rate of growth in the school's African American student population became the second fastest in the county.

He and his vice principal, Renee Shimko-Daye, sought to address the changes proactively in order to build on and maintain diversity at the school. Cole and Shimko-Daye have formed meaningful relationships among their different stakeholders through a combination of accessibility, sweat equity, openness, inspiration, and patience. The two combined their office in 2018, reinforcing the sense that they were on the same page. And they've believed in empowering others, with Cole saying they think about "creating ownership, using key people, building relationships . . . [that's how] you can help guide [the culture]." He acknowledged that it took some time for him to realize he didn't have to do it all himself, that it was important to create other leaders.

Early in their tenure, in 2014, Cole and Shimko-Daye conducted a needs assessment with their staff, the parent teachers association (PTA), and other stakeholders. It was guided by questions like, "What are we really lacking? What are we doing and how could we do it better?" Armed with data from the assessment, the leadership team set about creating their own centralized in-house community resources, reaching out to various stakeholders, and advocating for Title I funding. Cole isn't shy about borrowing ideas from other schools and organizations. Ecoff's Empowerment Zone is a room filled with information about community partners, along with parenting tips and the best ways for families to access resources. It's modeled in part on the Harlem Children's Zone (HCZ), a place-based effort to wrap community supports around vulnerable students and families using schools as an anchor point.[32]

HCZ, in turn, is a well-known model within an evidence-based community schools movement that seeks to integrate student supports, engage families and communities, expand learning time, and demonstrate collaborative leadership and practices.[33] To date, the movement has been concentrated in segregated areas and schools struggling with concentrated poverty and systemic racism. Importantly, Ecoff's efforts point to the idea that the community school and the school integration movements are not mutually exclusive.

The Empowerment Zone is one piece of the larger Ecoff story. A read-through of the school's brochure gives prospective families a sense that the school is fundamentally committed to improving academic achievement through social and emotional learning (SEL) or, as the text says, "educating the whole child." Ecoff was the first pilot SEL school in Chesterfield, according to Cole, and he has used the school's marketing materials to celebrate and showcase it. Cole also mentioned the images in the brochures, saying that "they speak volumes, because they represent all of our diversity." SEL has provided an affirmative way to talk about the school's diversity, allowing Cole or Shimko-Daye or the teachers to speak easily about students crossing lines of difference to form relationships and solve problems. This is what the students will be required to do as adults in a diverse society, they say, so why not start young, in elementary school? When it comes to external integration, SEL is Ecoff's programmatic draw and identity—the thing that sets it apart, despite its status as a neighborhood public elementary school.[34]

Modeling Interaction Across Racial Lines to Build Trust

I asked Cole if there has been any pushback related to the school's swift demographic changes from the white families assigned to Ecoff. Cole nodded in the affirmative. He said concerns from white families are often delivered via coded language such as, "We just moved from a west end school and Ecoff just doesn't 'feel' the same way." He's had good conversations as a result, "to where people have stayed," and has been guided by a sense that you have to address families' concerns, coded or otherwise. Though some have left, Cole told me, "[W]e still maintain what we do and set a good example. We talk about inclusive schools a lot and we put it right out there that we celebrate our diversity."

"What are some of the things you say, like how do you hold up diversity as a strength?" I wondered, because managing these fears is crucial for creating external integration in a resegregating suburban system. White students have been the most isolated from other racial/ethnic groups in schools, which can render initial contact—for parents or children—fraught with anxiety.[35] And it's not just anxiety about contact with other racial groups; it's anxiety about the loss of status and privilege that comes with whiteness in our society. The suburban aftershocks of the Great Recession linger, with attendant concerns about scarce resources and opportunities. Whites "seek to monopolize access to high status schools, and when competing groups threaten their monopoly, they resist or flee," in the words of sociologist Jeremy Fiel.[36] Building and maintaining the trust of diverse families is key because, even though enrollment at Ecoff is governed by proximity to the school, escape hatches exist. Families with resources can opt out by moving to a different school zone, into a center-based gifted program (provided their child qualifies), or into private schools. School system waivers, available on a limited basis, offer additional options beyond assigned neighborhood schools.[37]

Cole took a minute to respond to my question. "I think it's almost, I think even more than what you say, it's what you do," he said quietly. He continued, "And people will watch you. So if, for instance, at a meet and greet function to start the school year off, if I'm interacting with each and every family the exact [same] way in terms of how I embrace them, welcome them or talk to them and everyone sees that . . . then it says to them that it's okay, right?"

Modeling how to have interactions across racial lines is one aspect of leadership in a diverse school. This is what "norm entrepreneurship" around integration looks like.[38] Lafayette, the head of the Richmond Association of Realtors and former Chesterfield resident, thinks that a crucial piece of the puzzle for creating a healthy, inclusive school is "finding a good principal that a diverse set of families will believe in." Cole worked hard to be that person, saying that "most of my day is spent helping people understand other people's perspectives . . . creating an environment where people can feel like it's okay to not know everything and learn and grow."

Forging Bonds Between Home and School

Ecoff committed to strengthening the bonds between the worlds of home and school in challenging economic times. This work was part of what makes the school attractive to families from the outset, in addition to contributing to a positive climate within the school. At Ecoff, relationships based on authenticity, a willingness to take school events to communities, a PTA that strives for inclusivity and wraparound services, and external partnerships all contributed to an atmosphere of welcoming and connection.

The changing context for home-school relationships at Ecoff is an important backdrop to the school's current efforts in that direction. The school still serves affluent students who live in $500,000 homes. But teachers and the school counselor described rapid shifts in the level of need, with many surprised by the number of families calling for food assistance. And need in this suburban school cuts across racial lines, similar to what we saw at Sprout but much more so than in the urban middle school explored in chapter 4. Roughly 47 percent of economically disadvantaged (ED) students at Ecoff are black, 30 percent are white, and 15 percent are Latinx.[39] This matters both for equal status interactions among different racial groups and for overcoming racialized perceptions of poverty that leaders and teachers may hold.

In partnership with the local church, Ecoff sends food home for some families on the weekends. Student homelessness has increased, according to the counselor, and a number of families are residing temporarily in motels. Methamphetamine has been an additional issue, so much so that Cole took to riding the bus home with students to "make the school's presence known and to get a feel for our communities and neighborhoods," in the words of one teacher. The emotional stress families confront has risen correspondingly, with parent-teacher conferences occasionally feeling more like impromptu therapy sessions.

Reaching out and connecting with all of the different families is very much an Ecoff value. Shimko-Daye, the assistant principal, feels that "courageous conversations and relationships" have been part of the school's strong foundations. In addition to having the principal and teachers ride the bus home to build relationships, Ecoff held family nights in an apartment complex near the school. There was pizza, a school supply raffle, and extra supplies for kids "just to engage the community and let families know we're here for you." Part of the motivation for the visit was an uptick in bus referrals for misbehavior along this particular route. The school worked to build a shared sense of bus expectations to reinforce the message at home and at school.

Ecoff's teachers and leaders also offer a back-to-school night and a back-to-school morning to reach more families. "Of course, it requires more teacher input and more hours on the teacher," said one faculty member, "but even those maybe three families, we're hoping that teachers will be able to understand that they were able to come [to the morning session] when they might have been working and couldn't get to the night one." Ecoff is persistent and consistent in trying to reach parents and guardians in any way possible. Cole said, "I'll call everybody, visit houses, whatever I've got to do. But the calls aren't just to them. I'll call the aunts, and uncles, grandparents, whoever I can find and say, 'Will you have [the parent or guardian] call me?'" And once he's made a connection with a parent and built trust, he sees word of mouth spreading, families letting other families know that "[i]t's all right, it's all right, you can call them."

There's targeted dialogue around school economic shifts, too. One example came in the form of a "Coffee and Conversation" about the implications of becoming a Title I school. Cole and Shimko-Daye worried about the misconceptions and stigma attached to qualifying for additional funding because of rising student poverty. So they sought to lead and shape the formation of knowledge about the Title I program. Cole was adamant, for example, that families understand that Ecoff was not a Title I school but a school receiving Title I funds. Though the phrasing was a matter of semantics, he was trying to avoid distilling everything about Ecoff down into the Title I label, focusing instead on what the additional funding could support at Ecoff, as well as the numerous other attributes of the school.

While most of the home-school connections have been driven by leaders and teachers, Ecoff's PTA also has worked to become more inclusive. The group welcomes all and values multiple forms of participation (e.g., not just fund-raising prowess). As a result, turnout for PTA-sponsored events reflects Ecoff's growing diversity, even if the makeup of the officers lags somewhat behind.

Intentional Diversification of Teachers at Ecoff

Because of the close relationship between student and teacher composition, diverse faculties signal to families that the students are diverse.[40] That's why an intensive—and slowly successful—effort to diversify the teaching staff at Ecoff is, as with Sprout at the Children's Museum, both an external and internal integration strategy. It helps attract and maintain a diverse student body, but it also contributes to diverse faculty teams and offers important role models for students in the building.

Teachers of color made up just 2 percent of Ecoff's faculty when Cole and Shimko-Daye first arrived; through turnover and transfer requests, today they make up 20 percent. Ecoff's success is partly attributable to the draw that an intentional focus on diversity and inclusion creates for faculty, not just for families. The principal indicated that, with "the reputation we've developed, teachers are interested in transferring [to us]." The brochure, with its images of racially diverse children and emphasis on the unique programming, is a good recruiting tool. Each year during the hiring process, Ecoff's leadership deliberately sought a diverse applicant pool and interviewed more people than in the past. And during interviews, Cole explained the school's changing demographics to applicants in order "to gauge interest in or experience in learning about that." Shimko-Daye agreed, adding that the leadership team has been purposeful in using turnover to help shape the school, because it's important that kids see themselves in their teachers. And it's good for the faculty, too. Cole gave a nod to research on the advantages of diverse teams, saying that leadership wanted "to bring in diverse minds, because different mindsets and thought patterns come from people who've had different experiences and often that comes with different racial backgrounds."[41]

The shift in teacher demographics is partially documented in a series of "teacher of the year" pictures, dating back to the early 2000s, that hangs in the front entry of the school. Two black women were recognized within the past three years, preceded by a long line of white women. One of the more gratifying outcomes of the recent diversification of the faculty, Cole said, has been the reaction of families. White families and families of color have noticed the shift toward more teacher diversity—and effort behind it—commending the leadership and clamoring to enroll their children in some of the new teachers' classrooms.

Ecoff and Internal School Integration

Cole gets on the intercom to make the morning announcements. "Today is Friday, May 25, 2018, the 160th day of the school year," he begins. He ticks through the weather forecast; birthdays for students, a teacher, and a cafeteria worker; and closes with "Thanks, all, for the teamwork."

At Ecoff, SEL provides a framework for the school's efforts to build teamwork, establish trust and relationships among stakeholders, create a healthy school climate, and emphasize the value of diversity and cultural competency.[42] SEL is also a tangible manifestation of equal status, shared goals, and leadership—all fundamental to realizing optimal conditions for positive contact between different groups.[43]

SEL, sometimes referred to as character education, soft skills, or social awareness, traces its origins to more holistic notions of education that value the creation of good citizens along with high-achieving individuals.[44] SEL became firmly embedded in the national educational consciousness in the mid-1990s, both with the publication of a popular book on the importance of emotional intelligence and when the Collaborative to Advance Social and Emotional Learning (CASEL) released a set of guidelines for educators.[45] Research regarding SEL and student outcomes trends positive: a meta-analysis of over 213 SEL programs found that participating students displayed improved social-emotional skills, attitudes, behavior, and academic performance (corresponding with an 11 percentage point gain in student achievement).[46] Nurturing SEL competencies like curiosity, focus, and resilience is linked to cognition, with some evidence suggesting these competencies are just as implicated in success as academic skills.[47]

SEL Helps Structure Healthy Contact Across Lines of Difference

After the announcements, Cole hurries to the Empowerment Zone. He has a Friday meeting with the seven-member SEL council, an intentionally diverse group of fifth-grade students selected to embody certain traits (e.g., self-control, gratitude, curiosity, optimism, grit) from *The Character Club*, a children's book written by Cole to promote schoolwide SEL efforts. The council is selected through an application process, during which the children describe prior leadership experience, how they bring a specific trait to life, and how they contribute to the team expectations at Ecoff. On Fridays, SEL council representatives visit classes to talk about the trait of the week and deliver badges signaling whether or not a class has demonstrated the trait. At the apex of Virginia's testing season, this week's trait is "zest." "Keep up the positive energy," SEL council representatives tell other students, many walking into classrooms that already have sticky notes of encouragement ("You can do it!") on the doors.

Morning meetings, or twenty-minute daily classroom gatherings, form the backbone of regular SEL programming at Ecoff. Shawn Franko, the pastor of the nearby church and parent of an Ecoff student, said that his son describes the meetings as times when teachers try to help students understand each others' needs. It's a space to "create an idea of community and mutual concern where [the class] talks about what affects them together and how they function." Cole concurred, explaining that classrooms discuss "SEL skills, how to get along better, whatever problems they are having." But he also insisted that SEL structures, implemented with conviction and patience, are about something much deeper: "the idea that we can be a harmonious society and a just system."

Here's what one third-grade morning meeting looked and sounded like. Ms. B, a recent African American teacher of the year at Ecoff, brings her class together with, "Sweet peeties, let's get started. We haven't done Suzies's friendship tunnel since last week." Suzie is a very small, blonde first grader who's had trouble consistently staying on track with Ecoff's behavioral expectations. This tunnel is part of a cross-age SEL effort, where classes of older and younger students are paired together for different activities.

The class of third graders lined up naturally in interracial pairs, facing each other, to form the tunnel. Ms. B runs a loving, highly structured classroom. She says to her students, "Tell Suzie how proud you are of her and think about how you want to motivate her by telling her how you want her to continue to rock the rest of the week." She places herself beside the tunnel to film the interaction for Suzie's mom. Suzie walks down the line, and the students sound off rapidly: "You're the best! You're intelligent. I'm really proud of you. Have a great winter break. You're doing a great job. I hope you do good in class. You're so amazing, I'm so proud. You're a good person." Tiny Suzie gazes up at their faces as she walks through the tunnel, which ends with Ms. B saying, "Suzie, I *know* you're making your goal today."

As Suzie trots off to her first-grade class, chin tilted upward suggesting a little more confidence, Ms. B's third graders move into their regular dialogue about the classroom community. They take turns—a student is orchestrating the discussion—volunteering strategies for meeting expectations in the cafeteria and during a classroom transition. Ms. B closes the meeting saying, "Okay, sweetie peas, listen to me. You guys are awesome. I know we talk about it all the time. Not about me telling you that, but I want that part of you believing, so you can show that you've learned expectations around work and behavior. Guess what? You're just that awesome."

The different SEL interactions I saw firsthand or heard about shared a common thread of affirmation—sometimes for an individual and sometimes for a group—friendship, and/or empathy. SEL naturally organized close interactions across lines of difference, in part because school administrators worked to ensure that each classroom serves a range of students from different backgrounds and abilities. And it provided a regular space for conversation about conflict, racial or otherwise, that could be infecting the class.

Faculty Training and Buy-in Around SEL

SEL goes beyond students, reaching Ecoff's teachers as well. Frequent dialogue about community among students has given faculty new insight into the lives and experiences of their charges. As one teacher observed, "I think SEL opened up the mindset of a lot of educators in the building, because that is not what they've been a part of in their own life." The school counselor agreed, noting that hearing about student experiences with trauma develops empathy among teachers. And it gives them day-to-day context for a child's demeanor, engagement, or behavior. Key to success with SEL, said Ms. B, was developing a family atmosphere in the classroom, "because kids are more comfortable sharing issues they may be having."

A teacher training opportunity focused on simulating poverty further nurtured empathy for the lived experiences of students and families. Teachers described an elaborate immersion experience, with faculty divided into families, and roles within those families (e.g., adult versus student). Different stations were set up, and adult members of families had to navigate lines for bus tickets or social services where people may not be able to assist in the languages spoken at home. "It was interesting," said one faculty member, "and if you took it seriously, it was stressful. And even if you didn't take it seriously, there were these bonding experiences." When teachers assigned to the role of student, who play-acted taking part in a regular school day, reflected on the simulation, they described a sense of being concerned about what their families were taking on while they were in school—and what was at stake in terms of financial or employment viability. They also reported wanting to get up and leave or not being able to concentrate on schooling and instruction. For well-off faculty new to teaching economically diverse students, this experience provided a brief but powerful opportunity to experience the world differently. Hearing about the simulation, I was reminded of a long article on the neuroscience behind empathy that appeared in the *New York Times* magazine a few years ago. Researchers found that relatively simple interventions, centered on sharing short stories about the life experiences of opposing groups, could help build empathy—and thereby reduce prejudice—between individual members of groups long mired in conflict.[48]

In interviews, faculty readily acknowledged Ecoff's progress—a strengthening sense of shared purpose, acceptance, and community—even as they lamented the challenges of teaching in a rapidly shifting environment. National, district, and school-level demands to adapt instructional practice, experiment with new reforms, navigate fluctuating accountability systems, counter external inequities, and serve as first responders to a shredded social safety net are overwhelming—and underappreciated. As one faculty member noted, with others nodding their heads in agreement,

> I think for some teachers coming into a very diverse school, where social, economic and racial divides and situations that are systematic and outside of the school are brought into school every day, depending on your background and depending on how willing you are, and even if you are willing, what kind of strategies and abilities do you have . . . there's so many changes, we're trying a lot of new things, and for a lot of people who are either new, maybe not experienced with those things, it becomes this pushdown that's overwhelming, and so even getting to the point of saying and knowing what you need is very difficult for those people, because they're just keeping their head above water. They're trying to just find the air.

Teachers spoke of the importance of taking care of themselves and each other. They reminded each other to relax on the weekends, to get support if needed, to remember to breathe. Alongside all of the new SEL-related endeavors at Ecoff, there was the ever-present pressure of a federal and state accountability system, under which student poverty and sanction often seem synonymous.

A Broader Vision for Learning That's Inclusive and Culturally Relevant
Ecoff's halls were preternaturally quiet; the intersection of the Zest and
Self-Control corridors still. (Each hallway at Ecoff is named for one of
the SEL character traits.) This was an SEL school knee-deep in testing
season.

I pondered Ecoff's commitment to SEL during a period of sharp
demographic transition and hard-nosed accountability. "Was it difficult to maintain focus on new programming within the constraints
of Virginia's accountability system?" I asked Cole. He answered readily, saying it had taken some courage to push for the innovation "with
watchful eyes on our scores." I heard echoes of this in a 2018 interview
with the former superintendent of Chesterfield, who'd been in place
when Cole first began as Ecoff's principal. "I think Ecoff would have
gotten a lot more attention [from the central administration] if they
had seen the current outcomes move a little bit more significantly early
on," the then-superintendent, Dr. Newsome, told me. "Now they are at
a place where they can tout that, but earlier on they couldn't."

Under a strict accountability paradigm, it's difficult to pursue anything other than high(er) test scores as school poverty intensifies—despite the benefits we've already seen linked to SEL at Ecoff. This stands
in contrast to more affluent schools, which do not face the same accountability pressures and have freedom to experiment with various
programs. Fundamentally, achievement expectations for Ecoff have
been based on the idea that higher standards and accountability can
solve issues rooted in (re)segregation and concentrated poverty. Integration, on the other hand, represents a much broader take on the purpose
and outcomes of schooling, one that includes individual test scores but
that also goes far beyond them.

Cole elaborated on Ecoff's accountability trajectory, explaining
that there were a few early years of "sneaking past cut scores for [Vir-
ginia's Standards of Learning, or SOL, tests] by a matter of a percentage
or two." He acknowledged the link between the opportunities students
have outside of school and their performance within them, saying,
"SOLs often correlate with your student demographics . . . [T]here's

been growth but there's still a gap. We don't have a magic answer."[49] According to Virginia's new school-quality indicators, which are far more
nuanced than in prior years, in 2018 achievement gaps between various
subgroups at Ecoff were almost all considered level one, which meant
they met or exceeded the state standards or demonstrated sufficient
improvement.[50] The achievement gap between students with and without disabilities was the one exception. In terms of accountability, Cole
has seen "the pendulum swinging" away from a laser focus simply on
test outcomes and felt as if Ecoff was ready, having already expanded its
vision for learning to include SEL and culturally relevant instruction.

Ecoff's broader vision for learning could be seen along the school's
fourth-grade corridor, which displayed students' engagement with early
Virginia history. Some of their key takeaways illustrated exposure to
the darkness and lightness of our state's origins—opening up the possibility for empathic classroom dialogue around those tensions. "Set-
tlers were able to control their own government, many of its programs
help people get treated with kindness," one student wrote. "When Africans arrived their families were split apart, daughters were sold [sic]
to other men. Women took care of the white people's babies while the
men did work. They lived in hand made wood houses. Africans were
treated worse than animals. America relied on its own slaves," continued another.

It's not only that students engaged with content that accurately
reflected the contributions and contradictions of our society, it's also
the way they learned it. Ecoff prides itself on an instructional model
that "emphasizes different teaching styles with a focus on relationships, cross-curricular integration and . . . equity checkpoints to ensure
culturally relevant instruction," reported Cole.[51] Those checkpoints in
the lesson plans are designed to prompt teachers to think about how
they're differentiating instruction to meet the needs of all students in
the classroom. Ecoff's leaders want their faculty to be explicit about
multicultural strategies. And the school doesn't stop there, emphasizing the five Cs (critical thinking, collaboration, creativity, cooperation,
and communication) to support project-based learning, leadership, and
goal setting.[52] SEL is woven in and out of these different instructional

efforts, as is attention to race and inequity, teamwork, and the main-streaming of students with special needs.

Inclusion of students with special needs in regular classrooms is an additional manifestation of Ecoff's commitment to diversity. On a mid-winter Friday afternoon, Ms. Miller's fifth-grade classroom is finishing up a geography quiz and moving into groups. There are two adults in the classroom of twenty-five or so kids, the teacher and a collaborative special education instructor. Once the students have left, Miller tells me she has a number of boys in the class with unmedicated ADHD. She works with the collaborative teacher to plan when time permits, relying on their personal relationship when it doesn't. A look at Ecoff's students with disabilities by race doesn't turn up glaring dispropor-tionality, unlike national patterns.[53] I bumped into one of the school's special education teachers in Miller's hallway, a young, African Ameri-can man. He said he pulls out of the classroom "maybe 15 percent" of his students for instruction; otherwise every effort is made to push in. He'd been at Ecoff for five years, describing it as warm, welcoming, and inclusive, both for students and for adults.

Ecoff strives to maintain a similar push in posture with students who've been identified as gifted and talented. One teacher per grade level is certified in gifted instruction and serves a cluster of students—usually numbering no more than five—within the classroom. But unlike trends for students with disabilities at Ecoff, sharp disparities by race in gifted identification are in evidence. According to the 2015 federal Civil Rights Data Collection (the most recent year for which figures were available), black students accounted for just 6 percent of Ecoff's gifted enrollment, though they made up about 32 percent of the overall en-rollment. White students, on the other hand, were overrepresented in Ecoff's gifted population—making up about 75 percent of it, compared to 50 percent of the school population. Gifted numbers for Latinx stu-dents were on par with their share of the enrollment.[54] Ecoff's gifted disparities by race or ethnicity closely mirrored the district's.

More equitable access to the gifted and talented program had the attention of the Chesterfield school board and central administration, meaning that some of Ecoff's work to improve access to the program was dictated by the systemwide efforts. [55] In 2018, all third graders in Chesterfield were being screened for the first time, a change from past practices when teacher, student, or parental referrals guided the testing process. Cole pointed to the difficulty of navigating complex systems governing gifted identification as one barrier for struggling families and to teacher bias as another. Research backs up those claims, particularly with respect to teacher bias. Teachers are significantly more likely to refer same-race students to gifted programming.[56] To remedy some of this, the county's gifted department has worked with teachers to broaden their referral focus to include military and minority students, as well as students with special needs who might be "twice exceptional."

Yet, obviously, issues remain. One of Ecoff's faculty members acknowledged the difficulty of opening up gifted programming to more students, especially because grades still play a role in the algorithm. She said, "When grades go into [the referral] that can be tough because grades can sometimes be subjective . . . they are dependent on what kind of assignments are given and whether those are accessible to all of the kids and their work habits."

Attending to Disproportionality and Positive Discipline

Ecoff began implementing a widely popular discipline program, positive behavior intervention support system, or PBIS, when Cole and Shimko-Day first came to Ecoff.[57] The school moved from what felt like a "free-flowing behavioral management system" to one with lots more structure. Shimko-Daye talked about an evolution in implementation, partly because PBIS requires a good deal of training on the part of teachers and staff. For the first few years, discipline numbers—and racial disproportionality—remained a concern.

Those trend lines have changed dramatically, however. The total number of students suspended out of school at Ecoff dropped from fifty-eight to sixteen between 2014 and 2016. In terms of students of color, thirty-nine were suspended out of school in 2015 compared to eight in 2016.[58] So racial inequity in discipline persists, but the overall numbers are much better.[59] Part of the improvement, according to Shimko-Daye, has been due to teacher turnover and, relatedly, the development of a shared school culture around discipline. With the hiring of new teachers, she saw "more faculty willing to try new things. [A sense of] this is how it's done here, rather than this is how it was done prior to [our] administration." Leaders and teachers also review discipline data, the collection of which is fundamental to PBIS, on a regular basis. A student-level data display in Cole and Shimko-Daye's shared office gets updated every two weeks and helps remind the administrative team who is struggling. And there's a monthly review of referral data so that adults can target interventions and support to students who need it the most. Sometimes this is a "check in, check out" person for an individual student, an adult who routinely establishes a quick connection point with a kid upon school entry and exit. The Chesterfield system also has the resources to provide therapeutic day support for students who need additional assistance.

All of this helps. But teachers, counselors, and school leaders additionally converged on the idea that the injection of social-emotional programming into PBIS facilitated the decline in suspensions. Adult conversations around the PBIS discipline data are "holistic," according to one teacher, in part because of contextual information gleaned from regular SEL meetings with students. And the Ecoff expectations are regularly woven into SEL structures like morning or "anytime meetings."[60] Cole said the latter works because "you can spend five minutes regrouping and working through an issue that might have happened. That's going to save you fifty-five minutes of math time versus a wasted hour." I saw this in action in one of Ecoff's fifth-grade classrooms.

It was early Friday afternoon and the students were squirrelly. They'd finished their formative assessments and were looking for the next activity. The teacher, brown hair pulled into a half ponytail, half bun, gathered the kids in. "If your area is cleaned up please join us on the floor for a quick touch base meeting," she said quietly. The students converged, two adult assistants in the background. "Okay," the teacher began, "I wanted to kind of reset our tone. We haven't had a five-point day [part of the PBIS system] in quite a while. I want to quickly run through things that we might need to change that we're capable of but haven't been doing lately."

She talked about the importance of positive solutions and having a growth mind-set, the idea that students are capable of achieving their goals with hard work and practice. The students became involved in the conversation, offering suggestions like "we need to stop arguing and yelling at each other." The teacher reminded them of the importance of ownership and not singling one another out for ridicule. She said, "We know each other, we know there are some things we might struggle with and that we might need some support. And if [the other students] aren't listening to our encouragement, then stop. Let someone else address it. Or maybe the kid is working on it, transitioning to stop it."

The term "transitioning" referred to a coping strategy used by several of the classroom's students receiving special education services. This was SEL used to refresh the expectations attached to PBIS (e.g., the five-point day), or SEL as preemptive discipline. The meeting was a reminder to students that they were working toward a common goal of having their collective behavior acknowledged and rewarded through PBIS—and what that might ask of each individual. Ecoff teachers felt as if the meetings attached to SEL provided a structure for relationship building (or repairing) when conflicts or behavior threatened to undermine the classroom community.

Addressing Race in an Increasingly Diverse Elementary School

When we left the Sprout students, who were nearing the end of their preschool experience, most were demonstrating a burgeoning awareness of race in terms of physical characteristics like skin or hair color. Elementary school–age children continue their racial identity development along a fairly predictable continuum. Between the ages of six and ten, students begin to associate race and/or ethnicity with culture, understanding, for instance, that Indian American children may speak Hindu or eat Indian cuisine. They start wrestling with the idea that individuals can hold membership in different groups, say, both Indian and American.[61] By age eight, or third grade, there's a growing awareness of race as a social construct—or the idea that race encompasses little to no biological significance but plenty of social meaning.[62] Two years later, in fifth grade, students can associate stereotypes with different racial groups.[63] School leaders and teachers should use this age group's commitment to fairness and orientation to peer groups to their advantage by offering, as Ecoff does, abundant opportunities for teamwork and collaboration. More broadly, elementary school culture—defined as the curriculum, faculty and student demographics, support for cultural pluralism, and teacher leadership—contributes to racial identity development.[64]

By the end of elementary school, ten-year-old students of color may begin to grapple with racial identity formation. Thorny "Who am I?" questions in a society still wracked with pervasive racial discrimination may be linked to the disintegration of earlier cross-racial friendships. Kids of color often begin to socially segregate into same-race groups, at least some of the time, to safely sort out together what their racial identity means in the context of broader hostility.[65] White children, who are traditionally the most racially isolated, sometimes don't grapple with identity and race until later. While that may not hold true in racially and ethnically diverse settings like Ecoff, initial white student reactions to the reality of racism may be rooted in defensiveness—later giving way, with appropriate support, to honest reckoning and an orientation toward more justice.[66] These shifts don't negate the reductions in prejudice linked to early contact and genuine friendships across racial and ethnic lines. However, they do spell the beginning of more complex interracial interactions and negotiations.

Observations and interviews across varying classrooms at Ecoff showed the racial identity continuum at work in elementary school. Easy relationships among students of different backgrounds were on display in younger classrooms, in the cafeteria, and outside on the playground. Teacher interviews backed up the observation data, with younger-grade faculty quick to describe close cross-racial friendships in classrooms that felt like family. A faculty member who works with seven- and eight-year-olds said, "I have an ESOL class [with kids from around the world]. They look out for each other, it's still very innocent at that age . . . [W]e're a family." But teachers, parents, and administrators all shared stories of more racially fraught conversations and feelings in fourth and, especially, fifth grade.

In 2018, Ms. Miller reported that her fifth-grade class friendships started to change. Biracial students began to grapple with their identities, feeling they had to choose between white or black friendships. Their families were worried and discussed arguments at home about race with the teacher. Miller said, "They've kind of settled in now. Some have found each other; others have picked black or white." I observed an African American girl in this classroom try to sit next to a biracial girl and a white girl. The biracial student said, "You can't sit here." The white student added, "You're making me mad." Though I didn't have the back story for the anger, the racial dynamics were hard to miss.

Another example was a fifth-grade conversation around an SEL-related video the class watched together. The character had to decide who, at a diverse dinner table, deserved to get the best meal. In the end, the character decided to split it up among all the diners. "That's not reality," said some of the fifth-graders in the classroom, leading to a longer discussion during which students particularly homed in on a black and white binary when it came to disparities.

Concerns about racial bias in discipline emerged from this age group of students as well. In the aftermath of the 2016 election, which routinely and overtly surfaced racial prejudice, teachers began hearing accusations of racist punishment from a set of African American male fifth-grade students and families. [67] One of the white teachers who met with the boys to talk about their distress said they "shared that some of their families are telling them, you need to watch out for this, you need to be on the lookout [because] white people are racist . . . [A] lot [of the discussions] end up being political conversations which have caused a huge divide last year starting around election time both with adults in the building and with students."

For these older black male students at Ecoff, a nationally toxic racial environment found its way into the building and infiltrated teacher, family, and student relationships. SEL wasn't able to fully counter or ameliorate the toxicity, but it did provide structures for talking openly about racial inequality. Miller pointed out that it was critical to have those conversations with older students in diverse schools; without them, the risk of forming negative stereotypes was too great. She said, referring specifically to white students, "If there is negative exposure . . . we need to provide some context and opportunities to make sure they really understand diversity . . . [Otherwise] it sets students up for kind of a close-minded stereotype and . . . reiterates any of those family histories or ideas that are . . . poisonous to young minds." She talked further about how a negative event like a fight or an incident with a weapon, tinged with racial overtones, spurs emotional reactions—for all kids involved—that the school needs to handle carefully. Fears unaddressed, in other words, shape prejudice.

I asked how the school responded to the racialized tension among the fifth-graders, mindful that conflict in diverse settings—any setting—is virtually inevitable, and what matters is how it's dealt with. Responses conveyed mixed reactions. On the one hand, adults in the building wanted students to take responsibility for actions that had resulted in discipline. Students would counter that "I only get in trouble or sent out [because I'm black]." And a teacher or counselor might reply, "Are there other black students in the classroom who aren't in trouble?" the implication being that if additional black students weren't being singled out, racism wasn't the problem. This indicated a misunderstanding of how racism operates; racially unfair discipline doesn't need to impact all black students in the school for it to be a disproportionate or systemic issue. But teachers and counselors also said they worked to affirm student feelings, telling kids that every feeling you have is "valid and appropriate" or "real and okay." They talked about the importance of sharing each other's truth and also underscored the idea of "no matter where you're coming from or what you think happened, we also need to consider other perspectives to make a final decision." And they discussed looking at patterns over time, trying to see if students' behavior had shifted when they transitioned from one classroom to another, in order to better ascertain whether a teacher or classroom might need additional support.

When they did find evidence of significant behavioral shifts, taking responsibility for those changes proved challenging for some white teachers. Despite the emphasis on courageous conversations and the professional development surrounding SEL and culturally responsive

practices, unwinding years of white isolation takes time and authentic
commitment. As a teacher, "when you're put in the spotlight or in those
conversations [about racism] and it's direct, whether it's from that student or otherwise, having that conversation is difficult," reported one
faculty member. Cole was blunter, telling me that the "central issue was
that some teachers were scared of the kids," and describing "white families who felt the administration was giving too much grace to black
kids." For these reasons and others, rebuilding trust was difficult in the
fifth-grade student-teacher and student-family-school relationships de-
railed by accusations of racism.

In addition to continuing to work with teachers, Ecoff sought to
provide additional supports to black male fifth-grade boys. These took
the form of weekly mentoring meetings, called the Boys to Men group,
with male role models, including those of color, in the community. The
group of twelve boys was intentionally diverse and didn't include all of
the struggling kids for fear of stigmatizing the group before it was even
formed (those not included received one-on-one mentoring). Pastor
Shawn, who was at some meetings, said that bonds among the mentors
and students had definitely formed, but that behavioral changes were a
work in progress. Ultimately, all of the kids did successfully transition
to middle school.

Ecoff's school-based leadership team has worked to nurture equity
and diversity amid explicit systemwide efforts to do the same. In 2016,
the Chesterfield school board hired a new superintendent, Dr. James
Lane. The transition plan accompanying his hire outlined six key areas of focus, one of which was equity.[68] The new superintendent swiftly
broadcast his commitment to equity by announcing a new position, the
director of equity and student support services. In the new position, Dr.
Tameshia Grimes worked in tandem with an equity committee focused
on disparities in opportunities and outcomes (e.g., access to gifted and
other advanced curricula, student achievement, discipline) for Chesterfield's students.[69]

Grimes exuded empathy, seeking connection to students and staff in a role that daily asked people to grapple with hidden and not-so-hidden biases. She occasionally drew on her own childhood—or the experiences of her children attending schools in Chesterfield—to illuminate the gap between how schools *should* serve students of color and students confronting multiple layers of disadvantage and how they *actually* serve them. Bottom line, Grimes said, is that "[c]hildren are different. Our expectations for success don't have to be different. But how we interact with children to build relationships, to build trust, has to be different." Equity initiatives in the division included using class-size reduction funds to target additional support for English learners and growing emphases on culturally relevant instruction, restorative discipline practices, social-emotional learning, and trauma-informed care.[70]

The more recent equity work built on school officials' earlier focus on the achievement gaps illuminated by No Child Left Behind (NCLB). In the mid-2000s, as racial and economic diversity gained steam in suburban Chesterfield, the superintendent at the time, Newsome, was carefully navigating what many school stakeholders found uncomfortable: open conversations about race, disability, gender, and inequity. Newsome, tall, impeccably dressed, with a deep, quietly resonant voice, was Chesterfield's second African American superintendent. He also was an early advocate of NCLB—which later gave way to his sense that the law was flawed—for two reasons. One related to accountability for inequality in urban school districts. "For me," he said thoughtfully, steepling his fingers, in his new perch as superintendent of a small urban district just south of Chesterfield, "Having done all of my teaching in DC, I worked in schools where students had almost no opportunity for quality education and a better life out of poverty. I saw potential in NCLB to at least hold people accountable that were not being held accountable."

The second reason connected to those open and sometimes uncomfortable conversations. NCLB gave educators a mandate—and a language—to talk about achievement gaps in suburban districts long accustomed to looking the other way. Newsome said, "When I first started talking about achievement gaps in Chesterfield, I phrased it around the definition outlined in NCLB. I think that opened the door for a lot of the work."

Part of that work involved technical shifts like ensuring that nearly all eighth-graders in Chesterfield had the opportunity to take Algebra I. This meant closing an opportunity gap that bled into an achievement gap, as some students were on track for advanced math—and hence a college-bound curricula—but not others. Another piece of Chesterfield's early equity work was more normative, laying the groundwork for teachers and leaders to better understand and relate to students from a quickly widening set of background experiences. Guided by the idea that school leaders were a critical point of leverage in normative change, the director of professional development began extensive equity and diversity training for the division's administrators. Ecoff's Cole was an early adopter who "really embraced" the equity work, in the eyes of Newsome.[71]

Which brings us back to Cole's efforts at Ecoff Elementary. The intentional efforts around diversity and equity slowly were paying off. SEL and the community schools approach reached diverse groups of students and families. Faculty diversity grew alongside explicit training around culturally relevant pedagogy, race, poverty, and equity. Exclusionary discipline declined sharply, and achievement gaps slowly narrowed. But, as always, the work is never ending. Judging by Cole's example, it requires courage and the occasional risk.

Let's end with a sense of how leadership around equity and diversity manifested at Ecoff—a reminder of the many layers of work required to build trust, empathy, and competency among faculty so they can better serve their students.

I could hear the teachers from down the hall. It was a Friday half-day for students, the afternoon reserved for staff professional development. Now, kids gone, a group of teachers is dancing through Ecoff's cafeteria, sparkles and confetti flying, surrounded by a tight circle of staff. Cole and Shimko-Daye are in matching super-hero T-shirts. Cole confided that the training will be the first time he's brought his external consulting work on culturally responsive pedagogy formally to his faculty.

Cole starts moving through his presentation in a quick cadence, reminding staff that at Ecoff, they seek to name their diversity and empower open-mindedness. He says he wants leadership and faculty to be aware of equity and inequity, to build relationships, to connect with student lives, to empathize with their experiences, and to give students a reason to care by developing good lessons they are interested in. Then he pauses, turning to a set of candy props. "Let's talk about race for a little bit." And he starts going through the candy, playfully naming its diversity: "People who look like me, white boys, we are M&Ms, Swedish Fish. African Americans, there's Special Dark chocolate. Intelligence, we've got Nerds, Airheads, Smarties, and Dum Dums. LGBT, Skittles, taste the rainbow."

I'm typing fast, a little worried about how this is going over with his staff. But they are laughing and clapping their approval. Cole brings it home with this: "There's candy diversity everywhere. So the question is, how do you identify yourself? What I want us to do today is tell our story. I want you to tell your own and listen to someone else's. This discourse matters, assumptions and beliefs matter. That's just the truth."

Cole speaks with the ease of a practiced teacher. He watches his audience carefully, looking for hints of boredom or unease. There's an intentional mix of goofiness and substance—candy and story—that brings most faculty into the conversation. He talks about implicit bias by referencing the eighties sitcom *Head of the Class*, saying, "We were subconsciously told from the get-go that an African American boy couldn't be in a gifted classroom." That he talks about it at all is key to developing the leadership aspect of Gordon Allport's conditions for positive intergroup contact.[72]

Per Cole's instructions, the teachers split into pairs, and chatter breaks out. I see a white and black faculty pair literally jog into the corner to talk. The groupings are heterogeneous for the most part, many interracial, some a blend of younger and older faculty. Shimko-Daye sits on the steps of the stage with a faculty member, gently tapping her partner's knee to emphasize her point. After a few minutes on the first prompt—talk about your own identity—the second one comes: talk about a time when you felt someone was being culturally insensitive to you or someone else.

When the paired talk begins to fade, Cole brings everyone into a large circle. Faculty share haltingly, but when they do, it's powerful. There's a woman who acknowledges the death of her son, a former student at Ecoff, and her subsequent desire to work in the community that helped take care of him. Another woman thanks her fellow faculty for their support in her first year of teaching. She says, "I know I dress different, I do have a wife, which is a thing that's part of who I am. I talked with leadership about how to handle this with my students and they said it's okay if I'm open. I've been in schools where being myself was not okay to do."

Gentle applause breaks out after people share, with Cole occasionally thanking someone for their vulnerability. He closes by reminding each person in the room that they're part of a team and encouraging them to reach out to have similar conversations with different teachers. "Our kids will feel it, even if they don't see it," he tells them.

CHAPTER 4

Binford Middle School

New Leadership and Arts Integration in Richmond's Historic Fan Neighborhood

I WATCHED BINFORD MIDDLE SCHOOL's dynamic principal, Melissa Rickey, make a practiced but heartfelt case for arts integration to a roomful of prospective families and students one November evening in 2018, three years into her tenure. She spoke of student preparation and affirmation through the arts, as well as the school's coveted Turnaround Arts distinction and related partnership with musician Jason Mraz.[1]

In addition to her rousing embrace of arts in education, Principal Rickey underscored the importance of the school "looking like the city," saying that twenty-two of twenty-six elementary zones were represented at Binford through its choice-based open enrollment policy. She walked her overwhelmingly white audience, packed into Binford's auditorium for a chance to see the quarterly arts showcase, through a series of frequently asked questions around the availability of honors courses ("they are offered") and how the school handles discipline ("middle school is messy, but we're improving").[2] One of Rickey's more powerful statements, uttered in this period of heightened accountability, competition, and parental anxiety was this: "School should be joyful. We believe that's a prerequisite for success." As she closed, I saw people turn to smile at one another.

Rickey's presentation capped a night filled with numerous demonstrations of arts integration in practice. The seventh-grade life sciences class, for instance, had written original song lyrics about cell formation. It was called "Cell-o," sung in rhythmic gospel style to the tune of Adele's "Hello" and accompanied by a carefully choreographed dance. Visitors to Binford's second floor came upon a racially diverse group of girls, arms linked, singing, "Hello, it's me, a cell . . . I tell a story with my DNA." Shadow dancers from the class were projected onto the wall above the singers, breaking apart and coming back together in true cell fashion. Learning standards linked to the project flashed discreetly across the screen once the dancers had finished.

When I was a student at Binford in the early 1990s, the school was about 75 percent black and 25 percent white in a city school system that was roughly 90 percent black and 10 percent white.[3] More than five hundred students attended Binford at the time, tumbling to about two hundred twenty-five years later. The share of white students shrank from 25 percent to 6 percent during the same period. Those declines occurred in response to a dwindling population of assigned students, transportation cuts for choice students, and competition in the form of new middle school programming offered elsewhere in the city. But enrollment trends had shifted quickly under Rickey's leadership and the new arts integration emphasis. Over a short span of two years, by 2017, Binford's student population had more than doubled and the white share had increased to 17 percent.[4]

Overall white student enrollment in Richmond Public Schools (RPS), the system that houses Binford, tanked in the decades after the courts limited school desegregation to a city already hemorrhaging white, middle-class families and tax dollars.[5] In the aftermath of the Great Recession, however, the city, like many urban centers in the United States, reported faster population growth than its suburban neighbors— for the first time in almost a century.[6] Driving much of that growth were young, white, well-to-do professionals and families.[7] White population increases also have very slowly translated to white enrollment increases in Richmond's public schools, bringing with them the renewed tax base and per-pupil funding that accompanies reinvestment.[8]

Binford offers a glimpse of how a middle school can make good use of the opportunities presented by urban growth, in part by attracting and retaining white, affluent families like the ones in the crowd for Rickey's presentation. Within a very short period of time, new leadership and curricular foci, along with additional resources, helped shift perceptions about Binford's desirability among these families. Yet as white and middle-class interest mounts, the school remains committed to equitably serving a student population that reflects the still overwhelmingly black citywide enrollment. Binford is attempting, in other words, to find a balance between gentrification and integration.

It's not an easy task. Around the country, middle school is a crucial falling-off point for existing white and middle-class enrollment in urban schools.[9] These families, willing to stay for the elementary years, exit in droves once the developmental bridge between childhood and adolescence is in sight. Those that remain often are concentrated in just a few schools. Middle school is an educational conduit between primary school and preparation for the more complex academic worlds of high school and beyond. Within-school segregation, in the form of racialized tracking into upper- and lower-level courses, often takes firm hold here. And middle school, according to many of the caregivers, teachers, and leaders I interviewed, can be miserable. So what does it take to create integration during this often thorny rite of passage?

What follows is the story of a city in the throes of a renaissance that hasn't reached everyone, and an arts-integration-focused middle school in the midst of that renaissance. Like the other examples in this book, Binford's story is one of intentional leadership around diversity and perseverance against stubborn systems of segregation, of the limits and possibilities of a single school's efforts within those broader systems.

Dynamics of Segregation in an Urban School System

When federal courts overturned Richmond's city-suburban school district merger in the early 1970s, limiting comprehensive school desegregation to RPS, the city's population and tax base shrank as the pace of white flight further quickened.[10] Easy avoidance of the social and racial upheaval that urban-centric school desegregation represented was too tempting. In crossing over the city boundary, whites moved down a government-smoothed path of a post-WWII boom in suburban housing construction, readily available mortgage financing, ample credit, and rapid commuting times.[11] White and middle-class disinvestment in the city hobbled the nascent power of black political leaders, rapidly draining away resources as concentrated poverty skyrocketed. A regional mind-set in tatters, suburban outsiders peered in at a struggling urban core. They adopted surface-level, racialized explanations for urban troubles (e.g., mismanagement, high crime, and poverty), ignoring the suburb's role in systematically divesting cities of their status and power.[12]

Richmond's failure to cooperate regionally rendered the city-only school desegregation efforts short-lived and controversial. By 1984, facing the demographic realities of a now overwhelmingly black district, the Richmond school board sought an end to mandatory desegregation. Two years later, in one of the earliest decisions releasing a district from court oversight for desegregation, US District Court Judge Robert Merhige determined that Richmond schools were unitary, meaning they had eliminated dual, segregated systems of schooling for black and white students to the extent possible. Merhige's decision heralded the end of court-ordered desegregation for RPS. The judge also ruled against a second lawsuit seeking additional funding for the racially isolated school system.[13]

Echoes of contemporary debates about better funding for urban school systems can be heard in Judge Merhige's rationale. He dismissed money as a source of inequality, noting an RPS per-pupil allotment higher than the state average. Merhige also pointed to neighborhood and community poverty as the larger issue, ignoring the close relationship between state-sponsored housing and school segregation. His unitary status and funding decisions helped usher in a new era of judicial rulings related to school desegregation.[14] Courts increasingly viewed their remedial role as time-limited, claiming that ongoing segregation was an inevitable product of demographic transition rather than a centuries-old product of public and private decision-making.[15] The irony was that Merhige had been the one to issue the groundbreaking city-suburban district consolidation ruling in the early 1970s. His decision then centered on an entirely different understanding of the judiciary's obligation to remedy school and housing segregation—one that would have checked, had it been implemented, the demographic transition he found so intractable just a little over a decade later.[16]

In the aftermath of unitary status, RPS officials turned to the task of administering student assignment without court oversight. Hoping to appease black families struggling with unfair transportation burdens related to desegregation, retain remaining white and middle-class families, and control costs across the system, the district committed to neighborhood-based school assignments in 1987.[17] At the same time, several open enrollment schools—meaning any family in the district could apply for admission—continued to operate in the district, soon to be expanded. Proximity and choice, introduced by Richmond's first black superintendent in the mid-1970s, governed student assignment. Both still do.

Origins of a Diverse Urban Middle School

"Model schools" represented a central feature of school choice in RPS. These open enrollment schools offered a specialized curriculum with a focus on critical and creative thinking. Beginning in the late seventies and continuing for over a decade, officials designated a handful of elementary school "model" institutions. Sited throughout the city, they were highly regarded and sought after by both black and white middle-class families.[18] In 1988, just before I enrolled, Binford became the first model middle school in RPS, part of a statewide priority around revamping middle schools. A year later, the Virginia Department of Education awarded Binford "vanguard" middle school status to honor its innovative approaches to program design and instruction.[19]

Richmond's superintendent at the time, Dr. Albert Jones, selected Binford Model Middle for his own daughter. Though Binford, like Richmond's other model schools, contained some elements of magnet school design, particularly with regard to innovative or specialized programming, it differed from traditional magnets in important ways. For one, Richmond's post-unitary status era model schools didn't operate under

explicit diversity goals, a central feature of the historical magnet concept.[20] Most of Richmond's model schools also were not sited in neighborhoods of concentrated poverty.[21] Officials instead located them in
the city's more affluent neighborhoods, where the open enrollment and
neighborhood school emphases could work together to hold surrounding families and attract others from more distant communities.

I rode the school bus to Binford from Richmond's Church Hill
neighborhood. It picked us up in all our flat-topped, feathered-banged,
overalled (one strap down à la the *Fresh Prince*) early nineties glory, busily
rolling through the heavily black and overwhelmingly poor East End.
Our route wound in and out of the city's downtown and up into what
was then a white working-class enclave called Oregon Hill, finishing up
in Randolph and Maymont, two black working-class neighborhoods.

Church Hill fell outside Binford's actual attendance boundary,
while downtown, Oregon Hill and Randolph were located within its
eastern perimeter. To the west, Binford's zone encompassed my current
neighborhood of Byrd Park, long known as a racially diverse, mixed-
income community, as well as most of Richmond's historic Fan neighborhood, the largest continuous span of Victorian homes on the East
Coast.[22] Built at the turn of the last century, Binford takes up a full city
block in the Fan, a towering old gray stone fortress amid more delicate
Victorian neighbors.

Once Binford received its model middle school designation, those
of us enrolling from beyond the borders of the racially and economically diverse neighborhoods captured by Binford's attendance zone
went through a careful screening and selection process. I wasn't fully
aware of how the admissions process worked until I interviewed one
of my favorite middle school teachers for this book. David Odehnal
taught Binford's eighth-grade civics classes for more than two decades
with a series of fast-paced, rib-tickling conversational sidebars and creative projects. (I remember proposing an elaborate plan for peace between Northern Ireland and Great Britain in his class, not to mention
intensively preparing for my role as the defense attorney in Lorena Bobbitt's trial.)[23] As middle-class white and black interest in the citywide
enrollment option began to tick upward during Odehnal's first several

years teaching at Binford, the school implemented a faculty-led review of out-of-zone student portfolios. Odehnal was on the review committee, which considered a combination of recommendations, student test scores, elementary school grades, and attendance. It also had an eye for musical talent—Binford had excellent band and harp programs. The committee broke into smaller faculty teams, and teachers would check their individual student ratings against other members of their team. If a set number of teachers voted to admit a student, the team would forward its recommendations to the school administration for a final decision. Odehnal remembered admitting roughly one hundred out-of-zone students per year early on, with these students automatically qualifying for Binford's rapidly expanding honors courses. About a hundred in-zone students also enrolled each year by virtue of where they lived. These students weren't guaranteed access to the honors track.

A few items of note arise from Binford's out-of-zone selection procedures back then. In a system struggling to retain white and/or middle-class families after a sharply curtailed urban desegregation process, the prestige associated with Binford's model school designation and competitive selection process may have helped generate demand from these families when it came to middle school. One former faculty member further pointed to the superintendent's decision to send his daughter to Binford as a turning point that coincided with the model school label. Binford became "the place to go" in the early nineties, highlighting a significant status shift for the school among several groups of middle-class families, which snowballed into interest from similarly situated families in other parts of the city. Yet enrolling at Binford from beyond its attendance boundary was far from an open process, since the school's interest in the student dictated admission, rather than the other way around. Disproportionate white and/or middle-class enrollment in Binford had a systemic effect on other middle schools, pulling the district out of balance. And it created two systems of education within Binford itself, as automatic assignment to honors courses for admitted out-of-zone students divided them from in-zone peers for most of the day.

Back then, the simultaneous expansion of honors courses and the hiring of a full-time gifted instructor (a position determined by the

number of students requiring gifted services, the provision of which began in the late 1970s as part of another RPS effort to hold the middle-
class and white families flowing away from the system), created a wide
range of teaching and learning experiences at Binford. [24] In a school
that was 75 percent black and 25 percent white, honors classes drifted
toward a 50 percent–50 percent split. And though data on the racial
and socioeconomic status of honors students were and are impossible
to access publicly, Odehnal remembered it this way: "My first class was
pretty small, I think I only had one honors class, but each year it built.
What I really liked about it was that as you know, there were a lot of
white students, and there were a lot of African American students. I
found that a lot of the African American students who were in the honors classes . . . their parents were professionals. They were lawyers, they
were doctors, they were dentists."

In essence, tracking into and within Binford created two experiences, one overwhelmingly working class or low income and black, comprising mostly in-zone students, and another overwhelmingly middle
class and racially diverse, comprising mainly out-of-zone students.

Numerous conversations with Binford stakeholders suggested that
the growing availability of honors coursework in the early 1990s, along
with the tracking it engendered, became a key strategy for creating external integration—at the risk of severely undermining internal integration.[25] In other words, honors courses initially helped attract white
and middle-class families to the school, but dictated different sets of
opportunities within the school.

This was not a trend limited to Binford. Tracking feels like the way
we have always done education, though its origins can be traced back
to reactions to immigration in the early twentieth century and, even
before that, to the end of slavery.[26] It's bolstered by assumptions about
race, intelligence, merit, and how to best challenge high-achieving students. While tracking often begins with ability grouping and disparate
gifted identification in elementary school, it takes firm root in middle
school, where curricular pathways get locked in at the tender age of
eleven or twelve.[27] Supporters tend to point to the idea that tracking
makes instruction easier on the teachers and gives students the oppor-

tunity to learn at a suitable, individualized pace.[28] In school systems defined by rapid racial change and/or scarce resources, tracking also becomes a way to stave off the exit of more affluent families.[29] Despite these arguments, a meta-analysis of five hundred studies on tracking found "minimal effects on learning outcomes and profoundly negative equity effects."[30]

Using the creation and expansion of honors and gifted courses as a blueprint for attracting affluent and/or white families to Binford eventually extended beyond the building into other RPS middle schools. In fact, competition from these other schools is part of what contributed to Binford's overall enrollment decline in the early 2000s, as well as its corresponding drop in white and out-of-zone students. In racially and economically isolated urban districts, a new programmatic offering, a small but perceptible shift in family interest, a transportation-related policy change, and/or gentrification each has the potential to limit diversity at one school while promoting it at another. For Binford, all four circumstances converged in the late 1990s and early 2000s.

Shifting Programs, Policies, Interests, and Neighborhoods

In 1999, Binford began losing students to a new Richmond middle school that opened south of the James River. A separate wing of the building was devoted to prestigious International Baccalaureate programming, the entrance to which was governed by a test. Interviewees and enrollment trends also indicated that successive waves of white, affluent families began opting into a different RPS middle school north of the river, one with a zone that incorporated some of the wealthiest and whitest parts of the city.[31] Then, significant fiscal pressures associated with the Great Recession, along with decreases in test scores, prompted the Richmond school board to cut transportation funding for Binford's choice students. Meanwhile, demographics within Binford's attendance zone, the borders of which have not shifted since I was enrolled, underwent tremendous changes. The significant and rapid expansion of Virginia Commonwealth University helped gentrify the formerly working-class neighborhoods of Oregon Hill and Randolph, pricing out families with school-age children and replacing them partly with college-age students. Housing prices in the historic Fan community skyrocketed in the wake of the Great Recession. Moreover, a recent elementary school rezoning process that maximized neighborhood enrollment at a sought-after Fan elementary school essentially eliminated the possibility of opting into it from other city communities. Affluent families buying a home in the Fan began to feel as though they were also buying seats at the desirable elementary school, but not necessarily at Binford, which had suffered a loss of status for all of the preceding reasons. The dearth of Fan neighborhood families at Binford was, in fact, one of the motivations for the recent push for new programming at the school.[32]

As early as 2011, Richmond's school leaders recognized the urgency of addressing Binford's declining enrollment in the context of diminished enrollment across all of the city's middle schools.[33] The superintendent at the time, Dr. Yvonne Brandon, set a goal of creating a system of theme-based middle schools, known as the Middle School Renaissance.[34] Community and business partners would provide volunteers, mentors, and other forms of assistance to boost thematic foci and opportunities for out-of-school learning time. For Binford, an art-based theme was a natural fit given its proximity to Virginia Commonwealth University's nationally recognized arts program.[35]

All of which takes us to the beginning of Binford's contemporary external integration work, as stakeholders intentionally have strived to bring a racially and economically diverse group of students together through the front doors of the school. The work has incorporated many dimensions. These include community feedback, new programming, leadership that's helped shift family perceptions of the school, an emphasis on neighborhood and citywide enrollment, implicit diversity goals, free transportation, and equitable admissions.

Binford and External Integration

In 2014, after a series of stakeholder conversations and a community survey about Binford's future, processes led by a newly appointed superintendent, the Richmond school board decided to adopt innovative curricular foci, along with revamped enrollment policies and a return to free citywide transportation.[36] The new superintendent, Dr. Dana

Bedden, emphasized a quick decision-making process given the urgency of underenrollment.

There were competing pressures. One was a desire to capitalize on Richmond's long-standing and well-known arts scene.[37] Yet another, according to Bedden, a former magnet school principal in Washington, DC, was a sense that the rigor associated with an Advanced Placement College Board SpringBoard curriculum would "create a unique pull . . . [and] have the community believe that there was something reputable about the school."[38] The school board initially decided on a "both/and" approach, adopting an arts integration approach and the College Board SpringBoard curriculum.

Despite conversation around readopting the criteria-based admissions reminiscent of my childhood experiences, a reflexive local antidote for low white, middle-class parental demand and perceived school status, the superintendent pressed for actual open enrollment into Binford. Bedden proposed "a straight-up lottery" for out-of-zone students, reversing the school's earlier 1990s-era screening process.[39] Under the new paradigm, the school board also reinstated free, hub-based transportation to Binford. Out-of-zone students could receive a ride to their zoned elementary school and then catch a second bus to Binford. That system saved the school district money, while still ensuring that families struggling to provide their own transportation could enroll their children.

The school board didn't adopt explicit diversity goals for Binford when it approved the new design. Still, leaders publicly emphasized they wanted "a school that looked like the city." Bedden expressed that sentiment early on, telling me, "That first year I walked into the auditorium and saw that mixture of people crowding the scene with white, black, Asian, and Hispanic, you know, and I'm like, this is representative of the city. That's what we were hoping to get." Binford had found a niche that included integration.

Contemporary Shifts in Leadership, Faculty, and Outreach

Implementing arts integration and the AP College Board SpringBoard curriculum with finesse meant considerable training for Binford's growing faculty. Even before training though, faculty and leadership needed to believe in the new initiatives. To facilitate buy-in—and to open the door for more hires as needed—Bedden met with the teachers, telling them, "[Y]ou can opt out but it's okay to stay in and say that you're learning and help build this great middle school." He indicated that district leadership would view early test results leniently to provide time for learning and improvement. Bedden also decided to hire a different principal, feeling that a specific skill set was required to successfully move the initiatives forward.

The district found that skill set and leader in Melissa Rickey. Those around her described her as passionate, engaging, visible, reflective, and resourceful. She started as a visual arts teacher in an affluent part of suburban Chesterfield, mentored by a dynamic principal who believed in identifying and nurturing talent. Her contributions in Chesterfield had been recognized by Binford's university arts partners, who encouraged her to apply when the principalship opened up. After getting the job, Rickey moved her family from the suburbs into the Fan district and enrolled her son at Binford for the first year of the new programming. He was joined by Bedden's daughter, with both leaders deliberately demonstrating support for the new initiative. It's hard to calculate the impact of this personal investment, which extended beyond Rickey and Bedden to university partners and Binford teachers who also enrolled their children, but it does send important signals about the programming and the confidence of the leadership behind it.

Rickey's passion for using art as a means to better engage students in learning is matched by a large-hearted bent toward equity and inclusion. She's the daughter of a white American nuclear geophysicist and a Brazilian art teacher. Rickey grew up translating for her mom (or watching her dad do so) during parent-teacher meetings, while her family navigated false assumptions about her mother's intelligence due to the language barrier. She knows it doesn't have to be that way, breaking into fluent Spanish during faculty meetings with virtually no Spanish-speaking staff present in an effort to affirm rather than detract from linguistic diversity.[40] Without exception, stakeholders described Rickey as key to Binford's transformation, inspiring confidence and trust from a wide variety of families, teachers, and partners.

In the late spring and summer of 2014, Rickey, with her biracial background, along with a new white assistant principal, replaced a black administration. Like Binford's students, the composition of teachers had shifted since the 1990s, tracking prior research showing that faculty and student segregation are often intertwined.[41] As the school's students resegregated in the mid-2000s, so too had the racially diverse faculty of my childhood. It's growing more diverse again today, alongside growing student diversity and the new arts focus.

Outreach has been central to Rickey's work over the years. Her presentation to different stakeholders around the city has been honed over many experiences. One of the earliest was an invitation to speak at the Fan Women's Club, "a social organization for ladies living in Richmond's historic Fan district." In a beautiful Fan house decorated to the hilt for the holidays, four Christmas trees twinkling in the background, Rickey fielded questions about programmatic changes underway at Binford. A member of the club said, "[Maybe it was the] arts integration hook or just the idea that this was a new *something* was kind of the hook that was needed. [The Fan] was obviously an area that was hungry for a good middle school option."

Changing Conversations, Changing School Status

The voices of current Binford families show how linkages between neighbors, colleagues, acquaintances, and friends shape opinions about schools.[42] The influence that social networks have on family school choices makes cultivating positive perceptions central to external integration. Like its earlier model school designation, or the reimagination of early-years education at the YWCA, Binford's new programming and leadership changed the basic content of informal conversations over cups of coffee, at the playground, or during neighborly visits, opening minds and shifting decisions along the way. In the city proper, where decades of disinvestment have led many to believe that quality school options are scarce—and where rising inequality accelerates the sense of competition surrounding those options—these conversations among affluent and/or white families begin early and don't let up.

Though the neighborhood elementary school was a given for many white and affluent families, some of whom opted to live in the Fan primarily *because* of the elementary school, the mothers I interviewed repeatedly said they heard some version of the following: "You'll have to do something else for middle school. You can't go to Binford." Over the past couple of years, as the first few affluent, white Fan families began opting in to Binford, the pressure to shift those conversations mounted. "Now when I go to parties," one mother told me, "it's the first question I get asked, like OMG your son's at Binford, how's it going?" She, along with other interviewees, talked about the weight of those conversations, the anxiety and bias lingering behind questions related to rigor or safety. They felt a sense of responsibility to the Binford community, striving to talk about its strong points in an effort to reinforce its changing reputation.[43]

One Fan resident, a white mother of three young kids, sensed a generational shift in the urgency around school selection. She's a graduate of RPS, an old friend of mine from our days at Binford twenty-five years ago. We hadn't spoken in some time when she agreed to be interviewed. She said:

> So my kids, we're in the same district [that I was] . . . honestly I don't know how much thought my parents put into it. I feel like our decision is more deliberate, but also more fraught with indecision. I mean, it's all anybody talks about in our neighborhood. Where are you going to middle school? I think the choice that comes from doubting the choice . . . [means] you obsessively have to talk about all of those options all the time . . . and there's so much judgment in what you do.

I'm wondering what else besides increased parental indecision, anxiety, and judgment—already a lot—might feel different about the current era of parenting versus the former. So I asked her what she thinks about inequality in the city, now versus then. Here's a piece of that conversation:

> *Fan resident:* I don't remember any white kids at Binford that were wealthy-wealthy. I mean my family was certainly more middle

class than most. But now, there are parents that I know in RPS
that are what I would consider wealthy-wealthy. I kind of think
back in our day, if you were that wealthy you just went to private school.

Me: What do you think [the presence of wealthy-wealthy families]
does to the school system?

Fan resident: It probably makes it more unfair . . . [W]e have this art
auction [at my Fan elementary school] every year. And it raises
a ton of money for the school, and the money goes to fund the
afterschool programs, which a lot of children are able to attend
through scholarship. So it goes for the good of the school but
. . . I don't know if it's always for the good of the system.

These observations provide a brief window into rising wealth inequality and its ripple effects in an urban school system. Greater wealth
contributes to indecision around schooling; more resources give families more choices in the form of either private schools or relocation
to another district. White, wealthy families that choose to stay in the
public school system tend to cluster in a select handful of schools, funneling into them private resources and political clout in the context
of a heavily under-resourced, nonwhite, segregated public district.[44]
Those resources, in turn, can help pay for meaningful interventions
in the form of additional staff, tutoring, quality afterschool programming, professional development, building repairs, or extracurricular
activities.[45]

The mothers here also shed light on the intense professionalization
of parenting that has come to define child-rearing in this individual-
istic and unequal era.[46] As the middle class shrinks, well-off parents
strive to maintain their children's advantaged standing through education and enrichment. Progressive social values, which frequently go
hand in hand with affluent white families' choice of urban schools,
can be in tension with the concerted cultivation directed toward their
children.[47] So there's critique and awareness in the midst of parental
anxiety.[48] One white Binford mother said she was talking with a family that had elected not to go to the school, rationalizing their posi-

tion with a statement to the effect of: "You know, [our kids] went to a diverse elementary school and feel like that's where [our kids] learned their empathy and now they need to focus on their academics." She shook her head incredulously and went on to say that some affluent families choosing urban schools see themselves as martyrs rather than "in community." These families feel they are "taking a risk" with RPS as opposed to engaging with RPS. And affluent families with numerous options wield the existential possibility of exit, threatening to diminish the already scarce resources they are vying for.

For the wealthy families that do choose to stay "in community," strong convictions about what their own children stand to gain from diverse schools affirm their decision. Reflecting on how she grew during her years at Binford, my old friend told me, "I learned how to be uncomfortable . . . [I]t's a normal feeling . . . [F]or me it means you're still growing and learning, and opening up your world." When I asked my dad what he thought my sisters and I had learned from Binford, he said he was "proud and satisfied that every one of you is directed towards helping others, not held back by bias or ignorance." And an affluent white mom of kids of color saw the gains in both directions. "For me," she said, "It's about having a less racist society for my children . . . and [there are] obviously all kinds of benefits from being around kids who look like them . . . [so they] don't feel singled out or isolated."

All of these sentiments reflect an understanding of the social value of integrated schools, though, as we saw in the first chapter, they fail to include mention of the very real academic value.

The Fan neighborhood wasn't the only affluent, largely white community interested in Binford. A string of neighborhoods on the city's north side, known for their happy mixes of cottages, Arts and Crafts bungalows, four squares, and Queen Anne Victorians, contained numerous residents seeking additional public options for middle school. Much of the Northside community had invested in its diverse local elementary school but remained dissatisfied with its highly segregated feeder middle school. This group of families was used to navigating the open enrollment process into other middle schools but was often shut out by a lack of available seats. Rob McAdams, a Northside resident and university partner in Binford's arts transformation, led several informal parent meetings about the school in his neighborhood. He described it as "just going to peoples' houses with a little presentation on my laptop," where groups of primarily white parents had gathered looking for information and encouragement. McAdams, as I realized quickly during our meeting, is an arts integration ambassador second to none. These living-room conversations, layered onto more formal information disseminated by Rickey and the school system, produced results: McAdams remembers about twelve mostly white Northside elementary families going to Binford in the first year of its new programming, followed by a larger group that went with his son in the second year. By the third year, almost thirty Northside families had signed on to Binford.

Surveying their success in shifting the nature of dialogue about Binford among white and middle- to upper-class families, measured by a sharp increase in the number of choice-based lottery applications, a marked uptick of interest from in-zone Fan families, and the rapid growth and diversification of enrollment, many stakeholders began to worry about an overrepresentation of white and middle-class families in the school. After just two years, a key question surfaced: would Binford become predominately white in an overwhelmingly black and Latinx school system?

Unequal Information in an Unequal System

Unequal flows of information among segregated social networks—absent tangible diversity goals—represented an underlying reason for well-placed fears of starkly disproportionate white and/or middle-class enrollment at Binford. The white, mixed-race, and affluent families that I spoke with all had stories of navigating a byzantine open enrollment process. Here's how a white Fan mom with an advanced professional degree explained it:

> I've been going to all the middle school nights for years . . . [W]e just sought out every opportunity . . . [T]here were nuggets of information on how to navigate the system that I learned with repeated

opportunities to talk, especially around what classes were important [for entrance to the specialty high schools] . . . I felt like there was no manual for this. I needed any opportunity I could to untangle it and there would be little insights that people would drop either in the questions or in the administrative responses that helped me navigate the system.

She wasn't the only person who felt that way. Months after our interview, I ran into my friend from middle school, whose oldest child is a third-grader, at the Binford art showcase and information session described in the opening. She was there to get a feel for the school several years before her child could enroll. Other families felt obligated to participate in the open enrollment process for middle school despite reservations about its implications. One told me, "I felt like I would be doing my kid a disservice if I didn't [go through open enrollment]" but went on to say that she couldn't discern substantive differences between Binford (her zoned middle school) and the open enrollment option to which she could apply, except that the latter was "whiter and the building was in better shape."[49]

Middle-class black families in the city relied on similarly privileged but somewhat different sources of information about open enrollment. I spoke to an African American mother, a former RPS teacher, who enrolled her son at Binford from an out-of-zone neighborhood. Backed by experience with the open enrollment process in elementary school, which she'd navigated with the help of a principal she knew, this mom had gone to all of the middle school open houses, completed the application process, and had options. The family's zoned middle school worried her, in part because it was an amalgamation of two schools that had merged due to facilities' issues and overcrowding. To her, diminished resources and gang violence seemed possible if not likely. She ultimately settled on Binford because her son loved the arts and because she, like the other families I interviewed, adored Rickey.

Of the twelve Binford family stakeholders that I spoke with, only one mentioned exchanging information about schools with someone of a different race. The description came from a white resident of a primarily black working-class neighborhood. Her neighbor, a middle-aged black woman, "[d]idn't hear about the opportunities I heard about. You knew when and how and where and went to see [middle school options]. This was a conversation for me in preschool, that information was passed down from the jump. [But my neighbor] heard about Binford from me."

The white mom said that the hub-based transportation was a barrier for her neighbor, who worried about safe passage for her son. This segment of our conversation closed with an acknowledgment that the city had been working on making the information and system fairer.

Current school board member Kenya Gibson shared similar concerns, acknowledging that, even with improvements, more work is needed. The application process for open enrollment is now online, and early iterations of the new computer-based system made it difficult to know whether or not an application had been submitted successfully. RPS did extend the open enrollment application window from ten days to ten weeks, considerably expanding access for families who receive information more slowly or who lack access to a computer. Robocalls alert stakeholders to deadlines and information sessions, though Gibson is quick to say that it's not the same "as someone encouraging you to consider all the options." Or, as we saw above, a group of similarly situated families discussing the process for years and sharing tips and strategies for moving through it. And despite earlier and recently renewed calls for more equitable access and systemic engagement with theme-based secondary schools, explicit diversity goals that ask schools like Binford to stay within some approximation of the system's overall enrollment remain elusive. [50]

Binford and Internal Integration

As Binford's enrollment expands and diversifies, Rickey and her team have worked intentionally to shape an inclusive, collaborative school culture. Race, class, and conflict surfaced regularly within the school, met with numerous initiatives that facilitate and nurture relationships across lines of difference.

Binford's current leadership is blunt about the challenges posed by rapid racial shifts among students, families, and staff—but is ready and willing to engage them. As in society, race remains an ever present issue at Binford. Rickey said, "Race comes up often . . . [I]t comes up when there's conflict, when a teacher says something and it's interpreted, and there's hurt behind what was said. When there's discipline. It comes up when we're having peaceful discourse, or when there is a joyful moment in our community, a community showcase."

The discussion of race—and conflict surrounding it—is not limited to any one group. Families bring it up, sometimes directly, as when a black family seeks a same-race, same-sex teacher for a child who needs help, and sometimes indirectly, as when a white family urges the administration to consider ousting a black out-of-zone student for behavioral issues without acknowledging the racial implications of the request. Students bring race up when a different-race teacher disciplines them; teachers bring it up when they feel as if staff conversations aren't probing deeply enough into the specter race casts over the school. There are racial overtones in tensions between older teachers, who tend to be African American, and newer teachers, who tend to be white, as they explore shared wonder about what the new arts integration model means for teaching and learning and what discipline should look like in a changing environment.[51]

How to navigate it all? A guiding principle for Binford's leadership, also employed at Sprout and Ecoff, has been to simply acknowledge racial conflict as an ongoing struggle. There's a posture of listening and empathizing with the many different perspectives in the school community. As one Binford leader explained in 2018, "We try to keep that conversation [about race] in the forefront . . . [A] lot of times people are afraid to have the conversation. It's kind of like the elephant in the room that nobody wants to say anything about. We will have that conversation. It just takes a lot. You just need to close your mouth and listen to what people have to say and understand differences."

There are also numerous strategies and structures designed to place conflict alongside collaborative understanding. These include creating a shared mission; forming systems to promote contact among students, teachers, and families; using an arts and justice orientation to nurture positive identities, relationships, and achievement; and offering a wide range of electives and clubs for students.

Bringing the School Together Around a Shared Mission

Developing a short, clear school mission and vision became one key strategy for uniting faculty around a common purpose, especially once school stakeholders decided to shed the dual, sometimes competing, foci of arts and College Board SpringBoard after the first couple of years. In 2018, Rickey and several members of her leadership team traveled to a conference sponsored by Turnaround Arts, a public-private partnership to improve low-performing schools. Brittany Packnett, a former Teach for America corps member and current Black Lives Matter activist, keynoted the event and advised the various school groups. She asked leaders to think carefully about what leading and teaching art through equity meant. Rickey distinctly remembered Packett saying, "Are you really teaching lessons that love your kids?"

The question resonated. Wrestling with the importance of communicating to students, as Rickey put it, "I see you and what you're bringing to my classroom is valuable," the team began to think about how to articulate those values in a mission or vision statement. All three members of the Binford group had the words "prepare" and "affirm" in their notes from the conference and brought their ideas back to the sixteen-member school leadership team. Then they showed the team and the entire faculty Packnett's keynote and used a protocol to get everyone's input. The mission and vision grew organically from that process. "Prepare and affirm students to be their authentic selves through the arts" is now on the top of every agenda, on classroom and bathroom doors, in the hallways, and in Rickey's presentations to the external community.

Creating an "Us" out of "Them": The House System at Binford

In 2017, two years into her principalship, Rickey set to work building Binford's "houses." The five houses are modeled partly after Harry Potter's Hogwarts and have created teams of teachers and students within the school. One of their primary purposes is to build and support community. There are house handshakes, chants, posters, colors and T-shirts. Many of these group rituals are developed during the summer arts academy, a multiday orientation to Binford with free transportation provided by the school system. Friendly competitions like the House Olympics encourage house team members to cooperate in service of shared goals like winning the House Cup or earning points toward a special prize. Noncompetitive, performance-based house activities also reinforce cooperation and equal status interaction, especially when it comes to producing the quarterly or end-of-year arts showcases.[52]

Binford's houses offer multiple student leadership opportunities. Teachers select captains for each house, identifying a group of students who can lead a meeting with large groups of peers, help in the hallways, and develop strategy around winning the arts-based competitions. Introverts and class clowns alike have been selected, according to Rickey. Midyear, existing student leaders have been asked to find two additional housemates to serve as coleaders, looking for characteristics like trustworthiness or ability to inspire. There are a total of twenty house captains at Binford; multiple stakeholders described them as diverse in terms of race, socioeconomic status, and in- and out-of-zone residence.

Families reported that their children identify strongly with their houses, making posters and trying to explain the system to friends outside of Binford. Many genuine interracial friendships—and some romantic relationships—have sprouted among Binford's middle school students, according to adult observers. Such opportunities stem partly from close contact. Binford's houses have their own hallways so that student and teacher teams have a certain proximity to one another.

Each Binford house contains an English, math, science, exceptional education, and history teacher, along with one or two elective teachers. They share planning time, with regular meetings. Rickey says it "helps meet the needs of the arts integrated piece because, before, [the elective teachers] were on different teams, or planning periods." The collaboration also nurtures relationships among what's become "a pretty diverse teaching staff as far as age, race and experience," as one faculty member noted. He went on to say,

Everyone brings different things to the table. We have teachers that were brought in for arts integration. They were passionate about that and that's why they picked Binford and applied to it but don't necessarily have the experience of teaching in an urban district. And then you have teachers that have a lot of experience teaching in an urban district but were teaching way before arts integration was our thing and have seen different things come and go. They're looking for that development or that passion also.

The house structure, in essence, facilitates frequent, contextualized professional development. Teachers learn with and from one another, creating interdisciplinary, arts-based units and showcase products, in addition to problem-solving attendance and discipline issues and wrapping around students who need more support. By 2018, the second year of Binford's houses, attendance rates had increased and discipline referrals—and suspensions—had dropped sharply.[53] Rickey attributes this partially to regular, intentional conversations, enabled by the frequency of faculty house meetings, about attendance, discipline, and trauma-informed care.

Once enough students enroll in Binford, the goal is to have grade-level houses (e.g., two sixth-grade houses, two seventh, two eighth). But as of 2018, with about ninety students in each of the five houses, one was split between seventh- and eighth-grade students. And since house assignment was driven by the master schedule the first year they were rolled out, some administrators and stakeholders raised concerns about the overrepresentation of honors or exceptional education students in certain houses. The master schedule revolves around "student need, meaning exceptional education and other combinations, and then course requests for electives," said one teacher. Without intentional efforts to nurture diversity, which came in the second year of the house framework, "what they did is put a color and a face to our master schedule," the same teacher indicated. Test scores looked different across some of the houses, as did discipline. The second, 2018 iteration of house assignments yielded more balanced groups, aided by teachers' willingness to take on multiple class preparation tasks and instruct a mix of regular and honors courses. When asked if teachers expressed resistance to the shift and additional workload, Rickey just said, "They didn't want to be the reason student opportunities were limited."

White Students Still Disproportionately Assigned to Honors Courses

As white enrollment in both the school and in honors courses swells, reminiscent of the earlier Binford era, administrators and teachers have begun taking a close look at how students are identified for advanced curricular opportunities. For incoming sixth graders, placements flow from an uneven combination of teacher and counselor recommendations, grades, and test scores. Procedures associated with placement vary across Richmond elementary schools, with parental pressure likely contributing to high rates of gifted and honors identification in whiter, more affluent settings.[54] Creating additional layers of stratification, class cuts more cleanly along racial lines within Binford now than it did when I was a student. The school reported zero white, economically disadvantaged students in 2016, while more than half of the black students were economically disadvantaged.[55] White overrepresentation in honors thus became middle- and upper-middle-class overrepresentation, too.

Once at Binford, identification for seventh-grade course placement begins with a data triangulation process. The leadership team considers student, family, and teamed teacher input, student growth and achievement as measured by standardized tests, individualized education plans, and class size. Identification for honors isn't rigid, meaning students can take an honors English class but a regular math class, and they can shift between honors and regular classes as they advance a grade level.

Though Binford's use of multiple data points and flexibility is in many ways aligned with best practice, the system itself produces winners and losers when it comes to access to advanced curriculum. And the honors and regular course labels interfere with students' perceptions of one another. Students try to make meaning of why they can identify the level of a classroom just by noting its racial composition— and they often come away with racialized ideas about ability or cultural explanations for poor performance.[56] Tracking in general subverts the optimal conditions for intergroup contact, undermining equal status, disrupting cooperation and shared goals, and putting leaders in the position of sanctioning and upholding a racially unjust, limited contact system.

Forming a Multiracial Empathy Advisory Committee

With so many different expectations of K–12 public schools, it's hard to find structured time for contact among diverse families. But that's exactly what Rickey took on in the spring of her third year at Binford. She created a multiracial empathy advisory committee of about twelve school stakeholders—a mix of parents, school leaders, teachers, and community members to nurture empathy among adults at Binford.[57] In some ways, it was reminiscent of the interracial committees formed in the early days of desegregation. A number of court orders included interracial advisory committees to monitor and mediate issues arising from desegregation and to signal the value behind honoring the contributions and concerns of different groups.[58] Rickey's committee participated in data-based discussions of bias in discipline and tracking, in addition to exploring strategies for building positive relationships across lines of difference. A biracial advisory group member valued the effort, saying, "In middle school in particular there are fewer opportunities for parents to get to know each other; parents by nature are cutting the cord a little bit by then so that we don't have the opportunity to see and get to know and appreciate what all the differences are. That's what the group is doing." Another added that hearing multiple perspectives nurtured good decision-making on Rickey's part as she led Binford through rapid demographic change.

The empathy advisory committee wasn't actually the first opportunity for families and other school stakeholders to engage one another in difficult topics. In 2015, Rickey and the chair of Virginia Commonwealth University's arts education department applied for a modest community engagement grant to help build an arts culture at Binford. The grant made it possible for each student, family, bus driver, cafeteria worker, volunteer, teacher, and leader to visit the Virginia Museum

of Fine Arts several times. Afterward, they would debrief in small, facilitated groups, using art to have conversations such as, "What do
you see? Tell me more about what you see. I don't agree with what you
see, and this is why." Or, "What does that mean about our own beliefs
when we're challenged and hearing someone different from us?" Rickey
explained the arc of the conversations to me, smiling and reflecting:
"Arts are such a great way [to have these conversations] because it can be
about art or about everything but the art." Participating families, a racially mixed group that skewed white and numbered about thirty-five,
agreed and were particularly engaged, according to the arts education
chair. One of the African American family members in the group told
the facilitator, "Ordinarily I would not have . . . reached a level of trust
so quickly. I wouldn't have listened to you in the way that the art experience encouraged us to listen to each other."

Arts with a Justice Orientation Helps Promote Positive Student Identities and Achievement

Jonathan Walker's sixth-grade honors English class radiates gentle purpose. He's a young, white male teacher with owlish glasses and discreet
authority. Walker graduated from the Richmond Teacher Residency, an
intense, school-based, teacher preparation program at Virginia Commonwealth University that pairs residents with a veteran teacher for a
year before they take on their own classroom in a high-needs, hard-to-
staff school.[59] I'd zeroed in on his classroom because several interviewees mentioned it to illustrate student engagement with arts integration.
Rob McAdams, who's overseen professional development for many of
Binford's teachers, talked about Walker's curriculum around the book
Refugee, a compilation of different child-centered refugee stories. Each
student had a piece of fabric related to a refugee experience on their
desk, and Walker asked them to "pick it up, feel it, look at it, maybe
smell it." Eventually, the Binford class made an object out of the fabric
pieces and wrote accompanying scenes or stories. The unit fostered empathy and perspective-taking through deep immersion in the stories of
a highly marginalized group of people. It also fostered critical thinking. Walker said he notices a difference in the quality and character of

discussion among his more diverse classes. In these settings, he can see students pausing longer to gather their thoughts, thinking carefully about how different classmates might perceive their contribution. This is the "going to the gym for your mind" process that makes diversity such an influential contributor to higher-order thinking.[60]

Arts integration explicitly incorporating justice—environmental, racial, social—characterized student work at Binford. And all students, regardless of the level of their coursework, had access to arts integration. For urban schools, hit hardest by the narrowing of the curriculum under the standards and accountability movement, broad exposure to a creative pedagogy grounded in the arts in and of itself is an accomplishment.[61]

The performance-based assessments on display during the quarterly showcases capture well Binford's efforts in this direction. A recent showcase opened with an eighth-grade house video addressing the negative environmental impacts of coal ash ponds littering the state. In sixth grade, history students read scripts of their ideas about new monuments for Richmond's Monument Avenue, weighing in on a deeply symbolic issue. Constructed around the turn of the last century, current monuments honor Confederate heroes like J. E. B. Stuart and Robert E. Lee. By contrast, Binford's students, black and white, suggested new tributes to Martin Luther King Jr., Harriet Tubman, and Katherine Johnson, the African American female mathematician who enabled NASA's first space flights. Seventh-grade history students were similarly immersed in concepts of racial justice, creating comic strips detailing the Reconstruction amendments to the US Constitution, underscoring the importance of outlawing slavery, and guaranteeing citizenship and legal protections for former slaves. Haiku poems demonstrating the push-pull factors related to immigration were displayed alongside the comic strips.

In Walker's room, a small group of students queued up audio recordings of one another reading "I am from" poems aloud, while simultaneously projecting intricate self-portraits on a large makeshift tented screen in the middle of the room. The poems have similar root prompts (I'm from . . . items, phrases, and foods) that, paired with the portraits, vividly captured the diversity and commonality of student experience in the room. Perhaps the pièce de résistance, though, could be found on Binford's third floor, up a series of steep ramps in a dimly lit hallway. The seventh-/eighth-grade house, Binford's most racially and academically diverse, had collaborated to produce a carefully orchestrated rap battle between significant historical and contemporary figures. Huge papier-mâché puppets, maybe nine feet tall, took lyrical turns describing their contributions to society. We heard from Chief Joseph, Crispus Attucks, Jason Reynolds, and Harriet Tubman, to name a few. It took two students to support each of the puppets; others gathered to change the prerecorded, student-devised and -produced rap songs.

As Binford's students enter the world of adolescence, regular opportunities to deeply engage with a diverse set of historical role models, as well as their own widely divergent backgrounds, create room for the development of healthy identities. For students of color, guided space to explore their culture and history within the regular curriculum provides for racial identity immersion, which later gives way to a willingness to form relationships with white peers ready to acknowledge their budding racial selves.[62] For white students, regular exposure to the realities of racism—through curricula, contact, and genuine intergroup friendships—moves them forward along the path of becoming an antiracist ally to communities of color.[63] These are processes, of course, and not necessarily linear. But having frequent occasions to grapple with race, identity, and history through art provides powerful motivation to understand oneself and one another in relation to our imperfect society and more perfect ideals.

More tangibly, test scores for Binford's arts integration students have trended positive. Just over two in five students were considered proficient in English in the eyes of the state in 2014, the year before arts integration was implemented. That number grew to two in three students in 2018. Similar improvement occurred in science and, to a lesser extent, in math. Yet despite progress for all groups of students, stark gaps between black, white, and economically disadvantaged student performance remain.[64] Binford's black and economically disadvantaged students perform below state averages in English, math, and science, for instance, while white students perform well above. Again, test scores reflect opportunities and advantages accrued over time beyond the realm of school, in addition to content learned within it.[65] Binford's white students hail from middle- to upper-middle-class households—remember, none were identified as economically disadvantaged in 2016—and don't shed their class and race advantage at the schoolhouse door.[66] The performance of Binford's white students relative to their peers in the school and state highlights two important realities: (1) racial achievement gaps reflect racial opportunity gaps, and (2) white, upper- to middle-class student achievement, as measured by test scores, remains high in schools where they are in the racial minority. Extensive prior research bears out both points, but they're often lost in debates about race, achievement, and desegregation.[67]

Electives, Clubs, and Extras Offer Additional Opportunities for Positive Interracial Interactions

Opportunities for empathic learning at Binford extend beyond core subjects to electives and extracurricular activities associated with arts integration. Students select from a robust list of arts, dance, and music classes, each providing natural opportunities for the conditions that facilitate positive contact. A peek into Binford's new basement dance studio, for example, reveals a group of girls, most but not all of whom are black, doing a "shake and relate" exercise. The instructor is telling students to explore positive and negative space by carefully juxtaposing their movements. The girls are laughing, hamming it up, but working together to create pictures with their bodies.

To further extend arts engagement at Binford, students select from a menu of thirty-six different teacher-led clubs like foreign movies, cooking, makerspace, or gardening. The clubs take place during the day to eliminate transportation issues once the school day has ended. Afterschool extracurricular activities like Higher Achievement onsite or at places like the nearby Visual Arts Center offer additional enrichment opportunities. These are critical moments of contact for diverse students; research indicates that the quality and sustainability of interracial relationships increases through informal or out-of-school activities.[68] While a lack of transportation after traditional school hours erects a barrier to participation, in 2018 the city announced a public-private initiative to increase access to afterschool programs. By 2020, every elementary and middle school will either offer programs on-site or provide transportation to afterschool activities.[69]

Signs of broader investment in afterschool opportunities are encouraging, but for the last several years, many of the extras have been unique to Binford. As one teacher familiar with other middle schools in RPS indicated, "[Binford's] electives are more available and abundant, those are just options that other middle schools in the district don't all have full-time staff for." Some of Binford's distinctive opportunities arise out of community partnerships linked to the arts integration focus. Others flow from resources brought in by the school's grant-writing capacity and/or its highly engaged Communities in Schools coordinator.[70] Binford's leaders present funding opportunities to teachers in an organized way, along with detailed descriptions of money available for clubs. Still other opportunities are a credit to Rickey's leadership and the relationships she's nurtured in the Fan and elsewhere. Her leadership team emphasized that external partners "can see her passion . . . [I]t's easy for a donor or a university to say, 'I want to align myself with this person. They are really trying to make a difference in a child, and it's not just about SOLs [Standards of Learning].'" Regardless of their source, Binford's extras highlight the social and resource benefits linked to school integration, as well as the more systemic inequities that emerge against a background of limited resources.[71]

Of the four schools I examine, Binford arguably is situated within the most challenging context. Richmond's urban school system continues to struggle against disinvestment and severely constrained resources, conditions that have been many decades in the making. Connected to that history, wealth inequality in the city has grown increasingly stark and parsed along racial lines. These realities exert heavy pressure on the district and its schools, leaders, teachers, families, and students, nearly all of whom are committed, in principle, to racial and social justice.

Yet more affluent and/or white families wield too much power over the system, at times warping it to serve their individual needs without considering broader communal impacts. They accumulate copious information, stored within segregated social networks, about important but limited opportunities like open enrollment, competitive admissions, and honors placement. Many are more than willing to build relationships and workarounds that unfairly influence those opportunities. And they have the financial wherewithal to move within or exit the system if they don't get what they want, eliminating resources associated with their children and cyclically contributing to outsized influence.

In late 2017, Richmond's school board hired a new superintendent, the first white male to lead RPS in generations. Like those who came before him, Jason Kamras is committed to building a more equitable school system. He also is unafraid to broach the subject of race, the city's legacy of segregation, or the multipronged gaps in opportunity that flow from it.[72] In an early interview with the local newspaper, Kamras proposed a systemwide set of themed magnet secondary schools, not unlike past visions, but this time directly in response to segregation within the district.[73] It is the first task outlined in RPS's new strategic plan, and he has billed it as "our pathway to integration."[74] Kamras's willingness to confront racial isolation and associated funding inequalities head-on is supported by teacher, parent, and community-led grassroots organizations.[75] Still, a school board decision to implement systemic choice with civil rights protections would protect Binford, as well as any other new theme-based schools, from significant white and middle-class overrepresentation. That kind of overrepresentation hasn't happened yet at Binford; there was plenty of room for rapid growth because the school was so underenrolled at the start of Rickey's tenure. But increasing interest without clear diversity goals (and supporting external integration methods for achieving them) virtually guarantees a school that won't look like the city in the near future.

Meanwhile, within Binford, leadership and faculty continue building a culture of arts, joy, and love. During the sixth-grade awards ceremony in June 2018, held just a few days after Jason Mraz played for the annual Binford arts and music celebration, otherwise known as Bamfest, Rickey, with her characteristic warmth and authenticity, opened the event, saying:

> We are so proud of you. Right now it's just time to be present to feel the love from your faculty and to feel pride in your accomplishments . . . Families let me thank you for letting us teach your children. We're hoping every moment they spend in this building, they're becoming a person filled with courage, love, compassion and forgiveness . . . and we're hoping every year to make the experience even better . . . [T]hese children are going to change the world . . . [T]he entire city has got your back.

Teachers lined the walls, smiling as their students trouped forward to receive awards. Students broke into chants and cheers for their peers. Families beamed proudly. The scene brought to life the lyrics of Mraz's song and video, filmed with Binford's students:

> Here's to the infinite possible ways to love you . . . I want you to have it all.

CHAPTER 5

CodeRVA High School

Innovation, Equity, and Cross-District Collaboration

In the shadows of a Richmond factory building abutting Interstate 95, a modest group had assembled to celebrate the culmination of several years of city-suburban cooperation. The occasion: a ribbon-cutting ceremony for CodeRVA, a lottery-based, magnet high school, focused on computer science and early college and career opportunities, that serves thirteen local school divisions. CodeRVA represents the first intentionally diverse *regional* school of its kind in an area still reeling, as we've seen, from its past failure to come together around equal educational opportunity.

Several local superintendents stood together on a makeshift dais, with CodeRVA's director and its five initial faculty and staff members. A camera crew captured the August 2017 scene from below. Dr. James Lane, superintendent of Chesterfield County Public Schools at the time, offered opening remarks. He highlighted three major foci—equity, workforce development, and high school innovation—that successfully knitted together a diverse coalition of stakeholders to help form CodeRVA. And he emphasized the vital role state grants played in creating the new school.[1] After brief comments from several other stakeholders, those on the dais gathered to cut the wide red ribbon draped ceremoniously across the front entrance. In a few short weeks, the first class of ninety-three students would troop through those doors.

Dynamics of Regional School Segregation

CodeRVA's nascent rise came at a critical juncture for Richmond—and for the nation. The regional scope of segregation is accelerating. The Richmond area, for example, has boasted five of the country's twenty fastest-mushrooming exurbs when it comes to white population growth.[2] These communities lie just beyond the diversifying inner-ring suburbs of Chesterfield and Henrico, potentially signifying white exodus to the region's farther-flung counties and school districts.[3]

Between 60 percent and 80 percent of school segregation by race can be attributed to school district boundaries—the lines between central city and suburb, for instance, or suburb and exurb.[4] In terms of income, school district lines increasingly play a role in sorting affluent families away from everyone else. Those at the upper end of the income spectrum, who've benefited most from growing inequality, are better able to buy access into exclusive districts.[5] Today, most children of different racial/ethnic and economic backgrounds attend separate schools because they're enrolled in separate districts altogether. Legal decisions like *Milliken* have rendered district boundaries nearly impermeable since the 1970s, solidifying their power to include and exclude.[6]

Highly sought-after schools boost home values, leading residents to view schools and their associated districts as commodities, whether or not they have children in the system.[7] Since local property taxes continue to make up the majority of education funding, opportunity is consolidated by sealing off the boundaries to affluent districts, making them accessible only to residents with the financial wherewithal to purchase homes in the area.[8] Sociologists have termed such phenomena "opportunity hoarding," calling, to my mind at least, a run on the bread and milk grocery aisles ahead of a storm by families who've already stockpiled such necessities.[9] This ripples back into the areas left behind, diminishing resources, political power, and our sense of collective responsibility for children and public education.

For the most well-off families, choosing a community—and the educational institutions with which it's linked—amounts to the most important school choice they'll make. From this fact flows two critical developments. First, it's politically difficult for policy makers to alter school-related boundaries that secure advantaged families' "rights" to certain schools.[10] Second, politicians of every stripe have supported the rapid expansion of alternative forms of school choice like charter schools, framed as a way to offer all families the right to choose. Yet charters, not to mention private schools and any associated vouchers, often lack an intentional focus on integration.[11] Partly as a result, research consistently finds that charters, private schools, and vouchers contribute significantly to school segregation.[12]

But what if stakeholders designed public regional schools of choice with an eye toward integration? Attractive offerings, diversity goals, thoughtful outreach, interest-based admissions, and free transportation, to name a few key external integration features, could entice families across calcified district boundaries into shared school spaces. Despite significant political and legal hurdles, regional magnet schools have met with success in a handful of places, including Connecticut, Rhode Island, and Texas.[13] In Richmond, the idea of a choice-based regional school explicitly designed to foster diversity seemed far out of reach before CodeRVA, particularly in light of our past resistance to regional school desegregation. Such efforts generally are rare, making it vital to understand why and how they come about.

Origins of a Diverse Regional Magnet School

CodeRVA sprang from a potent combination of trusting relationships among Richmond area superintendents, seed money from the state, an emerging educational focus on equity, and visionary, strategic leadership. The process of designing CodeRVA was not without its challenges, particularly around regionalism and financing, but the aforementioned combination helped overcome the hurdles.

Close Relationships Among Regional Superintendents and State Seed Money

CodeRVA began as a brainchild of Richmond area superintendents. They came into close contact through Virginia's "superintendent's regions" meetings, which structure regular conversations around shared educational issues and challenges. The Region 1 gatherings—encompassing all Richmond area school divisions—helped nurture the dialogue and trusting relationships necessary to carry forward an interdependent project like CodeRVA. Stakeholders associated with the school took note of the single-garment principles underlying their cooperation, with one saying, "What is so inspiring about CodeRVA is the fact that you have so many superintendents coming together not thinking about their individual needs or their individual egos or their individual school systems. They are 100 percent thinking about how do we do something good that really solves a big problem."

As Lane noted in his remarks at CodeRVA's ribbon-cutting ceremony, a Virginia Department of Education (VDOE) grant incentivizing high school innovation provided an initial impetus for the school. The sum for the planning grant was modest—just $50,000—but the prestige associated with winning one of the five grants offered additional encouragement. In the Richmond area, local superintendents didn't necessarily want to compete with one another for the grant. So at the invitation of Lane, a VDOE representative came to a regional superintendents' meeting to explain the purpose of the new grant competition. After the state official left, area superintendents started brainstorming. Initial ideas revolved around online coursework, community college partnerships, and internships.

By the time the superintendents submitted the grant proposal several months later, the programmatic vision had evolved considerably—shaped by input from influential education, business, and community stakeholders. Mounting interest in computer science as a core curricular component, as well as an ongoing emphasis on college and career readiness, informed planning conversations. Superintendents also borrowed ideas from schools they'd visited or heard about—San Diego's High Tech High, with its zip code–based lottery and project-based learning emphasis, being one example. As ideas took root, two early, core superintendent values remained. One was the regional approach. The second was an emphasis on equity.

CodeRVA was the only high school innovation application submitted by a regional consortium of districts. It was far from the only educational entity that Virginia superintendents worked together on, however. Across the state, regional models geared toward exceptional education and other specialized offerings in the arts, math, science, or technology are not uncommon.[14] Lane was familiar with these efforts based on his prior experience as superintendent of several smaller school districts. Rattling off a list of regional endeavors like the state Governor's Schools for gifted students, he said:

> I knew that we had a penchant for regionalism [in the Richmond area]. And then when I was at Middlesex, everything was regional. We built a regional tech center in New Kent while I was there. We also had a regional Special Education program that was way more developed than what we have in Richmond, and then a couple of other partnerships with community colleges. And we were starting to build up some community college stuff at Powhatan and then I thought, how can we take this regionalism leverage and do something for the entire [Richmond area]?

For small districts with a more limited tax base, regional cooperation represents an important way of offering students a more robust set of educational opportunities. For large districts, expanding specialized curricular options makes sense too. CodeRVA represented an opportunity for all Richmond area districts, large and small, to explore high school innovation and an equitable admissions model in a laboratory setting. It was a way to experiment with ideas that could be scaled up in the districts later.

Virginia's existing regional educational endeavors offered examples of how to coordinate governance, finance, and transportation among multiple school divisions.[15] In Richmond, the Maggie L. Walker Governor's School for Government and International Studies, an elite competitive admissions high school, made site selection and free transportation for the proposed school relatively straightforward. As long as the new school was within a few miles of the centrally located Maggie

Walker, districts could transport both groups of students together. Per-pupil funding followed students to existing regional collaborations; the same would be true for CodeRVA.

A Focus on—and Incentive for—Equity

What distinguishes CodeRVA from Governor's Schools like Maggie Walker—and virtually all other school choice models in the Richmond area—is its emphasis on equity. Multiple CodeRVA stakeholders indicated that perennial pushback against *inequity* in the admissions process for Maggie Walker nudged area superintendents to imagine a different kind of opportunity for students. [16] Said one, "You have to understand that the Governor's School parents start undue pressure on all areas of a school district beginning in kindergarten [with gifted identification] . . . [W]e were trying to create another opportunity for kids that perhaps public education hadn't [experimented with] yet."

Layered on top of those specific Governor's Schools concerns was growing commitment to tackling educational inequity more generally. One superintendent acknowledged, "There's a lot of conversation right now about equity and schools . . . so, the timing was just really good." Though local superintendents tended to define equity as providing all students with the resources they needed to succeed, school diversity and/or desegregation became a part of that equation, too.

Unrelated to the state high school innovation grant, but occurring during the lead-up to it, several local gatherings underscored the importance of regional cooperation around school desegregation. [17] Most area school leaders at the time had participated in Leadership Metro Richmond, an organization that works to address racial and gender divides in area leadership—and one that consistently emphasizes regionalism. [18] CodeRVA stakeholders also mentioned one university-sponsored lunch meeting for local superintendents as particularly influential. They had gathered to hear about the prospect of a multimillion-dollar federal grant from Scott Thomas, then the director of the Magnet Schools of America, a nonprofit that represents magnet school stakeholders. The Obama administration had looked favorably upon several regional magnet school applications in the 2013 federal grant cycle, a fact that was not lost on area superintendents. It also didn't hurt that many had prior experience with magnet schools. The superintendent of a suburban school division had once overseen Wake County, North Carolina's well-known system of magnet schools and in that role had successfully applied for the federal magnet school funding. Lane had been a student in the Wake County schools, and his first teaching position was in a magnet-like middle school. Several other area superintendents were familiar with the concept if not the funding source. Crucially, a well-developed school desegregation plan is one of the conditions for federal Magnet Schools Assistance Program (MSAP) funding. Interviewees agreed that the possibility of winning an MSAP grant helped incentivize the push for equity and diversity. Lane explained,

> [There was always the question of] how are we ever going to pay for this [at least in terms of start-up costs associated with the innovative programming]? Well, you guys should go for a magnet school grant . . . [W]hen we learned it was 6 million bucks, we were like, "man, we might be able to open up this school without any money!" . . . So, what we learned in applying for magnet school grants was there was this required focus on desegregation, so we built this equity piece in, very purposefully for the magnet grant on the front end.

Though CodeRVA's first application for MSAP funding wasn't successful, the prospect of a second round helped maintain a focus on school desegregation throughout the occasionally difficult planning process. In other words, when conversations veered toward identifying the best and brightest coders in the region, emphasizing the ongoing opportunity for the federal magnet school grant helped steer the group back to the leadership's emphasis on equitable access.

Visionary and Strategic Leadership Propels CodeRVA Forward

CodeRVA evolved with the help of a diverse set of K–12 and higher education leaders, business partners, and advocates. A number of these backers pointed to Lane's leadership as essential to developing the school, along with that of the initial project manager, Dr. Yvonne Brandon. Those around him describe Lane as highly visionary, strong, and strategic. Brandon's long experience in Richmond Public Schools, cul-minating in her hire as superintendent, meant that she "knew educa-tion, knew Richmond, and knew how to bring people together," said CodeRVA's grant writer. These complementary characteristics, along with the expertise of the school's advisory council, helped the school come to fruition.

The advisory council itself was an exercise in strategy. Formed dur-ing the planning process, it included all of the area superintendents, university professors, key business partners, community college of-ficials, and computer science experts.[19] Recruitment was targeted, ac-cording to Lane. "I wanted to put people who were so influential on the council, that people would be scared to let the school die," he said, specifically referencing a member with local media ties who helped keep the story of the emerging school in the news.

Council members cultivated ideas related to CodeRVA, deliberating over the computer science theme, curricular pathways, project-based learning, a guaranteed internship with a local tech company called Maxx Potential, a two-year degree, and the admissions process, among other issues. Leaders also worked to build on existing foundations; before the first CodeRVA meetings, a regional entity called Bridging Richmond had convened partners to submit a large workforce develop-ment grant. As the advisory group coalesced around key elements of the school design, both CodeRVA and a solid coalition of stakeholders emerged. "I mean, [the school] didn't just come out that way," said Lane. "[It] was brokered as an agreement to get everybody on board."

From that work, leaders developed a consistent message about the vision for CodeRVA. The school, as Lane often emphasized, revolved around three pillars. The first was "[creating] a really innovative school environment a la High Tech High . . . where the courses were woven to-gether and everything was done through project-based learning." The second was designing a school with a job focus important to business partners because "we heard over and over again that coding was an is-sue." Students would learn a skill set "essential for the next century," while the increasing popularity of computer science would help guar-antee interest. The third pillar was equity, framed as "intentionally building a school where any kid could be successful no matter their zip code," and where all had equal access to an innovative experience. In moments of tension—related to the admissions process, for instance, or funding for the school—those intertwined messages would be reiterated. They created a multipronged rationale that appealed to a diverse set of interests, making it difficult to refute.

Foundational components of CodeRVA emerged from the superintendents, various employees of participating school districts, and the advisory council. Lane and Brandon divided members of the council and local districts into subcommittees for finance, location and transportation, curricula and student admissions, and support, among others. They worked behind the scenes with the committees to ensure that each group stayed true to the vision hammered out by the superintendents and in the council. At key sticking points, particularly around designing a lottery weighted by income and, if need be, race, direct one-on-one conversations reinforced the idea that CodeRVA would be a school that reflected the rich diversity of students in the region. Lane and Brandon were quick to remind committee members of CodeRVA's core equity and innovation principles. Neither leader waivered on the equity pillar, and most stakeholders ultimately fell in line.

The subcommittees were led by school division employees, with larger area school divisions offering substantial backing in terms of personnel and time. If support waned, leaders were able to draw on the initial memorandum of understanding (signed in the state grant application) as a reminder that they had formally agreed to participate.

Even when the school's more official governance structure emerged—a regional school board made up of one member of each participating division, presided over by a local superintendent—the advisory council remained. It continues to serve as a nonpolitical body with key expertise and influence on matters like computer science, project-based learning, the associate's degree, and equity.

Origins Challenges for CodeRVA

When CodeRVA's leaders considered early challenges, they often mentioned two interrelated issues: garnering agreement from participating school boards and financing the school. Each superintendent had the responsibility of communicating about CodeRVA to their respective boards. Some kept their members abreast of key CodeRVA developments as they emerged; others waited until the plan was more fully formed. Superintendent turnover during the two-year planning process further complicated consensus-building. In certain instances, area board members took issue with the regional nature of the school, making the case that divisions could go it alone on a coding effort. Financing the school also met with opposition. As Dave Myers, a local superintendent, said, "Money still isn't growing on trees [in the wake of the recession]," and student enrollment in CodeRVA meant modest funding reductions for the home district.

To keep plans for CodeRVA on track, Lane and Brandon offered to visit and communicate with local school boards. Business and computer science advisory committee members exerted pressure behind the scenes. Lane asserted that the equity and innovation pillars helped convince those on the fence, saying, "If it was just a computer science program, I could create ten computer science programs in a large school division. But it was this equity model, it was this innovation, it was this laboratory that got people excited."

Lane also was particularly adept at helping skeptical audiences understand the value of diverse schools. His remarks on the subject often went something like this:

> School is the only opportunity that we have sometimes for kids to experience that most—and this is going to sound fluffy—but that broader spirit of what America is from a diverse standpoint. And I feel like in the computer science world for CodeRVA you're going to have the same thing. You're going to have people just doing data entry, you're going to have people that are coding . . . you're going to have people that are administrators, you're going to have HR people, you're going to have custodians in the building. And I feel like at some point, an intentionally diverse school teaches you how to get along with all people, which is going to make you better in the job world, which is ultimately one of our goals.

Preliminary media interest in CodeRVA, generated by the unique equity and innovation foci, as well as the regional structure, created a public stake in the school before it even opened. An informed and excited public meant additional pressure for reluctant boards.

The funding concerns didn't go away though. When it came time to firm up commitments for the number of student seats each division was willing to subsidize (with larger divisions securing, say, thirty seats, and smaller ones maybe three), the bonds between area superintendents briefly were tested. A lot rode on those earlier promises, because "if we didn't get people to commit to the [number of slots we'd originally started out with], we might have been dead on arrival with money," said one superintendent. But a pointed meeting of local leaders at a statewide superintendent gathering soon led to renewed efforts to bring participating school boards together around funding the necessary number of slots. One participant characterized the conversations as "very direct," enabled by the strength of underlying relationships in the room.

Financing systemic regional educational efforts is a key stumbling block in other parts of the country. Our existing patchwork of school districts sets up needless competition for resources; any effort to cooperate across them requires a willingness to volunteer within-district resources in service of mutual ones. CodeRVA overcame this hurdle by making a strong case that it wasn't possible for individual school districts to create a similar opportunity on their own. But one can imagine that a more systemic expansion of regional educational entities like CodeRVA would face increasing opposition as funding began to follow hundreds or thousands of students out of individual districts into regional schools.[20] One possible workaround, employed elsewhere, is additional financial support from the state.[21] As Myers, the local superintendent who headed up the finance subcommittee, pointed out, the original $50,000 state grant was only enough to germinate the idea of CodeRVA, the costs of actually opening and operating a regional school were much higher.

Hiring a Permanent Director for CodeRVA

With the programming, location, admissions process, and regional funding and governance broadly sketched out, CodeRVA needed a permanent director to perfect and execute the details—and lead the school once it opened. That person was Michael Bolling, a specialty program (e.g., the Governor's Schools) and math instruction expert for the state department of education. In his prior role with the state, Bolling reviewed CodeRVA's high school innovation application, drawn in by the regional vision and the proposed approach to high school. For Bolling, the timing was right for a shift to directing CodeRVA as he was looking for an opportunity to grow professionally. His lack of prior school administrative experience was an asset in the eyes of several superintendents, freeing him from traditional conceptions of the role in a setting that would be very different. Those superintendents credit him with the final, effective push to get CodeRVA up and running. "At the end of the day, it was Michael who had to take these ideas . . . [H]is collaborative style and 'get it done' attitude and mentality . . . is what actually made it happen," said one.

That's the unique, somewhat-nail-biting-but-ultimately-successful origins story for CodeRVA. Now open, what policies and practices are supporting the initial vision, particularly around integration? Let's first consider external integration, or how the school equitably draws in a diverse enrollment. Then we'll turn to internal integration, or how the school supports its diverse enrollment.

CodeRVA and External Integration

Central to CodeRVA's success in roughly mirroring the student demographics of the region it serves has been a virtuous cycle of clear diversity goals, attractive programming, lottery-based admissions (with weights for groups underrepresented in the pool of applicants), and strong outreach and communication. Each element supports others. Diversity goals signal the school's commitment to diversity, while outreach, programming, and communication generate and sustain extensive interest in CodeRVA. The weighted lottery helps ensure diversity goals will be met.

We saw earlier that federal magnet school funding incentivized the focus on an admissions process governed by lottery rather than testing—despite pushback from a region deeply unfamiliar with such an approach.[22] Adding weights to a straightforward lottery in the event of a lopsided applicant pool—more high-income students than low, for example, or more white students than black—represented an even further step on the path toward equitable access.[23] It's important partly because families receive and exchange information about schools in highly segregated networks, as previous chapters have shown. If information flows unequally, even with the best outreach efforts, it's hard to build an applicant group that represents a robust cross-section of a district or region. CodeRVA's emphasis on computer science meant that gender, along with class and race, became an issue. Females are decidedly underrepresented in coding and STEM fields, although they perform as well as their male counterparts in math and science.[24] Lopsided representation for women—as well as for underrepresented minority groups—means lopsided access to increasingly lucrative professional opportunities.[25]

While the Richmond area lacked a local example of a weighted lottery, key superintendents were familiar with similar efforts around the country. High Tech High in San Diego, which had already served as a model for innovative programming, relied on a lottery weighted by zip code to give students a fair shot for admission. Moreover, CodeRVA's stakeholders remained committed to applying for federal MSAP funding.

The 2016 round of MSAP applications under the Obama administration included competitive priority points for lottery-based admission, as well as a priority for strategies that increased racial diversity by taking into account SES diversity.[26] CodeRVA sought to meet those priorities by proposing a lottery weighted toward a variety of SES factors, including parent/guardian educational level, family income, and eligibility for free and reduced priced lunch.[27] As part of the region's commitment to sharing resources, Chesterfield's full-time grant writer—a rarity in more cash-strapped divisions—lent considerable time and expertise to the MSAP application efforts. Brandon attended the annual Magnet Schools of America conference in 2016, going to sessions geared toward providing technical assistance on the upcoming grant. An external consultant, Michael Alves, provided additional support regarding the weighted lottery and the desegregation plan—as did local professors like myself. The submission also included numerous letters of support from high-profile Virginia politicians and other luminaries. CodeRVA's second MSAP attempt was successful, which meant about $6 million to support diversity, equity, and innovation over a five-year period. It was the first school in the area to receive federal magnet school funding.

That CodeRVA garnered 756 applications for 93 slots in the first year—and easily met its goal of approximating (within 5 percentage points) participating districts' overall demographics without relying on weights by race/ethnicity—made it something of a rarity in the federal magnet school community.[28] The regional scope of the school lent it a deeply important advantage when it came to nurturing diversity since most federally funded magnet schools are located in racially and economically isolated central city school systems.[29] It can be hard to create and sustain a robust system of magnets within such highly segregated districts. And aside from its regional reach, CodeRVA had other important mechanisms promoting diversity. A crucial one was its ability to precisely target outreach, made possible by the services of Alves, the school's lottery consultant.

An Independent Consultant to Guide the Weighted Lottery Process and Extensive Outreach

Once discussions of the weighted lottery were in full swing, early CodeRVA leaders united around the idea of an external consultant to design and conduct it. They were largely prompted by the desire for an independent perspective, one that could withstand intense scrutiny, should demand for the school skyrocket. Experienced superintendents knew that pressure from well-connected individuals could sway ostensibly random lottery systems in favor of certain students.[30] CodeRVA's director, Michael Bolling, has been pleased with the result, saying that the "anonymity and independence of the contractor has been really important to the integrity of the process . . . for the general public." He worked hard to secure funding for the consultant in CodeRVA's initial year, before receiving the MSAP award.

Based on his experience with voluntary school desegregation efforts nationwide, Alves worked with CodeRVA's leaders to devise an application and weighting process. Interested families fill out a short application, clicking through several screens to provide things like contact information, household income, and educational attainment.[31] Applicants within each participating school district are divided into low-, medium-, and high-SES groups based on a combination of educational attainment and free and reduced priced lunch eligibility.[32] The system assigns points to those groups, in line with the number of seats offered by the students' participating district.[33]

The software associated with the lottery process gave Bolling the ability to see the applicant pool in real time—and target outreach accordingly.[34] A carefully planned marketing rollout in the school's first year meant he had already represented CodeRVA at major secondary school choice events in the region (e.g., fairs highlighting existing options like the Governor's Schools, city high schools of choice, or the specialty centers located in many local suburban high schools). These face-to-face events, an important component of outreach, were supplemented by print and online materials.[35] Newspaper stories also piqued interest. Area school counselors, who help guide eighth-graders' high school choice process, received fact sheets and participated in outreach sessions related to CodeRVA. A local computer science class designed the initial layout for CodeRVA's website; visitors were encouraged to sign up for email updates. Email blasts that started with ten people reached eight hundred by the time application season rolled around. Materials were distributed in multiple languages and later, with prompting from the US Department of Education's Office for Civil Rights, the website became ADA compliant.[36] Even with extensive outreach, though, there were surely holes. So once the six-week application period opened, the consultant's software showed Bolling where those gaps in applications were—too few students were submitting from Petersburg City schools for instance, or not enough from schools serving high numbers of Latinx students south of the James River.

With regular data on the number of applicants per division, their demographics, and their status in terms of completing the application process, Bolling used the ample lottery application period to arrange in-person meetings in areas underrepresented in the pool. He focused heavily on reaching girls when it became clear they made up a smaller fraction of applicants than their presence in the region. Ultimately, he sought to build a 5:1 ratio of applicants to slot numbers within small school divisions and a 10:1 ratio in larger ones.

How information about CodeRVA was disseminated obviously matters for equitable access and school diversity. So too does the nature of the information. CodeRVA leaders honed their "three pillars" messaging about the school early on, but Bolling was in charge of communicating specific details of the lottery process to crowds of curious and sometimes competitive families, all seeking better educational opportunities for their children. In a region unfamiliar with weighted lotteries, how would he help stakeholders understand its purpose in an accessible, inclusive way?

Transparent Communication About Equity and the Weighted Lottery

Bolling and I are sitting in one of the small CodeRVA classrooms lining the front of the school. Natural light flooding through the floor-to-ceiling windows illuminates a conference table and comfortable seats, with plenty of outlets for student and faculty electronics. My question about the weighted lottery and communication elicits a flood. This is something Bolling has thought about deeply, investing considerable time and effort on top of the many other duties associated with opening a school. With a friendly smile, he asks for my take at the end of his response, giving me a firsthand glimpse of the openness to feedback and collaborative nature that so many highlighted as his leadership style.

I glean from his comments that transparency has been central to the lottery dialogue. He has strived for open, direct communication, though initial exchanges may have been tinged with defensiveness. In the first year of recruiting for the school, Bolling would talk to interested families first about the gender weights, which seemed to go over the easiest. Then he'd describe the socioeconomic weighting process, which usually garnered more questions. Bolling said that when diversity came up, people would "automatically go to race," so he tried to emphasize all of the different ways CodeRVA wanted to represent the region. This seemed to him more politically palatable, perhaps a response to decades of color-blind law and policy making (including SES diversity priorities alongside the goal of reducing racial isolation in the federal magnet grant).[37] But those same tendencies toward color blindness also have made it more difficult for the public to see and understand the myriad ways race continues to influence opportunity.

Not everyone was resistant to the idea of a weighted lottery, but those who were struggled to understand the lack of rigorous academic requirements. For this group, oriented heavily toward merit—and often unable to see how deep-seated privilege fuels our definition of it—Bolling honed a reply along the lines of: "Students with parents that are as supportive as you, with the means that you have, who can send [your children] to summer camps . . . encourage reading and investigation and provide the resources to do so, your kids will be successful no matter what. This school is not specifically for that child but it will include that child."

Some in his audiences would move on after this, but others would probe. At one of the first sessions, a parent raised his hand and said, "So you want to fill the school with poor, black girls?" Bolling worried that his knee-jerk reply of "I hope so" had been perceived as flippant, perhaps undermining his message around CodeRVA's commitment to giving underrepresented students a fair shot. After some reflection, Bolling, who speaks to diverse crowds of interested families as a white, middle-aged father of a high school–age son, decided he needed to "drop the defense," telling himself that "what we are doing is in the best interests of kids . . . really serving the greater good and leading the way for other schools to provide more opportunities to other types of kids." He could rest assured.

With the second year of outreach and information sessions, Bolling experienced fewer instances of direct pushback around the weighted lottery. Perhaps word and understanding reached prospective ears once the school opened. Opposition now feels more covert, couched in race-neutral terms but still concerned with merit. Questions in this vein sound like "So how are you keeping the kids out that aren't going to take it seriously?" To which Bolling has replied, "While I wish every student had a passion, sometimes the parents know better than children when [a good opportunity arises]. If a student feels that way at first, I hope experiences here will nurture a love for the field the school's focused on."

CodeRVA seeks to do what non-choice-based public schools are responsible for every day: engage all students in learning, no matter their background or circumstance. Bolling became adept at making the case for CodeRVA's admissions, most often using a straightforward equity rationale. Occasionally he'd underscore the realistic preparation for the diverse world of work that CodeRVA offers students. Given the research on the academic benefits of diversity, a more regular combination of both may prove potent in years to come.

Using Multiple CodeRVA Pillars to Attract Diverse Families

External integration at CodeRVA is aided by the multiple draws, or pillars, embedded in its design. The school's three areas of foci attracted a diverse group of interested families. In addition to the equity frame, there's the magnetic pull of coding, as well as the innovative school design that includes online and face-to-face instruction and pathways to postsecondary education and/or the workforce. Professor Tom Shields, a member of CodeRVA's advisory committee, put it this way:

> The best thing about the school really is you can choose whatever you want to highlight, right? You can highlight the coding, the coolness of working online on virtual classes. You can highlight the individualized learning plans related to that. You can highlight the collaborative nature of [CodeRVA] as you go through the different ways they've set it up. Just overall with employer's need for coding ... Or you can highlight the diversity and equity that's built into the enrollment process. It allows the school and the board to highlight what they want with different constituencies which is not a bad thing to have in a school.

The persistent strength of the three pillars also can be seen in CodeRVA's application figures for the second year. Over four hundred students applied for roughly eighty-five freshman seats in 2018.[38] Though these numbers represent declines from applications in the first year, when the school's "new car smell" likely provided an additional boost of interest, they still indicated very high demand.[39]

Families affiliated with CodeRVA expressed a variety of reasons for coming. Some were looking for a better fit for introverted students; others wanted to cultivate an interest in computer science, get a jumpstart on college coursework, and/or prepare their children for life after high school. Several mentioned the intentional focus on diversity as an important selling point. These families also emphasized the early, close connections established with Bolling and the faculty as ethical to taking a chance on a new school. In the first year, the school counselor met with each incoming family one-on-one. Bolling and the school's administrator were in regular communication with them, talking personally to parents and guardians on the phone and assuring them that their "kids would be known."

Making that promise a reality would fall to the work of internal integration. CodeRVA's leaders and faculty have worked hard to support diversity through a combination of student and faculty inclusivity trainings, trust-building, responsiveness, collaboration, and continuous improvement around equity and inclusion.

CodeRVA and Internal Integration

The class of 2022 trickled in for their second day of orientation to CodeRVA. Groups fell in step together, spilling off buses from all points of the region. They walked into a long, calm, gray space that more closely resembled an office in a start-up tech company than a schoolroom, columns and sofas creating small pops of color throughout.[40] During a regular school day, the room is filled with tables of students quietly and independently doing online coursework, awaiting scheduled breakout sessions with CodeRVA teachers who extend and reinforce computer-based lessons.

A table with breakfast items greeted the new students, along with handouts explaining the nine topics orientation would cover. Sessions included self-motivation for a blended learning environment, goal setting, digital citizenship, inclusivity, and team building. Faculty, which had more than tripled in size since the first year, marked out places for various topics in the main room and in the numerous breakout rooms lining its sides. A racially mixed group of sophomores, mostly girls with a few boys sprinkled in, were assisting with the orientation activities. Bolling and the faculty solicited the involvement of the older grades in response to detailed student feedback on the prior year's outreach and orientation process.[41] I watched one sophomore approach a table of shy freshman, smiling warmly, to ask how they were feeling, followed by assurances about how great the school was. The school counselor connected with individual students beneath a large map of school districts participating in CodeRVA.

After breakfast, I headed toward the session on inclusivity, passing an icebreaker along the way. "Find someone who likes dogs," called a teacher, followed by, "now someone with the same birthday month as you." A group of students gathered nearby at a photo booth to document the first few days of their CodeRVA experience.

CodeRVA's two humanities teachers, one black, one white, jointly led the session on diversity and inclusion. Joy Beatty, in her second year teaching at the school, moved the activity along with practiced pacing and humor. It started with shared definitions of culture and diversity and then transitioned to carefully studying a picture of multihued crayons. Beatty asked the students what differences they saw. "Some are stubby," "Some are not as sharp as others," "They are different sizes," "Different brands," "Different colors," flew the responses. Beatty probed for commonalities after the differences. "All crayons," "All wax," "All make people's point of view pop out," offered the students enthusiastically.

The class was warmed up, ready for a short story called "The Crayon Box That Talked." At first, the crayons don't get along, but after jointly creating a picture, a better-together message starts to emerge. The students were quick to point it out, noting "strength in their being unified." The conversation moved to comparing the crayons to people, who at first could be "judgy" but who were more accepting after they got to know each other. Beatty wrapped up the exercise with a definition of inclusive—"starting to accept each other and valuing the strength of the individual colors."

Erin Hill, in her first year, took up the thread, showing a student-generated map of Virginia and CodeRVA's participating districts. "It's clear that we have geographic diversity, isn't it?" she asked the students, expanding the point with, "Aren't they greater when they are together? We could also say that when they work together, the things they do are more widespread and powerful. The act of each of you being here is one thing, but what we do with it and how it resonates across Virginia is special."

The session communicated both the value of differences and the power of unity. Students listened intently; two sophomore assistants modeling buy-in for the newcomers, all agreeing that CodeRVA is an intersection, a place for them to come together. The paired instructors smiled. It was time to rotate to the next section.

Diversity and Inclusion Within CodeRVA

The external efforts expended to create a racially and economically diverse CodeRVA—things like the weighted lottery and extensive outreach—laid the groundwork for intentional work within the school. The freshman orientation activity built on a sophomore seminar conducted by a local nonprofit focused on inclusion.[42] After their first year at CodeRVA, rising sophomores and juniors responded to a survey question, "What would a truly inclusive school look like?" with comments like "our school was built on diversity and we do projects with random groups," or "a lottery system to apply." From the outset, CodeRVA's initial group of students understood that equity was part of the school's mission. They heard about it at outreach and orientation events, could see it in the mission and vision, and knew that it was behind the design of the lottery-based admissions process.

Many students view CodeRVA's diversity as an asset. A focus group comprising all African American rising sophomore girls, yielded robust, positive attitudes toward increased opportunities for interacting with diverse peers and feelings of comfort in the setting.[43] Students in a racially heterogeneous focus group appreciated that CodeRVA was "more balanced" than their prior schools, and liked meeting people they wouldn't have otherwise. Teachers felt similarly; as with Sprout, Ecoff, and Binford, the focus on equity and/or diversity was a draw for many.

Teachers use the school's diversity to enhance learning and instruction. They deliberately pull students with different perspectives into the breakout sessions that bolster the online coursework. This makes for more robust conversations, according to a humanities teacher. Faculty also routinely emphasize "soft skills" like critical thinking, collaboration, and empathic listening—down to interpersonal attributes like good eye contact and strong handshakes.

In the school's first year, professional development at local businesses, which displayed the intensely team-based nature of today's knowledge economy, reinforced the importance of such skills for CodeRVA teachers. Midway through the second year, soft skills were seen as more essential than ever as juniors began moving through the school's eight-week internship component. Paired teams worked on common challenges in the information technology (IT) world, helping customers back up data before an approaching weather event, for example, or developing log-in and passwords functions. Students were supervised by CodeRVA's local business partner and were expected to give a formal presentation and complete an interview. A professional practice workplace simulator is planned, designed to measure and give feedback on soft skills like collaboration, communication, and presentation.

New Peers, Small Size, and Collaboration Promote Positive Identities and Relationships

Leaders, faculty, and students all were quick to report the presence of healthy intergroup bonds at CodeRVA—an important building block for social integration. In high school, particularly one that so heavily emphasizes postsecondary opportunities, diverse social networks expand access to informal but critical information related to college-going, internships, and careers.[44] Beatty, the humanities teacher, said, "You do have [diverse] couples . . . [K]ids here are extremely open, intuitive, reflective . . . [They get] to reset, start over, see different kids." She underscored how deliberately staff and stakeholders worked to create a climate to support student inclusiveness. There's also something to the idea that starting anew fosters more open attitudes.

In a typical high school, cohorts have been together for roughly eight years. There's only so much room to maneuver against individual or group-based perceptions formed by peers. The hard adolescent work of defining oneself is buffeted by prior judgments and experiences. Conversely, amid the safety of knowing peers for so long, risk-taking around identity may be more limited. In a new high school, though, with a wide range of peers from cities, suburbs, and rural areas, and racial/ethnic and economic groups, students may be more willing to experiment with different possible selves.[45] Perhaps as a result, more CodeRVA students responded favorably to the question, "I feel comfortable being myself at this school," (47 percent responded "very true") than a nationally representative sample of students (35 percent responded "very true.").[46]

Faculty have taken note, observing that the first group of CodeRVA students didn't surface race as frequently as students in other schools where they worked, that friend groups formed and dissolved more readily, and that gender and sexual identities seemed more prone to shifting. Teachers did see some signs of self-segregation by race, a regular component of racial identity development at this age.[47] As high schoolers of color grapple with race, among other aspects of their identity, a need to immerse themselves in group history and culture, supported by peers with similar interests, arises.[48] CodeRVA faculty often allow students to group with whoever they want at collaboration tables during parts of the day, but also encourage diverse interactions through breakout sessions. Besides the team-based internship opportunity for juniors, teachers have designed two schoolwide project-based learning opportunities for all students. These various opportunities are important because they offer structured opportunities for creating the conditions associated with optimal contact across group lines.[49]

In the first year, the small size of the school—just over ninety students in the entering class, a mix of freshman and sophomores—made it easy for students to form relationships with peers. As one explained to the magnet school evaluation team: "One thing about this school is you can get even closer with your friends quicker ... I've known my home school division friends, my middle school friends a lot longer than I have known people here yet somehow I am a little more close with the people here."[50]

Easily formed bonds among peers also extended to teachers. CodeRVA students said they trusted their teachers, reporting general feelings of being known and cared about.[51] One explained, "It's not just a job to teachers [at CodeRVA]" and "they really care if you learn or not." CodeRVA faculty felt similarly, saying that working at the school made it easier to build relationships with students.

When racial incidents do occur, the small, intimate school environment lends itself to quickly addressing them. One administrator mentioned a cross-racial conversation among two friends that went awry in the spring of the school's first year. A black student told a white student, "That's so *white*." The white student took offense, and faculty responded by addressing the concept of bigotry during the school's next morning meeting, providing students with concrete examples of what it sounded like and some possible responses.

Various potholes remain on the road toward inclusivity at CodeRVA, however. CodeRVA students express some of the same tensions and hesitations as their parents or guardians about the school's admissions process. And the introduction of an incentive-based assignment completion structure that sorts kids into groups called CEOs, vice presidents (VPs), or managers may reinforce notions about who does and doesn't deserve a place at CodeRVA.

Grappling with Equity in CodeRVA

A heterogeneous group of five students sat around a corporate-style conference table describing to me their initial experiences at CodeRVA.[52] Toward the end of the conversation, the school's admissions process and new CEO grouping system sparked robust dialogue—and some disagreement.

When it came to the lottery, one white male student communicated a desire for admissions requirements based on prior experiences with coding or an interest in computer science. Three other students, two black and one white, thought adding an interview component to the lottery process would help identify students who didn't want to attend the school but who were forced to by their parents. At the same time, they acknowledged that reluctant students might change their minds once they experienced CodeRVA. One white female worried that the weights in the lottery, including those for gender, privileged some at the expense of others.

CodeRVA leaders heard similar feedback from a handful of other students. Part of it, they thought, might come from sharing a bus with students attending the region's highly selective Governor's School. Informally contrasting two different systems of admission with peers on the bus might raise ideas about worth not grounded in an understanding of ongoing barriers to equal educational opportunity. One faculty member said, "I guess it would make them feel more valued if they got selected because of their merits." Another noted that students expressing the desire for more competition in the CodeRVA admissions process tended to come from more educated and affluent families. Given residential and social segregation by income, these households likely experience fewer occasions to witness how gross inequality undermines a meritocracy.[53] More deeply infusing an understanding of historical and contemporary inequities surrounding race, SES, and gender into CodeRVA's curriculum could contextualize and inform the dialogue.[54] Past research shows that increased diversity in adolescents' social worlds, in conjunction with curricular content directly focusing on inequity, is linked to heightened concern for social inequality.[55]

An initiative designed to help students stay focused as they work through a blended curriculum raised related issues within CodeRVA. In the opening months of the school's first year, faculty, staff, and administration came together to discuss student progress. The three core subject teachers often were in breakout sessions facilitating learning among small groups, leaving the director, counselor, and administrator to supervise all of the remaining students engaged in online coursework. CodeRVA's accelerated curriculum in the freshman and sophomore years meant students needed to stay on track if they wanted to take advantage of subsequent community college coursework and internship opportunities. But lacking concrete examples of students who'd moved through the entire CodeRVA sequence, those opportunities seemed

abstract and distant. This made goal setting and self-motivation essential when it came to completing the individualized computer-based
lessons.

A student rewards system that designated students as CEOs, VPs,
or managers, with attendant status and privileges, emerged from that
dilemma. The first iteration of the structure highlighted the school's
emphasis on preparation for the world of work and was built to reward
progress (e.g., completing online assignments for each subject), not performance, on coursework. "You just have to put the time in," said one
teacher. "[I]t's not based on grades at all." CEOs had to be current or
ahead in all of their classes, earning the right to sit where they wanted,
use their cell phone, participate in Google hangouts during individualized computer work and eat lunch outside on designated days, among
other privileges discussed between the students and administration.
VPs had to be current in all but one of their classes and earned a modi-
fied version of the CEO privileges. Managers were behind in two or more
classes and had the least freedom of movement in the bricks-and-mortar
classroom and in online communities like Google hangouts. The goal,
according to the school counselor, was for all students to become CEOs.
Regular evaluation of progress meant that students had numerous
chances for promotion (and demotion) among the three groups. Teachers hoped that students in the manager group would "look down the
room [to the CEOs] and see what they are supposed to do and how to
get there, with us providing the necessary supports." Manager supports
include preferred seating near teacher resources, regular meetings with
academic case managers, and clearly defined opportunities for becoming VPs.[56] Yet, many faculty and students expressed some reservations
about the system. They touched on similar themes—the prospect of racialized sorting, a mismatch between the vision of the school and the
system in practice, a sense of unfairness.

Students and teachers indicated that the first several rounds of the
student rewards system produced a CEO group that was whiter than
the VP or manager groups, perceptions at least partly backed by data.
In those initial assignments, white students were somewhat overrepresented in the top two groups. Meanwhile, black students made up

about the same share of the CEOs (one in three) as their overall enrollment in the school but were underrepresented in the middle VP group
and overrepresented in the bottom manager group. Latinx students
were more evenly distributed. The school's small Asian population almost entirely resided in the CEO group.

The racial breakdown of the three groups intersected with the privileges—or lack thereof—that came with them. One African American
student said, "I can't stand it. [The CEOs] are sort of looking down at
[the other kids] like they're sort of better than them. Cause you have
all this stuff and they don't." His sentiments spoke to the dangers of
a status hierarchy emerging in a school striving in so many other ways
for inclusion.

Faculty and leadership readily acknowledged the pitfalls of the student rewards system, while also noting that it provided a helpful framework for monitoring and evaluating students. As with many other
first-year challenges, they talked about the importance of balance and
of finding their way forward through mistakes. Bolling's willingness
to seek input and change course accordingly extended to his faculty.
A strong sense of collaboration existed among the initial six adults in
the building, supported by daily afterschool meetings when the school
first opened. Faculty, staff, and leadership would debrief about the day,
jointly working on solutions as they went. As one teacher remarked, "We
literally have a say in everything." They relied heavily on student progress and performance data, using them to track and support those in
danger of falling behind and to create subject-specific breakout sessions.

Continuous Improvement Around Equity and Inclusion

CodeRVA's faculty and staff grew exponentially in the spring and summer of the first year, from six adults in the building to twenty-two. Yet
the emphasis on continual improvement, especially around equity and
inclusivity, remained.

Helping struggling students through the condensed online coursework remained a key equity concern. Many of the new faculty and staff
positions were geared toward providing that support. An academic case
manager and English and reading intervention teacher came on board,

as did numerous tutors for world languages, history, and math. The case manager helped students set realistic goals and conducted regular check-ins; the reading intervention teacher created schoolwide student book clubs, and the tutors worked with any interested students, providing one-on-one support with their lessons.[57] All students garnered benefits from the new personnel, and students who needed more support received it. While federal magnet school funding initially enabled much of the faculty expansion, CodeRVA leadership plans to sustain key positions as the school's student enrollment increases.

Magnet school funding comes with a built-in evaluation component. A team of university-based researchers regularly interacts with the school, providing feedback tied closely to the performance and desegregation goals laid out in the magnet grant. These formative and summative assessments formalized first-year faculty and leadership efforts to bring in external perspectives on what was working well and what needed adjustment. It all adds up to a cycle of continuous improvement around equity and diversity—setting specific goals, collecting regular data from multiple sources to see what gaps emerge, planning interventions to address the gaps, acting, reflecting on feedback, and doing it all over again.[58]

Here's how that process continues to play out with the student rewards system. Based partly on student feedback that the emphasis on performance rather than progress incentivized rapidly clicking through online coursework, faculty redesigned the criteria for promotion to CEO. It's now a combination of making progress, passing courses, and being a leader. CEOs are trained in peer mentoring; they have a regular caseload of students they meet and work with. The external evaluator also monitors patterns of promotion and demotion for racial disparities. Bolling reported, "We are constantly aware of shifting groups and providing supports. We do believe that each group should be representative of the school's population, that's why we look at multiple characteristics." And he emphasizes the continual evolution too, saying, "We'll likely change it for next year, modifying as the culture of the school changes."

Beyond the student rewards system, CodeRVA has relied on the ex-panding number of adults in the building to provide more leadership and growth opportunities for students. There's a tech support desk run by kids and supervised by a faculty member. There's a student ambas-sador group that conducts tours for interested families. There are the step team, yearbook club, and anime club, extracurricular activities that have cropped up in the second year, offering students more infor-mal opportunities for interaction across lines of difference. And there's an increasing emphasis on supporting positive behaviors. Teachers have been instructed to write positive, not negative, referrals for students.[59] Students can be nominated for exemplary interactions with peers or faculty, improvement or achievement in schoolwork, or helpful actions that add to the school community.[60]

As CodeRVA begins to implement the community college course options for juniors and seniors, equity must remain front and center. Over their final two years at CodeRVA, students can take a full slate of free dual-enrollment courses (up to sixty-nine credits) or a mix of dual-enrollment and traditional courses. All students receive, at a mini-mum, three dual-enrollment credits for the internship.[61] After individ-ually conferring with the school counselor and academic case manager, about 70 percent of CodeRVA students elected to take the first round of dual-enrollment history and English courses offered. Performance on a standardized test that community colleges use informed the con-versation between school staff and students, but families make the fi-nal decision about community college coursework.[62] Though facets of the process follow best practices for detracking, it will be important to continually monitor course pathways by race, ethnicity, and SES.[63] If disparities emerge, additional outreach and support or changes to the advising process may be in order.[64]

Early outcomes related to internal integration are positive. Student interviews and surveys showcased feelings of belonging, connectedness with teachers, and general support for diversity and inclusion. Long-term outcomes like graduation and college matriculation will come later. For now, testing indicates high rates of passage—well above state averages for all subgroups—on required state assessments.[65]

✳

CodeRVA days begin with a fifteen-minute morning meeting, students grouped with faculty at various places around the school. It's springtime, and one of CodeRVA's new teachers is leading a gathering of about twelve students. She's certified in special education and English language instruction; her voice is gently accented as she greets the students—"Salud, salud"—and moves through the roll.[66] Students place lunch orders on their computers, listening to a donation reminder for the nearby SPCA. "Bring your gently used blankets, sheets, and towels," the teacher says.

The long room is moving at roughly the same speed; as announcements wrap up, faculty direct students' attention toward a PowerPoint. There's a brief presentation and discussion about defining collaboration, what it looks like and how it happens at CodeRVA. Students readily supply answers like "at the collaboration stations," "through project-based learning," "in the classroom during breakout sessions and lunch time." They talk about why collaboration is beneficial at the level of the individual ("increases student retention, self-esteem, and responsibility" and "higher-level thinking") and society ("exposure to and increased understanding of diverse perspectives"). There's a quick reminder to set goals for the day and week and to check calendar invites. The teacher closes with encouragement to do well on the state science test and a reminder of her willingness to provide assistance as students prepare for the Spanish test. "Have a great day," she says, releasing students to teacher-led breakout sessions or online coursework, all in the caring realm of CodeRVA.

CHAPTER 6

Lessons Learned from Contemporary School Integration

The ideas behind *A Single Garment* originated with the letter to my daughter, penned in the weeks leading up to the 2016 election. The preceding year had seen the Obama administration use its platform to bring school diversity back into our national consciousness after decades of federal neglect and judicial retrenchment. Though members of Congress have continued pushing the Strength in Diversity Act, a legislative version of the school diversity planning grant proposed by Obama's Department of Education, the Trump administration swiftly pulled the plug on executive funding for it.[1] The same administration later rescinded pivotal guidance on the use of race in voluntary K–12 school integration, even as federal legal challenges to integration and affirmative action mount.[2] Against this backdrop, trying to understand more localized efforts to advance voluntary school integration—the focus of *A Single Garment*—seemed more essential than ever.

Now, in the early spring days of 2019, I'm writing the book's conclusion in the wake of racial scandals enveloping Virginia's governor and attorney general. On Governor Ralph Northam's medical school yearbook page, the searing image of two white friends, one in smiling blackface, the other in sinister Ku Klux Klan robes, stands as a reminder that our history is always with us—and that honestly confronting it remains crucial to piecing together the single garment. Our public schools can and should play a central role in brokering that confrontation. Indeed, state education leaders have nodded forcefully to the idea that schools must facilitate learning around race and injustice, relying on the bully pulpit to explain their rationale and provide resources for doing so. A posting from Virginia Secretary of Education Atif Qarni pointed to the role of school segregation in nurturing our divisions: "Segregation has increased ignorance and intolerance . . . [C]hildren turn into adults and the chasm that divided them as children, only widens as they take different paths beyond high school."[3]

Shortly thereafter, in a memo sent to all Virginia superintendents, Dr. James Lane, who had been so instrumental in the development of CodeRVA and who is now the state superintendent of public instruction, provided a list of teaching resources to support dialogue on racism. Along with the list, he wrote:

> As educators, we are uniquely positioned to be leaders in this effort. In the coming days, I encourage us all to take time to reflect on these events and the conditions that exist within our culture and communities that created space and place for these hurtful symbols to be perceived by some as acceptable. As education leaders—we have the opportunity and an obligation—to facilitate meaningful dialogue on racism and bigotry with our students, staff, and school communities.[4]

Intensifying racial discord only magnifies the urgency of the external and internal integration strategies employed in the four Richmond area schools discussed here. Decades upon decades of social science research tells us that school integration promotes stronger learning and twenty-first-century skills for all students, in addition to reducing prejudice, expanding opportunities, and cultivating citizens prepared to navigate a multiracial democracy.[5] Done well and thoroughly, school integration brings diverse students together in the same schools—and then works to confer equitable status and resources upon all of them in a cooperative and supportive atmosphere. It's obviously not a panacea;

our history and the deep and interconnected dimensions of inequality that flow from it are too complex for a single institution to root out. But school integration is a start—an important one.

Standing squarely in the middle of continual progress and regress, hope and struggle, this chapter highlights important lessons learned from the essential work taking place at our four schools.

Intentional Integration Requires a Full Understanding of the Dynamics of Segregation

In different and significant ways, Sprout, Ecoff, Binford, and CodeRVA shed light on the forces that shape contemporary segregation. Our separation today flows directly from the intentional design of policy, law, and action; undoing it will require the same concerted intentionality focused in the other direction. With Sprout, we saw how a mixed preschool economy—public, private, and informal home-based providers all offering a patchwork of early-years care options—produces highly uneven access to quality, affordable preschool. Uneven access is, in turn, bound up in stark racial segregation for the youngest students during a critical social and intellectual period.

Within urban school systems, our not-so-distant past still troubles our present. A city-only school desegregation plan in Richmond exacerbated white and middle-class disinvestment, creating a legacy of isolation and vigorous competition for limited resources. Those trends, as the case of Binford illustrated, remain particularly pronounced for urban middle schools. Amid swift contemporary population growth, driven in large part by white professionals and young families, the blend of Binford's informal diversity goals, open enrollment and residence-based attendance policies helps sever the link between school and housing segregation in the city.

Across the city line, racial and economic disparities in the Chesterfield school system—the growing east-west divide that so concerned stakeholders—underscore the dangers of resegregation in rapidly diversifying suburbia. We saw how a mix of neighborhoods within Ecoff Elementary's carefully etched attendance boundary temporarily lends itself to school diversity, just when students stand to gain so much from exposure to racial and economic integration. But profit-hungry developers, eager to build near highly sought-after schools, together with increasingly disparate educational opportunities in eastern Chesterfield, contribute to Ecoff's precarious position.

Between city and suburban school systems, school district boundary lines continue to tear at the single garment. As Richmond's nearby suburbs grow more racially diverse, the farther-flung ones grow whiter. The expanding scope of metropolitan segregation draws our attention to the ongoing urgency of regional cooperation à la CodeRVA, an innovative high school that connects students across the Richmond metro area with postsecondary opportunities and rich social networks. The voluntary nature of that cooperation, decades after the courts knocked down mandatory metropolitan school desegregation in Richmond, makes CodeRVA all the more noteworthy—provided we pay close attention to the equitable design of regional school choice employed there.

The dynamics of segregation across our varied sites reveal highly political, systemic issues, constrained by a legal environment that increasingly refuses to recognize the urgency of race-based remedies for racial discrimination.[6] They show that effective solutions for contemporary K–12 segregation involve harnessing and stabilizing demographic shifts, coordinating school and housing policy, interrupting the school-housing relationship through equitable school choice, paying close attention to the shape of school attendance boundaries, and circumventing school district boundaries. In the early childhood sector, finding ways to partner across the public-private divide is critical, as are public funding strategies that promote integration rather than segregation. All require intentionality, transparency, and bold, adaptive leadership.

Our schools represent one-off attempts to build diverse settings within deeply segregated systems. Nevertheless, they begin to illustrate the ingredients of more comprehensive approaches. We'll expand on these ideas—and revisit the concept of systemic reform—as the chapter unfolds.

Nascent School Integration Efforts Leveraged Financial Incentives, Local Interest, and Strong Leadership and Networks

While the intentional focus on diversity evolved differently across our four schools, significant themes emerged. Financial incentives, family and community interests, leadership seasoned in diversity and equity efforts, strong networks and relationships, and shared best practices all contributed to the origins of intentional integration at Sprout, Ecoff, Binford, and CodeRVA.

Financial Incentives for Diversity

In several cases, the emphasis on diversity arose from an existential threat of school closure. Sprout, you'll remember, viewed growth and increased socioeconomic diversity among its small students as essential to remaining solvent. Binford Middle faced the very real possibility of shutting down after years of declining enrollment and disinterest from white and middle-class families. For these two schools, increasing student diversity became a fiscal necessity. CodeRVA's commitment to diversity and equity also came, in part, from monetary considerations. The prospect of a significant infusion of federal magnet school dollars helped leaders make a stronger case for building an intentionally integrated high school.

During a period of still-constrained resources, then, it's very possible for policy makers to incentivize diverse schools through grant-funding opportunities. Recent examples primarily come from the federal level—efforts like the long-standing Magnet Schools Assistance Program (MSAP), the competitive priority for diversity across other federal education grants under the Obama administration's Department of Education, the new rules allowing for more flexibility related to Head Start funding, and the thwarted Opening Doors, Expanding Opportunities school diversity planning grant discussed in the introduction. States and localities absolutely should learn from these federal incentivizing endeavors, adopting and tweaking them to meet their needs. If monetary incentives falter, motivating through recognition—think awards or special designations for successful work around intentional school diversity and equity—offers a strong step in the right direction.[7] Technical assistance will be important, as leaders must develop capacity around school integration in a new legal era that limits how districts can consider race and ethnicity.[8]

Tapping into Families' Desire for a Diverse, Well-Rounded Education

Money wasn't the only diversity motivator. Significant community and family interest in diverse learning opportunities also prompted the focus on integration. Sprout's survey of preschool wants and needs illuminated the desire for school diversity across a broad cross-section of families. Parents and guardians connected to Ecoff, Binford, and CodeRVA all expressed deep appreciation for schools that "looked like the real world." Family desire for diversity paired well with other motivations like school programming that seemed suited to their child. All four schools offered some kind of innovative, theme-based approach to education, whether it was Reggio, socioemotional learning, arts integration, or computer science. Each bucked the narrowing of curricula associated with the standards and accountability movement, reminding us in some way of the broader purposes of education.[9] Whether it was through an emphasis on child-centered discovery and community at Sprout, building vital relationships and an understanding of self at Ecoff, systematically infusing the arts into learning at Binford, or preparing students for work in a rapidly changing economy at CodeRVA, our four schools worked diligently to widen what's become a constricted view of what schools can and should do.

Long a magnet school hallmark, intentional diversity combined with specialized, popular programming created a multipronged raison d'être for the four schools, extending their coalitions of support.[10] This was particularly true for CodeRVA, the design of which brought together regional leaders from business, K–12, and higher education. So while stakeholders clearly valued diversity, it wasn't the only educational or social attribute they sought.[11] Designing voluntary school integration efforts accordingly makes sense. Intentional diversity plus a unique educational focus expands political will for integration. As such, providing schools and systems with the initial resources necessary to support the development of those foci, as MSAP does, becomes an important consideration. Holding schools that receive the money accountable for diversity and equity, as MSAP also seeks to do, is imperative.

Leaders Committed to Diversity and Equity

Leaders committed to diversity and equity were integral to the origins of our schools. A number were graduates of desegregated schools themselves. Lane, the superintendent who helped knit together the regional group that brought CodeRVA to fruition, attended Wake County, North Carolina, schools during implementation of a systemic racial desegregation plan and later taught in a magnet-like setting. Similarly, Dana Bedden, past superintendent of Richmond Public Schools and one of the original minds behind Binford's redesign, went to desegregated schools as a high school student in Florida and was principal of a magnet school in Washington, DC. Other leaders drew upon prior professional knowledge and experience with integration. Kathleen Eastman came to Sprout with experience braiding Head Start and non–Head Start students in preschool programs. Joshua Cole, the principal of Ecoff Elementary, had just finished writing a dissertation on school desegregation in Richmond when he took the position. Still others, like Melissa Rickey or Bedden, "walked the walk," enrolling their own children in diverse schools. The fact that so many leaders had some personal or professional experience with school desegregation reminds us of its enduring effects. Graduates of Sprout, Ecoff, Binford, and CodeRVA—and other schools doing the intentional work of integration—are being prepared to one day lead on this issue themselves.[12]

Capitalizing on Relationships and Networks

Just as the leaders were important, so too were the relationships they built across and within Richmond communities. The idea for the Sprout School's location at the Children's Museum grew from casual conversations between the directors of each institution, brought together by regular board meetings on early childhood education. Similarly, regional meetings nurtured the partnership among Richmond area superinten-dents that yielded CodeRVA. Our leaders of existing schools, Cole and Rickey, both formed close connections with external partners, among them churches, community-based organizations, museums, and uni-versities. Without those relationships, Ecoff's emphasis on wraparound services and Binford's focus on art integration would have floundered.

More extended relationships and networks, developed through conferences and site visits, also proved useful. These opportunities gave local leaders opportunities to learn about exemplar schools around the country, including a museum-based preschool in Portland, Oregon, re-gional magnet schools in Connecticut, and an innovative high school with a lottery weighted by zip code in San Diego. Even though CodeRVA and Sprout were entirely new concepts for the Richmond area, knowl-edge of existing models elsewhere helped pave the way for their estab-lishment here. The relationships and shared models that helped give rise to the four schools underline the power of regular convening and strong dissemination around best practices for school integration.

Intentionally Diverse Schools Require an Effective Loop of External Integration Strategies

Across Sprout, Ecoff, Binford, and CodeRVA, we looked at what it takes to bring students of different racial/ethnic and economic backgrounds together in the same schools. These external, or outward-facing, inte-gration strategies formed an effective loop of clear diversity goals, non-competitive admissions, desirable programming, good communication and information, free transportation, thoughtfully drawn attendance lines, and/or careful site selection.

Diversity Goals

With all four schools, we saw that stated diversity objectives were criti-cal to external integration. Sprout's leadership regularly reiterated its goal of enrolling one-third full-pay families, one-third partial pay, and one-third fully subsidized students. Ecoff, bound to Chesterfield's res-idence-based system of student assignment, actively communicated its growing diversity as an asset in an effort to hold middle- to upper-class families and/or white families who might otherwise exit. Binford's principal, with support from the superintendent who spearheaded the programmatic transformations, talked repeatedly about creating a school that "looked like the city." And CodeRVA set an explicit goal of mirroring the demographics of the region it serves within 5 percentage points. Black students made up about 36 percent of the region's enrollment, meaning that CodeRVA strove to ensure that black students accounted for between 31 percent and 41 percent of the school's enrollment. In keeping with current legal parameters, CodeRVA's lottery system is designed to attempt to achieve its racial diversity goals through race-neutral socioeconomic weights. [13] Thus far, it's done so, though Sprout illustrated that socioeconomic status isn't always an effective substitute for race.

From our specific examples, among others, we see that diversity goals can take different forms but need to remain flexible. They should be anchored to the overall demographics of a school system or a set of regional systems. Importantly, diversity goals make it easier to hold schools and systems accountable. In New York City, officials handed desegregation advocates an important tool when they set forth a policy statement prioritizing diversity, developed goals to indicate progress toward that priority, and requested an annual report to hold them accountable for making progress.[14] Without accountability, whether it comes from the local, state, or federal level, it's too easy for competing forces (e.g., financial pressures for Sprout or unequal information for prospective Binford families) to undermine stated diversity goals.

Accountability for diversity that addresses systems of schools, not just single schools within a system, also helps combat the siphoning-off of families with more information and resources and/or competition that can flow from one or two intentionally diverse schools operating in deeply segregated systems. Louisville–Jefferson County, Kentucky, for instance, carefully assesses the racial and socioeconomic characteristics of its neighborhoods and strives to ensure each school in the system reflects students from a mix of different types of communities.[15] The city-suburban school district uses a method of voluntary integration called "managed choice"; every family in the district submits a set of preferences to the central office, which then assigns students according to a number of different priorities. These goals include proximity, diversity, and stability. The *systemic* nature of choice is important in Louisville–Jefferson County; requiring every family to choose reduces the stratification that ensues when only the most informed and heavily resourced families choose.

Interest-Based Admissions

External integration lessons from our schools further remind us that policy makers must offer integrating tools to support diversity goals. For schools of choice, interest-based admissions, governed by lottery or weighted lottery if schools are oversubscribed, represent a fundamental integration mechanism. All three of our choice-based schools were oversubscribed. Sprout at the Children's Museum's first-come, first-served admissions policy is mediated by its socioeconomic diversity goals; the school maintains a dual wait list for families who qualify for subsidies and families who don't. The other two schools of choice, Binford and CodeRVA, relied on a lottery process to fill seats if more families wanted to enroll than spaces were available. This practice represented a notable change of course for a region long invested in K–12 competitive admissions criteria—usually some combination of grades, teacher recommendations, and/or test scores. Lottery-based admissions open up access to schools of choice, allowing students to enroll based on interest rather than past opportunities and achievements. Weighted lotteries, as in the case of CodeRVA, go even further, ensuring access for students who may not be well represented in the applicant pool.[16] CodeRVA also reminds us that application processes should be easy to navigate with ample time built into deadlines so that families subjected to more outreach barriers still are able to participate.[17]

Extensive and Targeted Outreach

Disparate information about schools, distributed within deeply segregated social circles, sets up obstacles to accessing high-opportunity settings. That's why each of our four schools worked diligently to reach as many families as possible. Sprout drew on its diverse YWCA,

Head Start, and museum partnerships to cast a wide net of information about its programming. Despite not being a school of choice, Ecoff disseminated a glossy information brochure describing its SEL and community school emphasis to build and maintain diverse interest in residing within its attendance zone. Binford's leadership held numerous informational sessions in every sector of the city, in addition to offering open houses and student-led tours of the school. And CodeRVA relied on various forms of print and electronic communication (available in multiple languages) to spread the word about the new computer science opportunity. CodeRVA also used lottery software to target information to districts and groups not well represented in the applicant pool. Magnet school funding later made it possible for CodeRVA to hire staff focused explicitly on outreach.[18] This kind of person-to-person contact matters; research shows that counseling coupled with nuanced information about schools can shift decision-making processes.[19]

Multidimensional Information About Schools

The *content* of information about our four schools mattered, along with the extensive *delivery*. Ensuring that people receive multifaceted information about schools of choice has to be a core component of outreach. Information should include statistics not only on achievement but also on diversity, specialized programming, school climate, and family and/ or student satisfaction.[20] In the previous section, we reviewed the role that specialized school programming played in the origins of our four intentionally diverse schools. It obviously deserves mention here as an external integration strategy. The infusion of new school programming like Reggio, SEL, or arts integration helped remove stigmas associated with past segregation or current resegregation. It offered an affirmative way to talk about the school's purpose, drawing in families and vital partnerships. And programming helped shift the way our schools were discussed during casual conversations among families, friends, and acquaintances. It gave networks a chance to speak specifically about the educational characteristics of the school, countering racialized labels like whether it was good or bad.[21] Recall the living-room conversations exploring the arts integration changes underway at Binford or the

Sprout families attracted by some combination of the Children's Museum setting and the Reggio instructional approach. Discussion of new programming, in other words, can help supplement the less-detailed, racially coded information passed along through social networks.[22]

Integrating Social Networks

One could imagine more wide-scale efforts to change the content of information about schools. A Richmond-specific example of this comes in the form of a group called StayRVA. It's a grassroots movement of "parents and neighbors who want to help Richmond's public schools thrive."[23] The racially and ethnically diverse leadership organizes events encouraging families to become involved in and informed about their local schools. StayRVA actively tries to counter negative information about Richmond Public Schools by setting up times for families to volunteer or tour schools, meeting principals and teachers along the way. It sees urban population growth as a chance to boost school enrollment growth with the right support and knowledge. We need more civic organizations like StayRVA that can catalyze the contact and trust building underlying more integrated social networks. Virginia's shifting state accountability system may also help. Moving beyond a singular binary of accredited/unaccredited schools toward more detailed information may fuel more nuanced school conversations among networks—and, as a result, may also promote school choices that relate to more housing integration.[24]

Leaders Adept at Communicating the Value of Diverse, Equitable Schools

Leaders counted too, of course, when it came to the external work of attracting and retaining a diverse set of stakeholders. They had to become adept at authentically communicating the value of diverse, equitable schools and navigating smoothly across lines of difference. Sprout's director cultivated this skill at multiple school sites, speaking in heartfelt ways about the importance of exposure to diverse classmates in preschool. Ecoff's leadership worked hard to model close, trusting interactions with all families, hoping their example would illuminate the path for others. Cole also developed relationships with hard-to-reach families by creating the Empowerment Zone resource center, taking Ecoff's mobile office to apartment complexes in the attendance zone and pushing inclusivity with the PTA. At Binford, the leadership team addressed race head on, using the arts as a vehicle for opening up difficult conversations with students, teachers, and families. It also shared tracking and discipline data broken out by race with the empathy advisory group. Families of all backgrounds referenced a personal, trusting relationship with Rickey as they described their decision to opt into Binford. CodeRVA leaders relied on the three pillars—innovation, workforce development, and equity—to build broad-based support for the regional school. Bolling, for instance, would clearly articulate the value of equity in his informational presentations about the weighted lottery. Importantly, all of these leaders took time to develop and hone their messages. We heard Bolling talk about the evolution of his CodeRVA presentations, and Rickey speak openly about the tension that often came with conversations about race.

Leaders need more opportunities to practice these skills in low-stakes settings—master's and doctoral coursework and professional development both come to mind. Effective communication about race and difference flows in part from prior experience and in part from a strong understanding of the racial, social, and cultural contexts surrounding schools (e.g., the dynamics of segregation) that must be captured during pre- and in-service leadership training.[25]

Training must also recognize that strong leaders seek—and are offered—opportunities for wider impact. Given the centrality of leadership, rapid transitions at the school and district levels can produce instability and undermine integration work. Growing an effective pipeline of leaders trained in diversity and equity thus becomes critical.

Racially Diverse Faculties

Racially diverse faculties were crucial to the outward-facing task of building trusting relationships with diverse families. In the context of a national dearth of teachers of color, our four schools deliberately worked to build more diverse faculties. This helped signal that the schools welcomed and had the capacity to serve families and students of all backgrounds. It also reinforced the relationship between faculty and student integration. For all of the schools, an intentional external emphasis on student diversity helped pave the way for more faculty diversity. Faculty applicant pools tended to be more diverse than usual because potential teachers were drawn in both by the programming and by the emphasis on diversity and equity. This kind of branding around diversity, equity, and specialized programming is an evidence-based strategy for attracting more faculty of color, as is supportive school leadership.[26]

Dismantling the School-Housing Relationship

Given that the school-housing relationship remains a fundamental driver of segregation, external integration at Sprout, Ecoff, Binford, and CodeRVA involved careful attention to dismantling it. The shape of attendance boundaries for schools relying on residence-based assignment—Ecoff and Binford, in part—created opportunities for school diversity by encircling diverse neighborhoods. Nationwide, school zoning or rezoning (sometimes called redistricting) with an eye toward underlying neighborhood racial and/or economic diversity is one of the most common voluntary integration strategies.[27] So are transfer policies, which allow students to move out of their assigned zone school to different schools.[28] A handful of Ecoff's families attended the school through Chesterfield's transfer policy. Note, though, that the policy didn't include a specific focus on whether or not a transferring student promoted diversity. While the courts now prohibit districts from using the race of an individual student to make transfer decisions, officials can still consider students' SES, achievement, and/or the racial and economic makeup of the schools or neighborhoods involved in the transfer.[29] State guidance or oversight related to integration and school rezoning and transfers would likely prove useful, since both processes tend to be highly political at the local level.

The neighborhoods within Ecoff's and Binford's attendance zones are diverse—for now. But remember that rapid racial and economic changes defined the communities around both schools. Wealthy new developments in the western part of Chesterfield, coupled with more plentiful affordable housing in suburban Ecoff's eastern attendance zone, may undermine Ecoff's diversity in the future.[30] Swift gentrification in urban Binford's zone raises the threat of resegregation in the other direction. External school integration efforts must be paired with housing integration strategies like inclusionary zoning if stable diversity across both sectors is a goal.[31] In cities, this might look like setting aside affordable housing units in new apartments or condos, eliminating single-family zoning requirements, and maintaining affordable housing in rapidly gentrifying neighborhoods through a combination of land trusts, rent control, and tax adjustments. In suburbs like Chesterfield, officials might consider creating financial incentives for new mixed-income developments in struggling areas (attractive schools obviously make this easier) and setting aside a percentage of all new development in more affluent areas for affordable housing.

Free Transportation

Free transportation to K–12 schools of choice like CodeRVA and Binford (which enrolled students by lottery from all over the city and by priority from within its attendance boundary) helped ensure equitable access. Without transportation to sever ties between school and residential segregation, schools will simply reproduce neighborhood demographics.[32] Research has found that transportation increases student access to high-quality schools of choice, with particularly large impacts on black and Latinx students. These students were 30 to 40 percentage points more likely to attend significantly better schools (measured by proficiency outcomes on standardized tests) than their same-race peers not using transportation.[33]

Voluntary Regional School Integration

For CodeRVA, the ability to transport students across not just attendance lines but also across district lines created more meaningful opportunities for diversity, severing the school-housing relationship on a

much larger scale. As we've discussed, the 1974 *Milliken* decision, born
largely from a sense that the political climate for school desegregation
had shifted, not from consistent application of legal precedent, exempted
most suburban communities from school desegregation underway in
their neighboring central cities.[34] An easily available suburban alternative to massive shifts in the urban racial order accelerated white and
middle-class flight from central cities.[35] *Milliken* is partly responsible for
the fact that most school segregation today lies across school district
boundaries—making endeavors that draw students across different districts imperative. These efforts generally have taken two forms: smaller-
scale interdistrict transfer programs that allow some students to traverse
the city-suburban boundary, as well as large-scale city-suburban school
district consolidation, accompanied by desegregation, that impacts all
students residing in the new metropolitan district.

Interdistrict transfer and magnet programs have formed in metros across the country, including Boston, Massachusetts; Omaha, Ne-
braska; St. Louis, Missouri; Indianapolis, Indiana; Rochester, New York;
Hartford, Connecticut; and East Palo Alto, California. They grew out
of circumstances as varied as their locations—state law in some cases,
federal court orders in others.[36] The ones that continue to operate must
navigate the hurdles of regional power and resource sharing, accountability, and transportation.[37] Though reliable numbers are difficult to
obtain, the best estimates suggest that roughly forty thousand students
participate in interdistrict programs each year, with many more seeking
to gain entry.[38] The interdistrict choice and magnet programs in Hartford are by far the largest of the eight, using lotteries to admit city and
suburban kids into specialized magnets, suburban students into city
schools, or city kids into suburban schools. The best programs provide
comprehensive supports and counseling to participating students, in
addition to professional development for participating teachers, to ease
the transition between two worlds.[39] A seminal study of the nation's interdistrict programs, conducted by Kara Finnegan and Jennifer Holme,
found they have helped thousands of students across the city-suburban
boundary, opening up access to higher-opportunity domains along the

way. At the same time, these small-scale programs haven't systemically addressed regional educational inequity, just as regional equity efforts haven't typically included education.[40]

As Judge Merhige recognized long ago when he ordered the merger of Richmond, Henrico, and Chesterfield, consolidating separate school districts into broad metropolitan systems—and desegregating schools across them—represents the most comprehensive approach to integration. Unlike interdistrict transfer and magnet programs, all students and schools in the metro area are impacted. Various studies link metropolitan school desegregation to low and stable levels of black-white school segregation as well as faster declines in housing segregation.[41] Erasing the boundaries between city and suburb, desegregating all schools, and ensuring that families can make residential decisions disconnected from schooling ones helps open up the metropolitan housing market to more integrated decision-making.

School Location

Finally, the location of our schools also enabled external integration. Sprout at the Children's Museum's central city site, easily accessible via public and private transit, rendered it convenient for multiple families. CodeRVA's close proximity to another regional school enabled the two programs to collaborate when it came to transporting students. And Binford's and Ecoff's locations near racially and economically diverse parts of their respective city and suburban systems made it possible for officials to draw attendance boundaries in an integrating way. While the location of our four schools nurtured diversity, siting decisions for new schools can also exacerbate segregation. Growth in western Chesterfield offers a good example of the latter—the construction of exclusive new neighborhoods attract affluent families with children, forcing new school construction.[42] In these instances, officials should seek, where possible, sites that maximize proximity to a range of neighborhoods. State departments of education often sign off on school construction, offering an important opportunity for external review of potential impacts on segregation.

Integration Requires Continual Attention to Internal School Strategies

Effective external school integration bled directly into the hard, continuous work of internal, or inward-facing, integration in our four Richmond area schools. These different yet intertwined internal efforts included leadership passionate about the school's thematic or curricular focus; diversity and equity; strong teacher training and buy-in; efforts to ensure increasingly diverse faculties; programming that focused on holistic education and lent itself to the conditions for positive intergroup contact; leadership and teachers openly addressing race and conflicts surrounding it; curricula that supported that work; careful attention to tracking issues like identification for exceptional education and advanced coursework; monitoring of discipline disparities; and robust family and community engagement.

Leadership for Internal School Integration

Leaders have been at the forefront of each dimension of school integration—garnering political support during the origins periods connected to our four schools, communicating effectively about their schools' value as part of external integration efforts and now inspiring and structuring their internal communities to embrace diversity, equity, and related programming.

To begin the internal work, our leaders established or emphasized a strong vision with an explicit focus on race, diversity, equity, or unity. Sprout's, you'll recall, derived from the parent YWCA organization's emphasis on "empowering women and eliminating racism." Leadership and faculty fully embraced the mission, regularly circling back to it to explain the focus on intentional diversity and quality preschool. Ecoff's "everyone empowers everyone" motto served as an overt reminder of the single garment's emphasis on interconnectedness. Binford communicated its focus on joyfully loving children for who they are and want to be—using art to more fully understand those identities—with "preparing and affirming students to be their authentic selves through the arts." The school's collaborative process for developing that mission also offered a blueprint for creating shared purpose and ownership. Leadership that unites school communities around unambiguous moral or inspirational goals lends deeper meaning to the work of education and sets up one of the conditions for positive intergroup contact.[43]

When called upon to navigate thorny internal school conflicts related to difference, also central to establishing optimal conditions for contact between groups, our leaders strove to do so directly, fairly, and empathically.[44] To unpack tension surrounding race and discipline at Ecoff, Cole's school community developed the Boys to Men mentoring meetings for students, in addition to conducting one-on-one conversations with teachers. CodeRVA responding quickly to a racial incident at a morning meeting represented another example, as did Rickey's empathy advisory committee. The latter effort brought together a group representative of diverse school constituencies. Among other attributes, these kinds of committees help signal the value a school places on the contributions and concerns of different groups.[45] Such an approach also is in keeping with research on the benefits of diverse teams.[46]

Faculty Buy-in and Training for Diversity

Faculty buy-in and training for specialized programming and student diversity was essential to the success of our four schools. Leadership played a role here, too, by facilitating professional development on bias, affirming the cultures and backgrounds of various groups, overseeing instructional approaches that facilitate positive contact, and offering conflict resolution. Special programming at our four sites aligned with the focus on equity and diversity, making it easy for faculty to connect the dots within their training or PD. Reggio's focus on community, for instance, meant that meetings with the instructional consultant could naturally veer into discussions of how to handle conflict within the school. The poverty simulation and Cole's culturally responsive pedagogy training at Ecoff were, in some ways, an extension of the SEL work being done with students. An early grant that sponsored regular trips to the Virginia Museum of Fine Arts for all of Binford's community introduced a variety of school stakeholders to the new arts integration programming, illustrating how art can unlock different perceptions and difficult conversations. CodeRVA's faculty visited a tech company in the first year of the school to see soft skills at work in the knowledge economy; they've also experienced regular training on diversity through the Virginia Center for Inclusive Communities.

Building Diverse Faculties

In tandem with diversity training, leadership at Sprout, Ecoff, Binford, and CodeRVA worked to ensure that teachers and staff were themselves diverse.[47] When it comes to internal integration, diverse faculties give all students the opportunity to look up to, identify with, and be cared for by faculty and staff who both share and don't share their own background. Remember, too, that teachers of color can offer specific benefits to same-race students, serving as protective factors against unfair discipline or gifted and talented identification practices.[48] Leaders at our schools included explicit discussion of working with diverse students in interviews with prospective teachers, and prospective teachers spoke in turn about their desire to work with diverse populations. At each of the four sites, teachers described the ways in which faculty diversity contributed to effective, informal professional development around race. School structures that nurtured collaboration among faculty members—team teaching at Sprout, grouping teachers by grade level at Ecoff and in the Binford houses, and/or scheduling regular time for teams to interact in all of our schools—came into play. In addition to facilitating the development of healthy relationships across diverse teachers, which gives students concrete, normative examples of how they might do so with diverse peers, close collaboration helped faculty grow as instructors and added coherence to teaching in the school.[49]

Organizing Schools and Developing Instruction for Diversity

When it came to students, programming, instructional practices, and school organizational features worked together to facilitate positive contact across racial/ethnic and economic groups. We witnessed numerous occasions for students to meet on equal footing—both formally and informally—in cooperative classroom groups and houses, or during summer orientations, regular morning meetings, clubs, or afterschool activities.[50] These memberships provided opportunities for students to identify with new, larger groups beyond their own—an important component of reducing prejudice.[51]

Equal status contact opportunities often were paired with pedagogy that honored the contributions of different cultures and challenged past and present injustice. Think back to the fourth-grade history display in Ecoff's hallway or Binford's art showcase. Pedagogy of this sort contributes to equal status by taking an asset-based view of students.[52] It nurtures student appreciation of their own and others' cultures, develops ethical consciousness, and provides opportunities for connecting class material to real life.[53] We have good evidence that ethnic studies and/or culturally relevant pedagogy are linked to heightened learning experiences and stronger outcomes like more credits earned, higher achievement, and increased motivation.[54]

We also saw that classroom diversity enriched the learning of all students. At Binford, for example, Jonathan Walker reported robust and critical discussions in his racially and economically diverse English classes, witnessing mental workouts in action as his students paused to carefully consider the implications of their words and one another's perspectives.[55] Sprout's teachers noted a similar phenomenon among the youngest students, as peers shared expressive language across racial and economic lines.[56]

All of this again carries important implications for pre- and in-service training for teachers and leaders. Schools of education and professional development providers must present ample opportunities for educators to understand the sociocultural aspects of schooling and curricula, as well as explicit training in how to harness and address racial diversity for deeper learning and understanding.[57]

Addressing Race in the Classroom

Numerous examples of race surfacing in classrooms emerged from our four schools. We heard about the two-and-a-half-year-old white student at Sprout wanting to look like her black teacher and about the fifth-grade classroom at Ecoff debating whether a video accurately depicted race and equity. We learned of students grappling with refugee experiences in a Binford classroom, along with students (and families) struggling to understand the racial and equity implications of the weighted lottery at CodeRVA. Our educators responded in various ways, depending partly on students' developmental stage and partly on their own comfort talking openly about race. That comfort has been informed by educators' experiences with segregation in K–12 education. Separation breeds anxiety. While many leaders and teachers in our four schools reported prior experiences with diversity, that's not the norm in a segregated society. Too often educators fall back on a color-blind mentality, missing key opportunities to affirm and respect differences among students.[58] An accurate accounting of race and its continued impact must be woven into teacher and leadership training. This training would help educators understand that, though race is a social rather than a biological construct, past and present discrimination means that race remains very related to educational opportunity and outcomes.[59] From this shared point of understanding, leaders and faculty can begin having what Glenn Singleton calls "courageous conversations." Using data that speak to the school experience—ability grouping or course taking by racial/ethnic and economic subgroup, for instance—faculty should regularly engage in facilitated conversations that adhere to norms like "stay engaged, expect discomfort, speak your truth, and expect and accept a lack of closure."[60]

Monitoring and Tackling Tracking

Careful attention to racialized sorting of students within schools and classrooms is central to internal integration. That's because tracking can so easily undermine equal status contact, in addition to exposing students in lower-level courses to inadequate, disengaging curricula and the least experienced teachers.[61]

Sprout sought to head off these issues early with the implementation of "braiding." Kathleen Eastman worked hard to ensure that students receiving public or private subsidies were educated in classrooms alongside their nonsubsidized peers. Too often this isn't the case in preschools; different accountability requirements attached to federal and state subsidies mean that students are siphoned into separate classes or schools. Eastman overcame those obstacles by ensuring that the curriculum and nutrition for all students met whatever the highest programmatic standard demanded, ironing out the rest as it came.

In elementary school, attention to student sorting by race often involves monitoring identification for exceptional education, to include gifted and talented programming. Ecoff reported significant white overrepresentation in its gifted program. Systemwide efforts to educate teachers around multiple forms of giftedness and to screen all Chesterfield County third graders for giftedness were just taking root and may yield progress. Ecoff's administration did work to create classrooms that served a variety of students at the beginning of every year, and the school was deeply committed to including students with disabilities in regular classrooms.

In middle school, as Binford illustrated, tracking tends to become more rigid. Recommendations for sixth-grade honors classes followed students from Richmond's elementary schools, based in part on earlier gifted identification, along with test scores and/or teacher recommendations. Each of these criteria was and is subject to bias.[62] Once at Binford, Rickey and her team strove to make access to honors coursework as flexible as possible, triangulating data on performance, interest, and need and ensuring that honors or regular course identification in one subject didn't lock students into the same track for all courses. Still, significant racial disparities in honors placement were beginning to emerge at Binford, suggesting that more intentional action to level the playing field would be needed.

CodeRVA employed tactics similar to Binford's in order to ensure equitable access to its dual-enrollment offerings, the completion of which has important implications for college admissions and affordability. The high school had just begun implementing the community college curriculum at the close of the study, such that data on advanced course-taking by race or SES were not yet available.

We saw that the schools struggling with racial inequities in access to advanced coursework were committed to regularly examining related data and designing interventions accordingly. They continually explored some version of the following questions, neatly synthesized by education researcher Bill Hawley: "Do [grouping practices] result in sorting by race or ethnicity? How specific and well defined are the learning needs being addressed? How much of the day do students find themselves learning with the same group? Do student groupings remain stable over time and from class to class?"[63] In many ways, their work reflected an "equity improvement cycle" by gathering multiple sources of data, drawing on different perspectives, developing structured processes and systems to address equity issues, and continuously reflecting on progress and challenges.[64] What none had tackled—as of yet—was detracking students altogether.

We do have successful examples of systemic detracking, Rockville Centre School District in New York being one of the better known. As described in several noteworthy publications, a stubborn and pervasive pattern of underrepresentation among black and Latinx students receiving advanced diplomas animated the detracking efforts in Rockville. School officials set goals and started slowly, first eliminating the lowest-level courses—the ones that didn't prepare students for the examination associated with the advanced diploma—altogether.[65] The superintendent then opened up advanced math coursework to all students beginning in middle school. Struggling students were provided with additional support in the form of afterschool tutoring and math workshops.[66] Universal acceleration in other subjects like social studies and English was phased in gradually, with the same strong supports in place for students struggling to grasp material.[67]

The detracking efforts paid off. Controlling for prior achievement, socioeconomic status, and special education identification, researchers studying Rockville Centre found that black and Latinx students in detracked cohorts of students were 8.4 times more likely to earn a Regents diploma than if they were in tracked cohorts. White and Asian students were five times more likely to do so.[68] In other words, all groups benefited from detracking, with the students needing the most help receiving the most benefit.

General elements associated with successful detracking in Rockville Centre included leadership stability, a hiring emphasis on teachers and administrators who believed in equity and excellence, an initial focus on simply eliminating the lowest track, followed by methodically paced implementation of a high-level curriculum for all, with lots of support for teachers and students. The district also tied the rationale for detracking to external accountability policies. It was transparent in dealing with families who opposed the reform but didn't allow resistance to halt forward progress. Regular analysis of achievement data also helped make the case for ongoing detracking efforts.[69] Detracking, then, should take center stage as intentionally diverse schools move forward along the integration continuum.[70]

Monitoring and Confronting Racial Disparities in Discipline

As with tracking, racial disparities in discipline can undermine equal status and seriously disrupt learning opportunities for historically marginalized students. Leaders at all of our schools emphasized discipline focused on prevention, reparation, and/or rewards for good behavior, crucial elements in the fight to reduce inequities.[71] While these efforts haven't eliminated entirely racial disproportionality in discipline, they have moved the focus away from punishment that excludes students from the school learning environment. Interventions included an emphasis on creating community at Sprout, SEL paired with robust implementation of positive behavioral support interventions (PBIS) at Ecoff, regular teacher house meetings focused on wrapping supports around students and trauma-informed care at Binford, and positive behavioral referrals at CodeRVA. Ecoff and Binford, which initially struggled the most with inequitable and exclusionary discipline, rapidly reduced their total number of suspensions. They did so through committed leadership, regular sharing of data disaggregated by race and other subgroups, strong interventions, appropriate supports, and investment in implementation. The fact that the schools moved the needle on racially inequitable discipline—which is intimately related to segregation and bias—shows us that progress is possible with the right set of tools.[72]

Inclusively Connecting the Worlds of Home and School

Last but not least, all of our schools focused on making strong connections between students' home and educational lives. There were the obvious steps, like establishing expectations for structures (e.g., family events held during different times of the day, front office signs and protocols, dissemination of information in multiple languages) that allowed for multiple points of access and input into the four sites. But school leaders and teachers also constructed ways for families to meaningfully engage, whether through traditional avenues like field trips, visits, and PTAs, or nontraditional ones like Ecoff's Empowerment Zone or Binford's empathy advisory committee. Such efforts nurtured positive feelings and care between families, communities, and schools and served as opportunities for families—not just students—to come together under optimal contact conditions. This matters because positive interracial relationships among families model the importance of those bonds for children and can help reduce bias.[73]

A few last words while we're on the subject of families. My letter to Posey outlined some of the ways our white family has benefited from systems designed to maintain white supremacy and explained why we believe sending her to diverse schools is to her individual and our collective benefit. Throughout *A Single Garment*, I've endeavored to illustrate how the individual choices families make—especially families with the most information, resources, and political power, all of which have accrued unevenly to whites because of racial discrimination—fuel the dynamics of school segregation. Though many of the voluntary integration lessons flowing from our four schools relate to educational policy or leadership, efforts in those realms won't move to scale without significant political backing from families and the broader voting public.

We have to fight for intentional school integration. We have to see it as beneficial to our own kids, as essential for all of our students, as a remedy for past injustice, and as an antidote to an increasingly divided society. Our four schools show us that if we work hard enough, school integration can be all of those things.

Research Notes

I spent two years, spanning 2017–2019, conducting seventy-one interviews and/or focus groups with school and community leaders, families, teachers, and high school students connected to Sprout, Ecoff, Binford, and CodeRVA. I supplemented the interviews with observations and a review of documents related to the schools. Two central research questions guided the interviews, observations, and document review:

1. What kinds of policies and practices facilitate external integration in the context of historical and systemic segregation?
2. What are the opportunities and challenges for leadership and practice around internal school integration?

Gathering Data
Sample

I generated a list of possible interviewees for each school through several avenues. Once district and school-based leaders granted access to the four sites, I based an initial round of interviews and focus groups on a judgment sample of those who could provide significant insight into the policies and practices that promote intentionally diverse schools. These included school superintendents, principals, board members, teachers, and families. I closed each of those early interviews with the question, "Who else should I speak with?" I then turned to snowball sampling, so named for the way each new referral gained momentum (or snow) that led me to additional stakeholders. Snowball sampling has drawbacks, one of which is its heavy reliance on established social networks—particularly significant for a study related to school segregation.[1] Using an initial judgment sample informed by my prior involvement in the schools partially offset that weakness, as did specific requests for racially, ethnically, and economically diverse perspectives to principals willing to help form focus groups. Two of the four schools, Sprout at the Children's Museum and CodeRVA, were so small during the study time period that I was able overcome the limitations of snowball sampling by interviewing all leaders and teachers.

These endeavors ultimately led to a participant sample ranging from fifteen to twenty-three interviewees per site (see table 1). I conducted the most interviews and focus groups at CodeRVA, in part because high school students were included in the sample.[2] Participants of color accounted for between about 30 percent and 40 percent of the interviews or focus groups at each school. To protect confidentiality, I masked the specific racial/ethnic identities of the small number of participants not identifying as black or white.

In a region reporting fast-growing but highly concentrated Latinx and Asian populations, the lack of multiracial diversity in the participant sample represented another study limitation. Though Sprout and Binford almost exclusively served black and white students, Ecoff and CodeRVA reported enrollments with substantive shares of Latinx and, to some extent, Asian students. While the sample was not entirely without Latinx, Asian, and biracial perspectives, further exploring how racial/ethnic groups outside of the South's historical—and still, in many ways, paramount—black and white binary is an area ripe for further research.

Interviews and Focus Groups

I conducted semistructured interviews and focus groups with key stakeholders involved in Sprout, Ecoff, Binford, and CodeRVA. Semistructured protocols gave me the opportunity to loosely follow a questioning script (more on how this was generated below), at the same time remaining flexible when it came to new information.[3] Semistructured interviewing also permitted deviations in question order so that the flow of conversation could unfold more naturally. Most interviews took

Table 1 *Characteristics of participant sample*

SCHOOL	CHARACTERISTICS OF RESPONDENTS	NUMBER OF RESPONDENTS
Sprout (*n*=15)	**Role**	
	Leader	5
	Educator	7
	Parent/Guardian	5
	Race/Ethnicity	
	White	9
	Black	4
	Other	2
Ecoff (*n*=15)	**Role**	
	Leader	7
	Educator	3
	Parent/Guardian	4
	Race/Ethnicity	
	White	10
	Black	4
	Other	1
Binford (*n*=18)	**Role**	
	Leader	9
	Educator	4
	Parent/Guardian	13
	Race/Ethnicity	
	White	13
	Black	3
	Other	2
CodeRVA (*n*=23)	**Role**	
	Leader	11
	Educator	5
	Parent/Guardian	7
	Student	5
	Race/Ethnicity	
	White	14
	Black	8
	Other	1

Notes: Because a number of interviewees reported dual roles (e.g., leader and parent/guardian of student enrolled at a site), total numbers for the role and racial/ethnic categories do not always align. "Leader" includes school principals, superintendents, central office administrators, school board members, nonprofit leaders, and community organizers. "Other" race/ethnicity includes biracial, Latinx, and Asian.

place at either the schools or nearby coffee shops. Each lasted about an hour to an hour and a half, and focused on questions related to external and internal school integration.

Interview protocols for different stakeholder groups were developed from intensive study of social-psychological, sociological, legal, political science, and education policy literature related to school desegregation. Earlier versions of protocol questions for leaders, stakeholders, or teachers have been piloted and used in several national studies of magnet schools that I was involved in as a research associate with the UCLA Civil Rights Project. The results from one of those studies have been published in a Civil Rights Project manual on school choice and equity and will also appear in a forthcoming journal article with my coauthor Jennifer Ayscue.[4] The family protocol was informed by prior studies of school gentrification.[5]

I conducted a second round of interviews with leaders at the four school sites as the study came to a close. Questions dealt with the evolution of external and internal integration at the schools or with points of expansion or clarification that emerged from my initial review of the data.

All interviews and focus groups were audio recorded and transcribed directly after they occurred with assistance from Virginia Palencia, a graduate student researcher, or Rev.com. I also took nearly verbatim notes during each interview and added field and memo notes immediately after they concluded.

Observations

I supplemented interviews and focus groups with unstructured observations of schools and classrooms. Classroom observations provided insight into leadership and instructional practices (e.g., assigning students to diverse classrooms and groups, differentiating instruction, promoting equal status for students, designing cooperative rather than competitive activities that allow students to work toward common goals, and demonstrating support for cooperation across racial lines) that may promote positive intergroup contact. Broader school observations, which included recess and meals, assemblies, recruitment, and family events and field trips, provided additional opportunities to observe leadership and practice associated with intentionally diverse schools. I took extensive field notes during observations, capturing dialogue, instruction, and interactions that I witnessed.

Primary Documents

I additionally relied on primary sources such as newspaper articles, legal cases, and school-level data reports obtained from the Virginia Department of Education; national-level data obtained from the National Center for Education Statistics; school information brochures and websites; and school board documents and other policy documents from district and governmental bodies as applicable.

Analytical Method

Data collection and analysis occurred simultaneously, allowing me to engage in a reflexive and open-ended process.[6] I wrote several research summaries at different points in the study that guided my thinking around theory and emerging findings. The initial proposal for this book was one such summary.

I analyzed interview data and other documents collected using codes derived from the literature and theory on school desegregation, as well as additional codes that emerged from the data. Findings were checked and rechecked with participants to ensure that my interpretations were consistent with the data and that my conclusions were authentic.[7] Follow-up interviews with school leaders were particularly helpful in assessing the validity of emerging findings.[8] Leaders—along with numerous other participants—also reviewed and provided feedback on chapter drafts related to their school site.

I developed themes for different data sources (i.e., interviews, observations, and documents) and then compared these themes during the final component of analysis, which allowed me to triangulate information from the various sources. Data related to the four school sites were analyzed separately at first and then synthesized for cross-case themes.

Throughout my analysis, I considered whether emerging findings were consistent with existing literature on school segregation and desegregation, along with whether and how they expanded upon it.

Bias

As noted in the preface to this book, I wore a number of different hats when it came to involvement in the four schools. Strengths related to those multidimensional roles included access to the sites, trusting relationships that allowed for honest dialogue about sensitive topics like race and segregation, and the ability to ask more detailed questions about certain events or circumstances related to internal and external integration. Weaknesses included the potential for researcher bias in data collection and analysis. I sought to address those weaknesses by being transparent about which role I was playing at various intervals of my involvement with the schools (e.g., parent versus researcher) and by enlisting the assistance and perspective of a graduate student researcher new to the subject and sites. She and I worked independently to shape our notes around interviews and site visits, meeting regularly to review and discuss. Though I conducted all of the interviews, her independent transcriptions and accompanying memos served to either reinforce or negate my more entangled perspective. Checking themes and conclusions with numerous participants also confirmed and extended the validity of the research findings.

Confidentiality

This study dealt very particularly with a time and a place. I sought to understand not just internal and external integration strategies but how schools work to intentionally diversify within a segregated, metropolitan system. All of this made it important to be able to identify Richmond and the names of the schools. There is value in knowing who is doing the difficult but essential work of integration when it comes to sharing common challenges and triumphs. But while the region, the schools, and their leaders were identified, I protected the confidentiality of most teachers and families (unless they had specifically indicated a willingness to be identified), as well as all involved students.

Notes

Introduction

1. John King, "What We Ought to Be: Educational Opportunity, Civil Rights and the Every Student Succeeds Act" (speech, US Department of Education, Washington, DC, January 27, 2016), archived information, https://www.ed.gov/news /speeches/what-we-ought-be; John King, "Stronger Together: The Need for Diversity in America's Schools" (speech, US Department of Education, Orlando, FL, July 1, 2016), archived information, https://www.ed.gov/news/speeches /stronger-together-need-diversity-americas-schools.

2. Scott Page, *The Diversity Bonus* (Princeton, NJ: Princeton University Press, 2017).

3. Melanie Killen, David Crystal, and Martin Ruck, "The Social Developmental Benefits of Intergroup Contact Among Children and Adolescents," in *Lessons in Integration: Realizing the Promise of Racial Diversity in American Schools*, eds. Erica Frankenberg and Gary Orfield (Charlottesville: University of Virginia Press, 2007), 31–56; Thomas Pettigrew and Linda Tropp, "A Meta-Analytic Test of Intergroup Contact Theory," *Journal of Personality and Social Psychology* 90 (2006): 751–83.

4. Roz Mickelson and Mokubung Nkomo, "Integrated Schooling, Life-Course Outcomes, and Social Cohesion in Multiethnic Democratic Societies," *Review of Research in Education* 36 (2012): 197–238.

5. "Opening Doors, Expanding Opportunities" (Washington, DC: US Department of Education, December 2, 2016), https://www2.ed.gov/programs/odeo /index.html.

6. Emma Brown, "Trump's Education Department Nixes Obama-era Grant Program for School Diversity," *Washington Post*, March 29, 2017, https://www .washington post.com/news/education/wp/2017/03/29/trumps-education -department-nixes-obama-era-grant-program-for-school-diversity/?utm_term =.142719665c15.

7. Brown.

8. Representatives Robert C. Scott (D-VA) and John Conyers (D-Michigan).

9. I use the terms black and African American interchangeably throughout the book. The GAO report uses the term "Hispanic"; I use Latinx here for consistency with the term used throughout the book. Latinx is inclusive of more cultures than Hispanic and is also gender neutral.

10. United States Government Accountability Office, *Better Use of Information Could Help Agencies Identify Disparities and Address Racial Discrimination* (Washington,

DC: United States Government Accountability Office, GAO-16-345, April 2016), https://www.gao.gov/assets/680/676745.pdf.

11. Gary Orfield, *Must We Bus? Segregated Schools and National Policy* (Washington, DC: Brookings Institution, 1978).

12. James Ryan, *Five Miles Away, a World Apart: One City, Two Schools and the Story of Modern Educational Inequality* (New York: Oxford University Press, 2010); Gerald Grant, *Hope and Despair in the American City: Why There Are No Bad Schools in Raleigh* (Cambridge, MA: Harvard University Press, 2009).

13. Robert Pratt, *The Color of Their Skin* (Charlottesville: University of Virginia Press, 1992); Nancy Maclean, *Democracy in Chains* (New York: Viking Press, 2017).

14. Orfield, *Must We Bus?* If Southern leaders hadn't resisted *Brown v. Board of Education* so fiercely, spatial separation would've been less intense. When *Brown* was decided in 1954, nearly all urban school segregation flowed from the fact that black and white students attended separate schools within the same school systems. A decade and a half later, with the three branches of the federal government temporarily unified in their commitment to *Brown*'s implementation, steady white exodus from cities to suburbs meant that more school segregation now flowed from the fact that black and white students lived in separate school systems altogether.

15. Robert A. Pratt, "The Conscience of Virginia: Judge Robert R. Merhige Jr., and the Politics of School Desegregation," *University of Richmond Law Review Online* 29 (2017), https://lawreview.richmond.edu/2017/09/28/the-conscience-of -virginia-judge-robert-r-merhige-jr-and-the-politics-of-school-desegregation/.

16. Ryan, *Five Miles Away*.

17. Brown v. Board of Education of Topeka, 347 U.S. 483 (1954).

18. Richard Florida, *The New Urban Crisis* (New York: Basic Books, 2017).

19. Richard Florida, "Urban Neighborhoods, Once Distinct by Race and Class, Are Blurring," *CityLab*, February 19, 2019, https://www.citylab.com/life/2019/02 /city-race-class-neighborhood-white-black-rich-segregate/583039/.

20. Amy Stuart Wells, Lauren Fox, Diana Cordova-Cobo, and Douglas Ready, "A Shared Future: Addressing the Patterns of Resegregation in Urban and Suburban Contexts: How to Stabilize Integrated Schools and Communities Amid Metro Migrations" (Cambridge, MA: Joint Center for Housing Studies of Harvard University, Working Paper, 2018), https://www.jchs.harvard .edu/research-areas/working-papers/shared-future-addressing-patterns -resegregation-urban-and-suburban.

21. Martin Luther King, "The Ethical Demands of Integration," in *A Testament of Hope: The Essential Writings and Speeches of Dr. Martin Luther King*, ed. James Washington (San Francisco: Harper, 1986), 118.

22. john a. powell, "A New Theory of Integrated Education: True Integration," in *School Resegregation: Must the South Turn Back*, eds. John Boger and Gary Orfield (Chapel Hill: University of North Carolina Press, 2005), 281–304.

Chapter 1

1. E. Frankenberg and R. Jacobsen, "The Polls-Trends School Integration Polls," *Public Opinion Quarterly* 75, no. 4 (Winter 2011): 788–811.

2. 2017 National Phi Delta Kappan Poll, Communities in Schools (August 2017), https://www.communitiesinschools.org/press-room/resource/2017-national -pdk-poll/.

3. 2017 National Phi Delta Kappan Poll.

4. Robert Lount Jr. and Katherine W. Phillips, "Working Harder with the Out-group: The Impact of Social Category Diversity on Motivation Gains," *Organizational Behavior and Human Decision Processes* 103, no. 2 (2007): 214–24; Katherine W. Phillips and Denise Lewin Loyd, "When Surface and Deep-level Diversity Collide: The Effects on Dissenting Group Members, *Organizational Behavior and Human Decision Processes* 99, no. 2 (2006): 143–60; Katherine W. Phillips, Katie Liljenquist, and Margaret A. Neale, "Is the Pain Worth the Gain? The Advantages and Liabilities of Agreeing with Socially Distinct Newcomers," *Personality and Social Psychology Bulletin* 35, no. 3 (2009): 336–50.

5. Katherine W. Phillips, Gregory B. Northcraft, and Margaret A. Neale, "Surface-Level Diversity and Decision-Making in Groups: When Does Deep-Level Similarity Help?," *Group Processes & Intergroup Relations* 9, no. 4, doi: https:// doi.org/10.1177/1368430206067557.

6. Scott E. Page, *The Diversity Bonus: How Great Teams Pay Off in the Knowledge Economy* (Princeton, NJ: Princeton University Press, 2017); Scott E. Page, *The Difference: How the Power of Diversity Creates Better Groups, Firms, Schools and Societies* (Princeton, NJ: Princeton University Press, 2007).

7. For a summary, see Katherine W. Phillips, "How Diversity Makes Us Smarter," *Scientific American*, October 1, 2014, https://www.scientificamerican.com/article /how-diversity-makes-us-smarter/.

8. Tamara Wilder, Rebecca Jacobsen, and Richard Rothstein, *Grading Education: Getting Accountability Right* (New York: Teachers College Press/Economic Policy Institute, 2008).

9. Neil Rudenstine, "Student Diversity in Higher Learning," in *Diversity Challenged: Evidence on the Impact of Affirmative Action,* ed. Gary Orfield (Cambridge, MA: Harvard Education Press, 2001), 37.

10. Rudenstine, 37.

11. Patricia Gurin, *Defending Diversity Affirmative Action at the University of Michigan* (Ann Arbor: University of Michigan Press, 2004); Anthony Antonio et al., "Effects of Racial Diversity on Complex Thinking in College Students," *Psychological Science* 15 (2004): 507–10.

12. Sweatt v. Painter, U.S. 629 (1950).

13. Amy Stuart Wells, Lauren Fox, and Diana Cordova-Cobo, *How Racially Diverse Schools and Classrooms Can Benefit All Students* (Washington, DC: The Century Foundation, 2006), https://tcf.org/content/report/how-racially-diverse-schools -and-classrooms-can-benefit-all-students/?agreed=1.

14. Jeremy Franklin, William Smith, and Man Hung, "Racial Battle Fatigue for Latina/o Students: A Quantitative Perspective," *Journal of Hispanic Higher Education* 13 (2014): 303–22; Shaun Harper, Sylvia Hurtado, and Lori Patton, "Nine Themes in Campus Racial Climates and Implications for Institutional Transformation," *New Directions for Student Services* 120 (2007): 7–24; Sylvia Hurtado and Deborah Faye Carter, "Effects of College Transition and Perceptions of the Campus Racial Climate on Latino College Students' Sense of Belonging," *Sociology of Education* 70, no. 4 (1997): 324–45; Angela Locks et al., "Extending Notions of Campus Climate and Diversity to Students' Transition to College," *Review of Higher Education* 31, no. 3 (2008): 257–85; Tara Yosso et al., "Critical Race Theory, Racial Microaggressions, and Campus Racial Climate for Latina/o Undergraduates," *Harvard Educational Review* 79, no. 4 (2009): 659–90.

15. Jessica Guyen, "Exclusive: Google Raising Stakes on Diversity," *USA Today*, May 6, 2015, https://www.usatoday.com/story/tech/2015/05/05/google-raises-stakes-diversity-spending/26868359/.

16. Jeanne L. Reid, "Racial/Ethnic Diversity and Language Development in the Preschool Classroom," in *School Integration Matters: Research-based Strategies to Advance Equity*, eds. Erica Frankenberg, Liliana Garces, and Megan Hopkins (New York: Teachers College Press, 2016), 12.

17. C. Schechter and B. Bye, "Preliminary Evidence for the Impact of Mixed-Income Preschool on Low-income Children's Language Growth," *Early Childhood Research Quarterly* 22 (2007): 137–46; Jeanne L. Reid and Douglas D. Ready, "High-quality Preschool: The Socio-economic Composition of Preschool Classrooms and Children's Learning," *Early Education and Development* 24, no. 8 (2013): 1082–111.

18. Reid, "Racial/Ethnic Diversity and Language Development in the Preschool Classroom."

19. Elizabeth Cascio, "Does Universal Preschool Hit the Target? Program Access and Preschool Impacts," NBER Working Paper No. 23215 (Washington, DC: National Bureau of Economic Research, 2017), https://www.nber.org/papers/w23215.

20. Richard D. Kahlenberg, *All Together Now: Creating Middle-class Schools Through Public School Choice*. A Century Foundation Book (Washington, DC: Brookings Institution Press, 2001).

21. Gregory J. Palardy, "High School Socioeconomic Segregation and Student Attainment," *American Educational Research Journal* 50, no. 4 (2013): 714–54.

22. Russell Rumberger and Gregory Palardy, "Test Scores, Dropout Rates and Transfer Rates as Alternative Indicators of School Performance," *American Education Research Journal* 41 (2005): 3–42; Christopher Jencks and Susan Mayer, "The Social Consequences of Growing Up in a Poor Neighborhood," in *Inner City Poverty in the United States*, eds. L. E. Lynn Jr. and M. G. H. McGeary (Washington, DC: National Academy Press, 1990).

23. Robert Linn and Kevin Welner, eds., *Race-Conscious Policies for Assigning Students to Schools: Social Science Research and the Supreme Court Cases* (Washington, DC: National Academy of Education, 2007); Robert Garda, "The White Interest in School Integration," *The Florida Law Review* 63 (2011): 605; Roslyn Mickelson, *School Integration and K–12 Outcomes: An Updated Quick Synthesis of the Social Science Evidence* (Washington, DC: National Coalition on School Diversity, 2016).

24. David Armor and S. Watkins, "School Segregation and Black Achievement: New Evidence from the 2003 NAEP," in *The Benefits of Racial and Ethnic Diversity in Elementary and Secondary Education*, US Commission on Civil Rights, 2006: 28–49; April Benner and Robert Crosnoe, "The Racial/Ethnic Composition of Elementary Schools and Young Children's Academic and Socioemotional Functioning," *American Educational Research Journal* 48, no. 3 (2011): 621–46; Martha Bottia et al., "Distributive Justice Antecedents of Race and Gender Disparities in First-Year College Performance," *Social Justice Research* 29, no. 1 (2016): 35–72; Mickelson, *School Integration and K–12 Outcomes*; Carl Bankston and Stephen J. Caldas, "Majority African American Schools and Social Injustice: The Influence of De Facto Segregation on Academic Achievement," *Social Forces* 75, no. 2 (1996): 535–55; Mark Berends and Roberto Penaloza, "Increasing Racial Isolation and Test Score Gaps in Mathematics: A 30-Year Perspective," *Teachers College Record* 112, no. 4 (2010): 978–1007.

25. Robert Putnam, *Our Kids* (New York: Simon & Schuster, 2015).

26. See, for example, Mickelson, *School Integration and K-12 Outcomes*.

27. Katherine Magnuson and Jane Waldfogel, eds., *Steady Gains and Stalled Progress: Inequality and the Black-White Test Score Gap* (New York: Russell Sage Foundation, 2008).

28. Jaekyung Lee, *The Anatomy of Achievement Gaps: Why and How American Education Is Losing (but Can Still Win) the War on Underachievements* (London: Oxford University Press, 2015).

29. Socioeconomically disadvantaged schools were defined as schools in the bottom 25% of the national distribution of the school-level economic, social, and cultural status (ESCS index). Socioeconomically advantaged schools were among the top 25% of the national distribution of the school-level ESCS. Similar logic applied to the definition of individual student socioeconomic disadvantage or advantage. See Organisation for Economic Cooperation and Development, *Equity in Education: Breaking Down Barriers to Social Mobility PISA* (Paris: OECD Publishing, 2018), https://books.google.com/books?id=hWV0D wAAQBAJ&source=gbs_navlinks_s.

30. James S. Coleman et al., *Equality of Educational Opportunity (Coleman) Study (EEOS)* (Washington, DC: National Center for Education Statistics, 1966); Geoffrey Borman and Maritza Dowling, "Schools and Inequality: A Multilevel Analysis of Coleman's Equality of Educational Opportunity Data," *Teachers College Record* 112, no. 5 (2010): 1201–246.

31. Sean Reardon, "School Segregation and Racial Academic Achievement Gaps" (working paper no. 15-12, Stanford Center for Education Policy Analysis, Palo Alto, CA, 2015), http://cepa.stanford.edu/wp15-12.

32. Amy Stuart Wells, Lauren Fox, and Diana Cordova-Coba, *How Racially Diverse Schools and Classrooms Can Benefit All Students* (Washington, DC: The Century Foundation, 2016), https://tcf.org/content/report/how-racially-diverse-schools-and-classrooms-can-benefit-all-students/?session=1.

33. Tara Yosso, "Whose Culture Has Capital? A Critical Race Theory Discussion of Community Cultural Wealth," *Race, Ethnicity and Education* 8 no. 1 (2005): 69–91.

34. A. D. Coppens et al., "Learning by Observing and Pitching In: Benefits and Processes of Expanding Repertoires," *Human Development* 57 (2014): 150–161; Shirley B. Heath, *Ways with Words* (Cambridge, UK: Cambridge University Press, 1983); D. L. Medin and M. Bang, *Who's Asking? Native Science, Western Science and Science Education* (Cambridge, MA: MIT Press, 2014); B. Rogoff, M. Correa-Chávez, and K. Silva, "Cultural Variation in Children's Attention and Learning," in *Psychology and the Real World*, eds. M. Gernsbacher et al. (New York: Worth, 2011).

35. Sonia Nieto, *Affirming Diversity: The Sociopolitical Context of Multicultural Education* (White Plains, NY: Longman Publishers USA, 1996), 259.

36. Peter Wood and Nancy Sonleitner, "The Effect of Childhood Interracial Contact on Adult Antiblack Prejudice," *International Journal of Intercultural Relations* 20, no. 1 (1996): 1–17; Maureen Hallinan, "Diversity Effects on Student Outcomes: Social Science Evidence," *Ohio State Law Journal* 59 (1998); Sandra Graham, Anke Munniksma, and Jaana Juvonen, "Psychosocial Benefits of Cross-Ethnic Friendships in Urban Middle Schools," *Child Development*, 2013, doi:10.1111/cdev.12159.

37. Stephen C. Wright et al., "Including Others in the Self," in *The Social Self: Cognitive, Interpersonal, and Intergroup Perspectives*, eds. Joseph P. Forgas and Kipling Williams (New York: Psychology Press), 343–64.

38. Walter G. Stephan and Cookie White Stephan, *Improving Intergroup Relations* (Thousand Oaks: Sage Publications, 2001), 29.

39. Brown v. Board of Education of Topeka, U.S. 438 (1954).

40. Richard Kluger, *Simple Justice: The History of Brown v. Board of Education and Black America's Struggle for Equality* (New York: First Vintage Books, 1975), 317.

41. Kenneth Clark and Mamie Clark, "Segregation as a Factor in the Racial Identification of Negro Pre-School Children," *The Journal of Experimental Education* 8, no. 2 (1939): 161–63.

42. Marian Radke and Helen Tager, "Children's Perceptions of the Social Roles of Negroes and Whites," *The Journal of Psychology* 29 (1950): 3–33.

43. Erica Frankenberg, *Segregation at an Early Age* (State College: Penn State Center for Educational and Civil Rights, 2016), https://cecr.ed.psu.edu/sites/default/files/Segregation_At_An_Early_Age_Frankenberg_2016.pdf.

44. "Understanding Racial/Ethnic Identity Development: An Interview with Dr. Sandra Chapman," by Melissa Giraud and Andrew Grant-Thomas, Embrace Race.org, May 23, 2017, https://www.embracerace.org/blog/recording-and -resources-understanding-racial-ethnic-identity-development.

45. Giraud and Grant-Thomas.

46. Steven Roberts, Amber Williams, and Susan Gelman, "Children's and Adults' Predictions of Black, White, and Multiracial Friendship Patterns," *Journal of Cognition and Development* 18, no. 2 (2017), doi: https://doi.org/10.1080/152483 72.2016.1262374.

47. Louise Derman-Sparks and Julie Olsen Edwards, *Anti-Bias Education for Young Children and Ourselves* (Washington, DC: NAEYC, 2010). See summary here: Louisie Derman-Sparks, "Stages of Children's Racial Identity Development," https://www.earlychildhoodwebinars.com/wp-content/uploads/2016/02 /Stages-of-Childrens-Racial-Identity-Development.pdf.

48. Dr. Martin Luther King Jr., "Letter from a Birmingham Jail," The Martin Luther King, Jr., Research and Education Institute, Stanford University, 1963, https://kinginstitute.stanford.edu/king-papers/documents/letter-birmingham -jail.

49. Charles Lawrence, "One More River To Cross," in *Shades of Brown*, ed. Derrick Bell (New York: Teachers College Press, 1980), 50.

50. Elizabeth Anderson, *The Imperative of Integration* (Princeton, NJ: Princeton University Press, 2010), 123.

51. Thomas Pettigrew and Linda Tropp, "A Meta-Analytic Test of Intergroup Contact Theory," *Journal of Personality and Social Psychology* 90, no. 5 (2006): 751–83.

52. Based on prior research conducted with the desegregating Merchant Marines and with desegregating housing projects. Gordon Allport, *The Nature of Prejudice* (Boston: Addison-Wesley, 1954).

53. Prudence Carter, "Student and School Cultures and the Opportunity Gap," in *Closing the Opportunity Gap*, eds. Prudence Carter and Kevin Welner (New York: Oxford University Press, 2013), 143–55.

54. Pettigrew and Tropp, "A Meta Analytic Test."

55. Pettigrew and Tropp.

56. A. Voci and M. Hewstone, "Intergroup Contact and Prejudice Toward Immigrants in Italy: The Mediational Role of Anxiety and the Moderating Role of Group Salience," *Group Processes and Intergroup Relations* 6 (2003): 37–54.

57. James Banks et al., "Diversity Within Unity: Essential Principles for Teaching and Learning in a Multicultural Society," *Phi Delta Kappan* (November 2001): 196–203.

58. E. Harmon-Jones and J. J. B. Allen, "The Role of Affect in the Mere Exposure Effect: Evidence from Physiological and Individual Differences Approaches," *Personality and Social Psychology Bulletin* 27 (2001): 889–98; A. Y. Lee, "The Mere Exposure Effect: An Uncertainty Reduction Explanation Revisited," *Personality and Social Psychology Bulletin* 27 (2001): 1255–66.

59. Pettigrew and Tropp, "A Meta Analytic Test."

60. Pettigrew and Tropp, 766.

61. G. Rhodes, J. Halberstadt, and G. Brajkovich, "Generalization of Mere Exposure Effects to Averaged Composite Faces," *Social Cognition* 19 (2001): 57–70.

62. A. Dijker, "Emotional Reactions to Ethnic Minorities," *European Journal of Social Psychology* 17 (1987): 305–25; W. Stephan et al., "The Role of Threats in the Racial Attitudes of Blacks and Whites," *Personality and Social Psychology Bulletin* 28 (2002): 1242–54.

63. Sandra Graham, Anke Munniksma, and Janna Juvonen, "Psychosocial Benefits of Cross-Ethnic Friendships in Urban Middle Schools," *Child Development* 85, no. 2 (2014): 469–83, doi:10.1111/cdev.12159; Sandra Graham, "Race/Ethnicity and the Social Adjustment of Adolescents: How (Not If) School Diversity Matters," *Educational Psychologist* 53, no. 2 (2018), doi: https://doi.org/10.1080/0046 1520.2018.1428805; Joanna L. Williams and Jill V. Hamm, "Peer Group Ethnic Diversity and Social Competencies in Youth Attending Rural Middle Schools," *The Journal of Early Adolescence* 38, no. 6 (2018): 795–823.

64. Jaana Juvonen, Kara Kogachi, and Sandra Graham, "When and How Do Students Benefit from Ethnic Diversity in Middle School?" *Child Development* 89, no. 4 (2017): 1268–82.

65. Juvonen, Kogachi, and Graham.

66. Graham, "Race/Ethnicity and the Social Adjustment of Adolescents."

67. Amy Stuart Wells and Robert L Crain, "Perpetuation Theory and the Long-Term Effects of School Desegregation," *Review of Educational Research* 64, no. 4 (1994): 531–55; Jomills Henry Braddock II and James M. McPartland, "Social-Psychological Processes That Perpetuate Racial Segregation: The Relationship Between School and Employment Desegregation," *Journal of Black Studies* 19, no. 3 (1989): 267–89; Jomills Henry Braddock II, "Looking Back: The Effects of Court-Ordered Segregation," in *From the Courtroom to the Classroom: The Shifting Landscape of School Desegregation*, eds. Claire Smrekar and Ellen B. Goldring (Cambridge, MA: Harvard Education Press, 2009).

68. Roslyn Mickelson, *The Reciprocal Relationship Between Housing and School Integration: Research Brief No. 7, Updated* (Washington, DC: National Coalition on School Diversity, 2011).

69. Richard D. Kahlenberg et al., "What Do School Tests Measure?," *Room For Debate: A New York Times Blog*, August 3, 2009, https://roomfordebate.blogs.nytimes.com/2009/08/03/what-do-school-tests-measure/#richard; Maria Krysan and Kyle Crowder, *The Cycle of Segregation: Social Processes and Residential Stratification* (New York: Russell Sage Foundation, 2017); Annette Lareau and Kimberly A. Goyette, eds., *Choosing Homes, Choosing Schools* (New York: Russell Sage Foundation, 2014).

70. Robert Jones, Juhem Navarro-Rivera, and Daniel Cox, "In Search of Libertarians in America," *PRRI*, 2013, http://www.prri.org/research/2013-american -values-survey/.

71. Daniel Cox, Juhem Navarro-Rivera, and Robert P. Jones, "Race, Religion and Political Affiliation of Americans' Core Social Networks" (Washington, DC: Public Religion Research Institute, 2016), https://www.prri.org/research /poll-race-religion-politics-americans-social-networks/; Lisa Windsteiger, "How Our Narrowing Social Circles Create a More Unequal World," *The Guardian*, June 27, 2017, https://www.theguardian.com/inequality/2017/jun/27/people -like-us-why-narrowing-social-circles-create-more-unequal-world.

72. John Dewey, *Democracy and Education* (New York: McMillan, 1916).

73. Robert B. Reich, *The Common Good* (New York: Knopf, 2018).

74. Rebecca Jacobsen, Erica Frankenberg, and Sarah Winchell Lenhoff, "Diverse Schools in a Democratic Society: New Ways of Understanding How School Demographics Affect Civic and Political Learning," *American Educational Research Journal* 49, no. 5 (2012): 812–43.

75. M. Kurlaender and J. Yun, "Measuring School Racial Composition and Student Outcomes in a Multiracial Society," *American Journal of Education* 113, no. 2 (2007): 213–42; M. Kurlaender and J. Yun, "Fifty Years After Brown: New Evidence of the Impact of School Racial Composition on Student Outcomes," *International Journal of Educational Policy, Research and Practice* 6, no. 1 (2005): 51–78.

76. Joseph E. Kahne and Susan E. Sporte, "Developing Citizens: The Impact of Civic Learning Opportunities on Students' Commitment to Civic Participation," *American Educational Research Journal* 45, no. 3 (2008): 738–66.

77. Roslyn Arlin Mickelson and Mokubung Nkomo, "Integrated Schooling, Life Course Outcomes, and Social Cohesion in Multiethnic Democratic Societies," *Review of Research in Education* 36, no. 1 (2012): 197–238.

78. Dick Stanley, "What Do We Know about Social Cohesion: The Research Perspective of the Federal Government's Social Cohesion Research Network," *Canadian Journal of Sociology* 28, no. 1, Special Issue on Social Cohesion in Canada (2003): 5–17.

79. Braddock, "Looking Back.

80. Reich, *The Common Good.*

81. Amy Stuart Wells, Jennifer Jellison Holme, Anita Revilla, and Auro Atanda, *Both Sides Now* (Berkeley: University of California Press, 2009).

82. Anderson, *The Imperative of Integration.*

83. Jessica YiYi Li and John Mannes, "How Greater Diversity Can Improve Montgomery's Magnet Schools," opinion, *Washington Post,* July 22, 2016, https:// www.washingtonpost.com/opinions/how-greater-diversity-can-improve -montgomerys-magnet-schools/2016/07/22/8e58592a-4923-11e6-acbc-4d4 870a079da_story.html?noredirect=on&utm_term=.910ec05aff8b.

84. Li and Mannes.

85. "Better Use of Information Could Help Agencies Identify Disparities and Address Racial Discrimination," United States Government Accountability Office (GAO) Report, 2016, https://www.gao.gov/assets/680/676745.pdf.

86. "Better Use of Information."

87. Roslyn Arlin Mickelson, "Subverting Swann: First- and Second-Generation Segregation in the Charlotte-Mecklenburg Schools," *American Educational Research Journal* 38, 2 (2001): 215–52; Jeannie Oakes, *Keeping Track: How Schools Structure Inequality*, 2nd ed. (New Haven, CT: Yale University Press, 2005).

88. Kevin G. Welner and Carol C. Burris, "Is American Education on a Bad Track?," *National Education Policy Center* (NEPC) summary, August 13, 2013, https://nepc.colorado.edu/publication/american-education-bad-track; Carol C. Burris, Kevin G. Welner, and Jennifer Bezoza, "Universal Education to a Quality Education: Research and Recommendations for the Elimination of Curricular Stratification," National Education Policy Center (NEPC) summary, December 14, 2009, https://nepc.colorado.edu/publication/universal-access.

89. Frederick M. Hess, *Common Sense School Reform* (New York: Palgrave Macmillan, 2004).

90. Susan Eaton, *The Children in Room E4: American Education on Trial* (Chapel Hill: Algonquin, 2007), 197.

91. Jack Schneider, *Beyond Test Scores* (Cambridge, MA: Harvard University Press, 2017).

92. Center on Education Policy, *Instructional Time in Elementary Schools: A Closer Look at Specific Subjects* (Washington, DC: Author, 2008).

93. Diane Ravitch, *The Death and Life of the American School System* (New York: Basic Books, 2015), 249.

94. Matthew Chingos, "Who Opts Out of State Tests?," Brookings, June 18, 2015, https://www.brookings.edu/research/who-opts-out-of-state-tests/.

95. Linda Darling-Hammond, "Keeping Good Teachers: Why It Matters, What Leaders Can Do," *Educational Leadership* 60, no. 8 (2003): 6–13.

96. Afra Hersi, "Darling-Hammond: The Flat World and Education: How America's Commitment to Equity Will Determine Our Future," *Journal of Educational Change* 11, no. 3 (2010): 291–95.

97. Corey Koedel and Julian R. Betts, "Re-Examining the Role of Teacher Quality in the Educational Production Function" (working paper, Department of Economics, University of Missouri, 2007), http://economics.missouri.edu/working-papers/2007/wp0708_koedel.pdf.

98. Charles T. Clotfelter, Helen Ladd, and Jacob Vigdor, "Who Teaches Whom? Race and the Distribution of Novice Teachers," *Economics of Education Review* 24, no. 4 (2005); Donald Boyd et al., "The Narrowing Gap in New York City Teacher Qualification and Its Implications for Student Achievement in High Poverty Schools," *Journal of Policy Analysis and Management* 27, no. 4 (2008): 793–94; on experience, see Hamilton Lankford, Susanna Loeb, and James Wycoff, "Teacher Sorting and the Plight of Urban Schools: A Descriptive Analysis," *Educational Evaluation and Policy Analysis* 24, no. 1 (2002): 37–62; on qualifications, see Richard Ingersoll, "The Problem of Underqualified Teachers in American Secondary Schools," *Educational Researcher* 28, no. 2 (1999): 26–37.

99. Robert Hanna, Max Marchitello, and Catherine Brown, "Comparable but Unequal: School Funding Disparities" (Washington, DC: Center for American Progress, March, 2015), https://cdn.americanprogress.org/wp-content /uploads/2015/03/ESEAComparability-brief2.pdf; Frank Adamson and Linda Darling-Hammond, "Addressing the Inequitable Distribution of Teachers: What It Will Take to Get Qualified, Effective Teachers in All Communities" (Palo Alto, CA: Stanford Center for Opportunity Policy in Education, December, 2011), http://www.boldapproach.org/uploads/db_files/SCOPE%20 teacher%20salary%20brief.pdf; Kacey Guin, "Chronic Teacher Turnover in Urban Elementary Schools," *Education Policy Analysis Archives* 12 (2004): 42; Charles T. Clotfelter, Helen F. Ladd, and Jacob L. Vigdor, "Are Teacher Absences Worth Worrying About in the U.S.?," *Education Finance and Policy* 4, no. 2 (Spring 2009): 115–49; IDEA, UCLA, "Separate and Unequal 50 Years after Brown: Racial Opportunity Gaps in California's Schools" (Los Angeles: UCLA/ IDEA, 2004), http://idea.gseis.ucla.edu/publications/files/brownsu2.pdf.

100. Charles T. Clotfelter et al., "Do School Accountability Systems Make It More Difficult for Low-Performing Schools to Attract and Retain High-Quality Teachers?," *Journal of Policy Analysis and Management* 23, no. 2 (2004): 251–71.

101. C. Kirabo Jackson, "Student Demographics, Teacher Sorting, and Teacher Quality: Evidence from the End of School Desegregation," *Journal of Labor Economics* 27, no. 2 (2009): 213–56; Douglas Massey and Mary J. Fischer, "The Effect of Childhood Segregation on Minority Academic Performance at Selective Colleges," *Ethnic and Racial Studies* 29, no. 1 (2006): 1–26.

102. Erica Frankenberg, "The Segregation of American Teachers," *Education Policy Analysis Archives* 17, no. 1 (2008).

103. Green v. County School Board of New Kent County, U.S. 695 (1968).

104. Roslyn Mickelson, Stephen Smith, and Amy Nelson, eds., *Yesterday, Today and Tomorrow: School Desegregation and Resegregation in Charlotte* (Cambridge, MA: Harvard Education Press, 2015).

105. Mickelson, Smith, and Nelson; Jennifer Ayscue et al., "Segregation Again: North Carolina's Transition from Leading Desegregation Then to Accepting Segregation Now" (Los Angeles: UCLA Civil Rights Project, May 14, 2014), https://www.civilrightsproject.ucla.edu/research/k-12-education/integration -and-diversity/segregation-again-north-carolina2019s-transition-from-leading -desegregation-then-to-accepting-segregation-now.

106. Kirabo Jackson, "Student Demographics, Teacher Sorting and Teaching Quality.

107. Central to meeting conditions for intergroup contact, see, e.g., Gordon W. Allport, *The Nature of Prejudice* (Cambridge, MA: Addison-Wesley Publishing Company, 1954).

108. Scott E. Page, *The Diversity Bonus: How Great Teams Pay off in the Knowledge Economy*. Our Compelling Interests (Series) (Princeton, NJ: Princeton University Press, 2017).

109. C. E. Sleeter, "Preparing Teachers for Multiracial and Historically Underserved Schools," in *Lessons in Integration: Realizing the Promise of Racial Diversity in America's Schools*, eds. G. Orfield and E. Frankenberg (Charlottesville: University of Virginia Press, 2007).

110. Seth Gershenson, Stephen Holt, and Nicholas Papageorge, "Who Believes in Me? The Effect of Student Teacher Demographic Match on Teacher Expectations" (working paper, Upjohn Institute for Employment Research, Kalamazoo, WI, 2015), doi:10.17848/wp15-231; Thomas Dee, "Teachers, Race, and Student Achievement in a Randomized Experiment," *The Review of Economics and Statistics* 86, no. 1 (2004), doi:10.1162/003465304323023750; Alice Quiocho and Francisco Rios, "The Power of Their Presence: Minority Group Teachers and Schooling," *Review of Educational Research* 70, no. 4 (2000): 485–528; "Does Student Race Affect 'Gifted Assignment?," AERA, November, 2015, https://www.aera.net/Newsroom/News-Releases-and-Statements/Does-Student-Race-Affect-Gifted-Assignment/Discretion-and-Disproportionality-Explaining-the-Underrepresentation-of-High-Achieving-Students-of-Color-in-Gifted-Programs.

111. Damira S. Rasheed, Joshua L. Brown, Sebrina L. Doyle, and Patricia A. Jennings, "The Effect of Teacher–Child Race/Ethnicity Matching and Classroom Diversity on Children's Socioemotional and Academic Skills," *Child Development* (2019), https://onlinelibrary.wiley.com/doi/abs/10.1111/cdev.13275?af=R.

112. Vanessa Siddle Walker, *Their Highest Potential: An African American School Community in the Segregated South* (Chapel Hill: University of North Carolina Press, 1996); Vanessa Siddle Walker, *The Lost Education of Horace Tate* (New York: The New Press, 2018).

113. Owen Thompson, "School Desegregation and Black Teacher Employment" (Washington, DC: National Bureau of Economic Research, Working Paper No. 25990, 2019), https://www.nber.org/papers/w25990?utm_campaign=ntwh&utm_medium=email&utm_source=ntwg20.

114. Frankenberg, "The Segregation of American Teachers."

115. Alice Quiocho and Francisco Rios, "The Power of Their Presence: Minority Group Teachers and Schooling," *Review of Educational Research* 70, no. 4 (2000): 485–528; Farah Ahmad and Ulrich Boser, "America's Leaky Pipeline for Teachers of Color: Getting More Teachers of Color into the Classroom," Center for American Progress (May 2014), https://cdn.americanprogress.org/wp-content/uploads/2014/05/TeachersOfColor-report.pdf.

116. Pamela Grundy, *Color and Character: West Charlotte High and the American Struggle over Educational Equality* (Chapel Hill: The University of North Carolina Press, 2018).

117. Grundy, 79.

118. Peter H. Irons, *Jim Crow's Children: The Broken Promise of the Brown Decision* (New York: Viking, 2002), 33.

119. Noliwe M. Rooks, *Cutting School: Privatization, Segregation, and the End of Public Education* (New York: The New Press, 2017).

120. Nathan Margold, *Margold Report* (NAACP, 1933).

121. Richard Kluger, *Simple Justice: The History of* Brown v. Board of Education *and Black America's Struggle for Equality*, rev. and expanded ed. (New York: Knopf, 2004), 293.

122. James E. Ryan, *Five Miles Away, a World Apart: One City, Two Schools, and the Story of Educational Opportunity in Modern America* (Oxford; New York: Oxford University Press, 2010).

123. john a. powell, "A New Theory of Integrated Education: True Education," in *School Resegregation: Must the South Turn Back?* eds. John Boger and Gary Orfield (Chapel Hill: University of North Carolina Press, 2005).

124. Rucker Johnson, "Long-run Impacts of School Desegregation & School Quality on Adult Attainments" (working paper series, NBER, 2011).

125. Johnson.

126. For a detailed summary of the short- and long-term benefits of desegregation for black students, see Braddock, "Looking Back."

127. Rucker Johnson, "The Grandchildren of Brown: The Long Legacy of School Desegregation" (working paper, Goldman School of Policy, Berkeley, CA, March 2012).

Chapter 2

1. Erica Frankenberg, *Segregation at an Early Age* (State College: Penn State/Center for Education and Civil Rights, 2016), https://school-diversity.org/wp-content/uploads/2016/10/Segregation_At_An_Early_Age_Frankenberg_2016.pdf.

2. I use "early years" care to mean care for children between the ages of 0 and 4. Pre-school or early childhood education is included in this range but typically refers to a narrower band of children ages 3–5 attending school before kindergarten.

3. Marcia K. Meyers, "The ABCs of Child Care in a Mixed Economy: A Comparison of Public and Private Sector Alternatives," *Social Service Review* 64, no. 4 (1990): 559–79, doi: 10.1086/603796.

4. Quality is generally defined along the lines of class size; child-adult ratios; warm, strong child-adult interactions; and use of curricula—notice the absence of diversity. See Jeanne Reid et al., *A Better Start: Why Classroom Diversity Matters in Early Education* (Washington, DC: The Century Foundation, 2015).

5. Jacqueline Howard, "The Costs of Child Care Around the World," CNN, April 25, 2018, https://www.cnn.com/2018/04/25/health/child-care-parenting-explainer-intl/index.html.

6. Sean F. Reardon and Ximena A. Portilla, "Recent Trends in Income, Racial, and Ethnic School Readiness Gaps at Kindergarten Entry," *AERA Open* (2016), doi:10.1177/2332858416657343; Daphna Bassok et al., "Socioeconomic Gaps in Early Childhood Experiences: 1998 to 2010," *AERA Open* (2016), doi:10.1177/2332858416653924.

7. *From Best Practices to Breakthrough Impacts: A Science-Based Approach to Building a More Promising Future for Young Children and Families*, Center on the Developing Child at Harvard University, Harvard University, Cambridge, MA, 2016. See also "Ready Mind Project: Game-Changing Research," http://ilabs.washington.edu/game-changing.

8. Carlota Schechter and Beth Bye, "Preliminary Evidence for the Impact of Mixed-Income Preschool on Low-Income Children's Language Growth," *Early Childhood Research Quarterly* 22, no. 1 (2007): 137–46; Jeanne L. Reid and Douglas D. Ready, "High-quality Preschool: The Socio-economic Composition of Preschool Classrooms and Children's Learning," *Early Education and Development* 24, no. 8 (2013): 1082–1111.

9. The Reggio preschool approach is a student-centered pedagogical style rooted in relationship-driven learning environments. See Mary Ann Biermeier, "Inspired by Reggio Emilia: Emergent Curriculum in Relationship-Driven Learning Environments," *Young Children* 70, no. 5 (November 2015), https://www.naeyc.org/resources/pubs/yc/nov2015/emergent-curriculum.

10. Virtually all of the Sprout leaders and teachers I interviewed referenced these twin components of the organization's mission as they reflected on the origins and goals of the school. Their varied allusions to it reflected strong commitment to the work of the organization. It also made the decision to support an intentionally diverse preschool a clear fit for the YWCA. When I asked the director, Kathleen Eastman, if there was any internal tension around the emphasis on a mixed-income model, which also helped increase racial diversity in the school, she pointed to the YWCA's mission and said no. In fact, she went on to suggest that the organization should further extend its efforts, saying, "[W]e probably have not done enough with eliminating racism over recent years. We're trying to bring that back."

11. "YWCA History," Richmond YWCA, http://ywcarichmond.org/history/.

12. Head Start and Early Head Start serve more than a million low-income children and families each year in the US. The goal is to break the cycle of poverty through comprehensive educational, health, social, and psychological programming. See "History of Headstart," Office of Headstart, https://www.acf.hhs.gov/ohs/about/history-of-head-start. Around the same time that Linda Tissiere became CEO of the YWCA, three long-standing area preschools for low-income children were shuttered. In the wake of the recession, providing full-day/full-year care for Head Start families proved too heavy a lift. The YWCA had hung on longer, able to draw on a robust endowment that also funded its programs for survivors of domestic and sexual assault.

13. In addition to the gap, there was also the problem of underenrollment. When Tissiere arrived in 2012, the downtown YWCA's four Head Start classrooms were far from capacity, enrolling just 40 students. Three years later, the number had grown to 70, a marked improvement but not enough to sustain the program. More Head Start families had begun choosing the YWCA, and a

new, state-funded Virginia Preschool Initiative (VPI) classroom had opened in the building. Each of those five classrooms still exclusively served low-income families who qualified for the federal or state subsidies. Even with the new classroom, there was still room to expand in the downtown location, not to mention in additional sites. Growth wouldn't mean diminishment of services provided to low-income families but rather more services for a range of families.

14. Because Head Start targets low-income families, and because it comes with its own accountability paradigm, programs that serve both Head Start and non–Head Start students (which are rare in the first place) often separate the two groups into different classes. Eastman saw this practice in some of the wealthier suburbs of Boston. It bothered her.

15. A version of the sliding-scale idea actually caught on in the waning days of the Obama administration. During the fall of 2016, the US Department of Health and Human Services (HHS) issued new Head Start guidelines granting states and localities new flexibility—as long as they worked with research experts to evaluate their model—with regard to program requirements. These guidelines, which remain in effect, also supported the development of mixed-income preschool models in programs receiving funds from Head Start. See Head Start Performance Standards, Final Rule, United States Government Publishing Office, September 6, 2016, https://www.gpo.gov/fdsys/pkg/FR-2016-09-06/pdf/2016-19748.pdf. See also US Department of Health and Human Services, "1302.15 Enrollment," ECLKC, January 10, 2019, https://eclkc.ohs.acf.hhs.gov/policy/45-cfr-chap-xiii/1302-15-enrollment. Moreover, in 2016, federal preschool grants, jointly administered by HHS and the Department of Education, offered incentives for states proposing to increase socioeconomic diversity when developing or expanding preschool options. "Application for New Awards; Preschool Development Grans," *Federal Register* 79, no. 159, Department of Education and Department of Health and Human Services (2014): 48854, 48874, 48886, http://www.gpo.gov/fdsys/pkg/FR-2014-08-18/pdf/2014-19426.pdf. Under US Education Secretary John King, the Department of Education wanted to do even more to further preschool diversity, recognizing that it is a critical period for integration.

16. Elizabeth Anderson, *Imperative of Integration* (Princeton, NJ: Princeton University Press, 2011).

17. Convenience sample of 20 families. Twelve were middle to upper income (defined as making more than $60,000/year for a family of four) and 8 were middle to lower income (defined as making less than $60,000/year for a family of four). Racial/ethnic groups represented were black, East Asian, Latinx, South Asian, and white. Thirteen families were from the city, 5 from Henrico, and 1 each from Chesterfield and Hanover. Phillip Reese Consulting, "Care That Works: Qualitative Research to Capture Early Childcare and Education Needs of Richmond Area Families," Final Report of Findings Prepared for the YWCA of Richmond, Richmond, VA, April 10, 2015.

18. This finding tracks with sociological studies finding that working-class families tend to value more compliance than affluent families. Annete Lareau, *Unequal Childhoods: Class, Race and Family Life* (Los Angeles: University of California Press, 2003).

19. See, e.g., Jennifer Holme, "Buying Homes, Buying Schools," *Harvard Educational Review* 72, no. 2 (2002): 177–206.

20. Phillip Reese Consulting, "Care That Works."

21. The directors knew each another from serving on the board of Smart Beginnings, a regional early childhood advocacy group.

22. The Children's Museum saw an opportunity to expand into the preschool space, raise organizational awareness, and increase membership. There was also an existing model for a preschool-museum partnership at the Opal School in Portland, Oregon. The YWCA, meanwhile, saw an opportunity for expansion into a central, popular, and trustworthy community location that could facilitate its progressive new curriculum. Rupa Murthy's fund-raising prowess for the YWCA raised half a million dollars in a little less than a year, providing the resources needed to construct the two classrooms and hire and train teachers in the Reggio approach.

23. A primary external consideration for school integration is eliminating barriers to access like transportation. It's hard for families to access a school of choice if they struggle to get to it. About 10% of households in America's large metro areas lack access to a vehicle (see Adie Tomer, *Transit Access and Zero Vehicle Households*, Metropolitan Infrastructure Initiative Series [Washington, DC: Metropolitan Policy Program at Brookings, 2011]), the majority of whom are low income. The provision of transportation is expensive, however, making it difficult for early-care nonprofits already struggling to piece together per-child funding for full-day/full-year care. Unlike K–12 education, which almost universally offers free transportation to assigned regular public schools, the fragmentation of early-years care means families are not usually selecting between one option that provides transportation and another that doesn't. Sprout's partnership with Richmond Public Schools around the provision of Head Start *has* meant occasional free transportation to the downtown YWCA preschool. It's not offered at either Sprout school right now. Leadership and teachers acknowledge the lack of transportation could be a barrier to access, the teachers thinking in particular of one family that regularly navigates Richmond's limited and byzantine public transit system. But they also cite the central location of both preschools and the fact that they are on the bus routes. In fact, the Sprout schools are in very close proximity to Richmond's new rapid transit bus line.

24. Jennifer Ayscue et al., "Choices Worth Making: Creating, Sustaining and Expanding Diverse Magnet Schools" (Los Angeles: UCLA Civil Rights Project, 2017).

25. Amy Stuart Wells and Robert L. Crain, "Perpetuation Theory and the Long-Term Effects of School Desegregation," *Review of Educational Research* 64, no. 4 (1994), doi:10.3102/00346543064004531.

26. Green v. County School Board of New Kent County, 391 U.S. 430 (1968).

27. Erica Frankenberg, "The Segregation of American Teachers," *Education Policy Analysis Archives* 17, no. 1 (2009), doi:10.14507/epaa.v17n1.2009.

28. Scott Page, *The Diversity Bonus: How Great Teams Pay Off in the Knowledge Economy* (Princeton, NJ: Princeton University Press, 2017). See also Alison Reynolds and David Lewis, "Teams Solve Problems Faster When They're More Cognitively Diverse," *Harvard Business Review*, March 30, 2017, https://hbr.org/2017/03 /teams-solve-problems-faster-when-theyre-more-cognitively-diverse.

29. Marcy Whitebook et al., *Early Childhood Workforce Index- 2018* (Berkeley, CA: Center for the Study of Child Care Employment, 2018).

30. Whitebrook et al.

31. Enrollment data by income and race/ethnicity provided by the Sprout School.

32. US Department of Health and Human Services, "2017 Poverty Guidelines," https://aspe.hhs.gov/2017-poverty-guidelines.

33. All numbers in this section, unless otherwise indicated, provided by Sprout's director.

34. US Department of Education, The National Household Education Surveys Program, "Child Care: Percentage of Children Ages 3-6, Not Yet in Kindergarten, in Center-Based Care Arrangements By Child and Family Characteristics and Region, Selected Years 1995–2012," Federal Interagency Forum on Child and Family Statistics, http://www.childstats.gov/americaschildren/tables/fam 3b.asp?popup=true.

35. See, e.g., Parents Involved in Community Schools v. Seattle School District No. 1, 551 U.S. 701 (2007).

36. The downtown Sprout, where the plan has been to more gradually layer in the Reggio curriculum over the Head Start and VPI programming, is making progress toward the diversity goals. In 2017, nearly 70% of families at the downtown Sprout lived below the federal poverty level, and about 30% fell between 100% and 300% of it. Just 2% of families earned incomes that were 300% or more from the poverty line. In terms of racial diversity, 83% of students downtown identified as black, 7% as white, 4% as Latinx, and about 7% as mixed or other race. Most of the partially or nonsubsidized families and white families enrolled during the latter period of data collection, suggesting that interest from these groups is building.

37. Ziba Kashef, "How to Talk to Your Child about Race," *BabyCenter*, May 2017, https://www.babycenter.com/0_how-to-talk-to-your-child-about-race_3657102 .bc.

38. What the Sprout at the Children's Museum teachers are attempting to learn and do is supported by an influential preschool accrediting body, the National Association for the Education of Young Children (NAEYC). In a 2010 publication on antibias education for preschoolers, the organization recommended teacher-guided activities around bias, saying, "We do not wait for children to open up the topic of reading or numbers before making literacy and numeracy part of our daily early childhood curriculum. Because we have decided that

these understandings and skills are essential for children, we provide literacy and numeracy discussions and activities in our classrooms. The same is true for anti-bias." Louise Derman-Sparks and Julie Edwards, "Anti-Bias Education for Young Children and Ourselves," National Association for Education of Young Children, Washington, DC, 2010.

39. Kenneth Clark and Mamie Clark, "Segregation as a Factor in the Racial Identification of Negro Preschool Children," *The Journal of Experimental Education* 8, no. 2 (1939): 161–63, retrieved from http://www.jstor.org/stable/20150598.

40. Gordon Allport, *The Nature of Prejudice* (Reading, MA: Addison-Wesley Publishing Company, 1954).

41. Willis D. Hawley, "Designing Schools That Use Student Diversity to Enhance Learning of All Students," in *Lessons in Integration: Realizing the Promise of Racial Diversity in American Schools*, eds. Erica Frankenbeg and Gary Orfield (Charlottesville: University of Virginia Press, 2007), 31–56; Anthony Bryk et al., *Organizing Schools for Improvement: Lessons from Chicago* (Chicago: University of Chicago Press, 2010); James A. Banks, *Educating Citizens In a Multicultural Society*, 2nd ed. (New York: Teachers College Press, 2007).

42. Gary Orfield, John Kucsera, and Genevieve Siegel-Hawley, "E Pluribus . . . Separation: Deepening Double Segregation for More Students" (Los Angeles: The UCLA Civil Rights Project, 2012).

43. Amy Stuart Wells and Robert Crain, "Perpetuation Theory and the Long-Term Effects of School Desegregation," *Review of Educational Research* 64, no. 4 (1994): 531–55.

44. The social and civic aspects of racially diverse early educational experiences should not be overlooked. Preschool's emphasis on social skills like perspective taking, sharing, fairness, and cooperation makes it ideal for shaping future citizens and implementing the conditions that facilitate positive contact across groups. See, e.g., Frankenberg, *Segregation at an Early Age*.

45. Beyond skill diversity, a study also found that kids of all racial/ethnic backgrounds learned more expressive language skills in racially and ethnically diverse classrooms than in homogeneous ones. Jeanne L. Reid, "Racial/Ethnic Diversity and Language Development in the Preschool Classroom," in *School Integration Matters: Research-Based Strategies to Advance Equity*, eds. Erica Frankenberg, Liliana Garcia, and Megan Hopkins (New York: Teachers College Press, 2016).

46. For instance, one study from social psychology found that four- and five-year-olds with parents who had more diverse friendships displayed less racial bias than children with parents with fewer diverse friendships. Rebecca Bigler et al., "Children's Intergroup Relations and Attitudes," in *Advances in Child Development and Behavior: vol. 51, Equity and Justice in Developmental Science: Implications for Young People, Families and Communities*, eds. S. S. Horn, M. D. Ruck, and L. S. Liben (San Diego, CA: Elsevier Academic Press, 2016).

47. Across interviews with Sprout at the Children's Museum teachers, discipline emerged as a potential area for school-family disconnect. Black and white

teachers reported that the way Sprout and Reggio approached discipline—
natural consequences, providing a quiet corner for voluntarily having space
away from the group, a "work it out" crown to help mediate conflicts in the
community—was often at odds with a more authoritarian parenting style. In
general, Sprout teachers acknowledged that it might take time for children
to become accustomed to different discipline approaches but pushed back
against the idea that families should dictate how they handled situations at
school. One returned to the sense that the close team of diverse faculty was
valuable here, saying, "If you have teachers who are diverse in their knowledge
of discipline, you can open up your mind to say let's try something else." Even
if the inconsistency might feel confusing at times for the children, they too become exposed to different ways of handling behavior and feelings. At Sprout,
the staff to student ratio (1:5 in the older room, 1:4 in the younger) allows
teachers to pull students out of the room for a one-to-one conversation, or just
a break, when they are struggling. Faculty do not use suspension as a disciplinary tool for their young students, which seems common sense until a glance
at federal civil rights data illuminates the fact that racial disproportionality in
discipline begins at this tender age. Black students account for 18% of the public preschool enrollment but 42% of preschool suspensions. "Civil Rights Data
Collection—Data Snapshot: School Discipline," US Department of Education
Office of Civil Rights, March 2014, https://ocrdata.ed.gov/downloads/crdc
-school-discipline-snapshot.pdf.
48. Allport, *The Nature of Prejudice*.
49. For the most part, students in the Sprout schools have equitable access to rigorous curriculum, a critical feature of internal integration. However, two barriers—neither insurmountable—arose with the downtown Reggio expansion.
One barrier is that the downtown Sprout location came with an established
set of teachers used to instructing with the Head Start and Virginia Preschool
Initiative curricula. By contrast, teachers hired for Sprout at the Children's
Museum were at least partly selected on the basis of their interest in learning
about Reggio. As we'll see, this issue plays out in K–12 curricular reorienta-
tions, when a school's faculty has to orient to a new theme or programmatic
element—sometimes in addition to multiple other initiatives and policy shifts.
The process can take time, and not all teachers are willing adopters. Collaborative leadership that makes a strong case for the shift helps, as does support. At
Sprout, Kathleen Eastman and Mary Driebe, the program's committed Reggio
consultant, provide support and leadership, as do teachers who've worked at
both locations. The second barrier relates to the overlapping accountability
and curricular requirements. Eastman explains that they started Reggio at the
Children's Museum location because "we knew we had full control of this site.
It's all our funding, we do everything." (Recall that fully subsidized students at
the Children's Museum are funded through scholarships rather than state or
federal money.) The braided classrooms at Sprout downtown need to meet the

standards set forth by Head Start and VPI, while simultaneously adopting the Reggio approach. Those two needs aren't necessarily in conflict but do exert considerable demands on the downtown teachers. Eastman describes a steady Reggio infusion at the downtown location, working within the set curriculum, spurred by a toddler teacher's invitation to a Reggio conference and then by another teaching saying, "I want to learn more." Driebe consulted with those two classrooms, and then everyone noticed that the other classroom of three-year-olds had begun implementing similar strategies—seemingly by osmosis. Through that organic process, Eastman emphasized a sea change, with all downtown classrooms infusing Reggio into the curriculum, albeit at different levels of engagement. The downtown teachers are on board, in other words, with one saying, "I'll never go back to the way it was."

50. Cheryl Staats et al., "Race and Ethnicity: Views From Inside the Unconscious Mind," *State of the Science Implicit Bias Review* (2017), http://kirwaninstitute .osu.edu/wp-content/uploads/2017/11/2017-SOTS-final-draft-02.pdf; Robert Putnam, *Our Kids: The American Dream in Crisis* (New York: Simon & Schuster, 2015).

Chapter 3

1. James E. Crowfoot and Mark A. Chesler, "Implementing 'Attractive Ideas': Problems and Prospects," in *Effective School Desegregation*, ed. Willis D. Hawley (Beverly Hills: Sage Publications, 1981), 265–96.

2. National Center for Education Statistics, 2015–2016. Calculations by author. Virginia, Chesterfield, and Ecoff all report higher shares of black enrollment—and lower shares of Latinx enrollment—relative to the nation, though that's rapidly changing.

3. John Ramsey and Luis Lovillo, "Chesterfield County's Poverty Divide," *Richmond Times Dispatch*, June 14, 2014, http://www.richmond.com/news/local /chesterfield/chesterfield-county-s-poverty-divide/article_0f8b2da2-73cf-5693 -9aa0-46f6d9a451f5.html.

4. There are over 60 schools within Chesterfield County, making it one of the largest districts in the state and in the country. In 2015, almost half of the schools report that a majority of students qualify as economically disadvantaged (ED), the state's measure of student poverty. Yet more than a quarter are low-poverty schools where 25% or fewer students qualify as ED. Racial bifurcation exists, too. Nearly 50% of Chesterfield's schools report that the share of black students ranges between 60% and 89%, while about 15% of schools report that the share of black students ranges between 0% and 19%.

5. Chesterfield's eastern border actually abuts not one but four independent cities. Richmond is the largest, but there are also the three smaller urban communities of Colonial Heights, Hopewell, and Petersburg. Manufacturing and industry historically were located near these cities and along major railways, thoroughfares, and the river.

6. Vanessa Remmers, "'Neglected Far Too Long': Chesterfield Supervisors Require More of Businesses Along Northern Jeff Davis Corridor," *Richmond Times Dispatch*, September 5, 2018, https://www.richmond.com/news/local/chesterfield/neglected-far-too-long-chesterfield-supervisors-require-more-of-businesses/article_c58e2cb4-7ccc-59e3-9a1e-25fb7fc0c68b.html.

7. In September 2018, Chesterfield's Board of Supervisors sought to remedy that mistake by passing stricter requirements for new development along the corridor—basics like sidewalks, parking lots behind buildings, and landscaping. See Remmers, "'Neglected Far Too Long.'"

8. A concerted campaign tied to 2010 census data helped Chesterfield take stock of rapid demographic shifts and exposed a growing east-west divide. Lafayette describes a sense of awakening, though not everyone is participating in the conversation—or the action. On the municipal side, political recognition began with establishing a revitalization department of two personnel and limited resources. The department focused initially on challenges like a lack of sidewalks and streetlights in some eastern communities. In 2017, it morphed into the 18-person Community Enhancement Department, with a desire to serve as "neighborhood doctors" for struggling parts of Chesterfield. Real tension exists, though, around whether the department will focus on citing poor residents for violations or provide the support and resources needed to meet county requirements.

9. Douglas S. Massey, "The Legacy of the 1968 Fair Housing Act," *Sociological Forum* 30 (2015): 571–88, doi:10.1111/socf.12178.

10. Gregory Squires, *Why the Poor Pay More: How to Stop Predatory Lending* (Westport, CT: Praegar, 2004).

11. Richard Florida and Patrick Adler, "The Patchwork Metropolis: The Morphology of the Divided Postindustrial City," *Journal of Urban Affairs* 40, no. 5 (2017): 609–24, doi:10.1080/07352166.201.1360743; William Frey, *Melting Pot Cities and Suburbs: Racial and Ethnic Change in Metro America in the 2000s*, State of Metropolitan American (Washington, DC: Metropolitan Policy Program at Brookings, 2011).

12. Max Besbris and Jacob William Faber, "Investigating the Relationship between Real Estate Agents, Segregation and House Prices: Steering and Upselling in New York State," *Sociological Forum* 32, no. 4 (2017), doi:https://onlinelibrary.wiley.com/doi/abs/10.1111/socf.12378.

13. Amanda K. Hurley, "The Problem of Resegregation in Suburbia," *City Lab*, February 15, 2016, https://www.citylab.com/equity/2016/02/the-problem-of-resegregation-in-suburbia/462396/.

14. Myron Orfield and Thomas Luce, "America's Racially Diverse Suburbs: Opportunities and Challenges," *Housing Policy Debate* 23, no. 2 (2013): 395–430.

15. Jonathan Rothwell, "Housing Costs, Zoning and Access to High-Scoring Schools" (Washington, DC: Brookings, 2012), doi: https://onlinelibrary.wiley.com/doi/abs/10.1111/socf.12378. Solomon Green, "Zoning Matters: How

Land Use Policies Shape Our Lives" (Washington, DC: The Urban Institute, 2019), https://vimeo.com/336208270.

16. Ta-Nehisi Coates, "The Case for Reparations," *The Atlantic*, June 2014, https://www.theatlantic.com/magazine/archive/2014/06/the-case-for-reparations/361631/; Richard Rothstein, *The Color of Law: A Forgotten History of How Our Government Segregated America* (New York: Liveright, 2017).

17. Maria Krysan and Kyle Crowder, *Cycle of Segregation: Social Processes and Residential Stratification* (New York: Russell Sage Foundation, 2017).

18. Ann Owens, "Segregation by Household Composition and Income Across Multiple Spatial Scales," in *Handbook on Urban Segregation*, ed. Sako Musterd (Cheltenham, UK: Edward Elgar Publishing, forthcoming).

19. Myron Orfield, *Region: Planning the Future of the Twin Cities* (Minneapolis: University of Minnesota, 2010); Genevieve Siegel-Hawley, "Educational Gerrymandering? Race and Attendance Boundaries in a Racially Changing Suburb," *Harvard Educational Review* 83, no. 4 (2013): 580–612, doi:10.17763/haer.83.4.k385375245677131. A couple of decades ago, when Chesterfield's school enrollment was less diverse, high school attendance zones—which encompass larger geographic areas relative to elementary or middle school zones—tended to distribute students more evenly. This meant that high school zones each contained some neighborhoods closest to city boundaries, part of a slice that then radiated down and out to include more far-flung suburban and rural sections. Over time, as higher-end housing development targeted the western part of the county, feeder patterns changed and concentrated affluence in the west.

20. Salem Elementary, one neighboring school, was 58% white and 50% ED in 2017, while Gates, the other neighbor, was 60% white and 26% ED. Ecoff itself was 44% white and 44% ED.

21. Vanessa Remmers, "Redistricting Could Impact More Than 1,000 Students in Chesterfield County," *Richmond Times Dispatch*, January 23, 2018, https://www.richmond.com/news/local/chesterfield/redistricting-could-impact-more-than-students-in-chesterfield-county/article_cec276db-e1d4-5351-bc3a-b07abbb0ba50.html.

22. One study of suburban Connecticut found that the state's accountability system gave families and real estate agents a new, race-neutral vocabulary for discussing school quality simply on the basis of test scores. Jack Dougherty, "Shopping for Schools: How Public Education and Private Housing Shaped Suburban Connecticut," *Journal of Urban History* 38, no. 2 (March 2012): 205–24.

23. See Jennifer Jellison Holme, Anjale Welton, and Sarah Diem, "Pursuing 'Separate but Equal' in Suburban San Antonio," in *The Resegregation of Suburban Schools*, eds. Erica Frankenberg and Gary Orfield (Cambridge, MA: Harvard Education Press, 2012), 45–68; Kathryn Wiley, Barbara Shircliffe, and Jennifer Morley, "Conflicting Mandates amid Suburban Change: Educational Opportu-

nity in a Post-desegregation Florida Countywide District," in *The Resegregation of Suburban Schools*, eds. Frankenberg and Orfield, 139–62.

24. Carrie Coyner, "It Starts At Home," *Richmond Magazine,* June 20, 2018.

25. Demand for the school is corroborated by the number of waiver requests for admission to Ecoff, as well as by the dismay of families reassigned to other schools due to the recent rezoning process.

26. Jack Schneider, *Beyond Test Scores: A Better Way to Measure School Quality* (Cambridge, MA: Harvard University Press, 2017).

27. Kendra Taylor, "The Contribution of Attendance Boundary Segregation to School District Racial Residential Segregation in Large U.S. School Districts" (PhD diss., Pennsylvania State University, 2018).

28. Chesterfield County Planning Department, "Ecoff School Attendance Zone Profile: Demographics and Land Use," Chesterfield, August 2015.

29. Chesterfield County Planning Department.

30. One study found that roughly two-thirds of neighborhoods that were about 30% nonwhite in 1980 were predominately nonwhite two decades later. See Orfield and Luce, "America's Racially Diverse Suburbs."

31. I was not a faculty member at the time.

32. Paul Tough, *Whatever It Takes: Geoffrey Canada's Quest to Change Harlem and America* (New York: Mariner Books, 2009).

33. Jeannie Oakes, Anna Maier, and Julia Daniel, "Community Schools: An Evidence-Based Strategy for Equitable School Improvement," Learning Policy Institute, 2017, 1–26, https://learningpolicyinstitute.org/product/community-schools-equitable-improvement-brief.

34. Other distinguishing features flow into SEL. The community resources that come with the Empowerment Zone are part of surrounding the whole child with the supports he or she needs to succeed. An emphasis on Professional Learning Communities, or PLCs, hinges on the idea that teams of teachers, looking closely at numerous data indicators, can better support the whole child. Project-based learning and cooperative learning efforts also are part of SEL, as is character education and a commitment to creating a sense of family in the school.

35. Gary Orfield, John Kucsera, and Genevieve Siegel-Hawley, "E Pluribus . . . Separation: Deepening Double Segregation for More Students," (Los Angeles: The UCLA Civil Rights Project, 2012); Krysan and Crowder, *Cycle of Segregation.*

36. Jeremy Fiel, "Closing Ranks: Closure, Status Competition, and School Segregation," *American Journal of Sociology* 121, no. 1 (2015): 126–70.

37. Another route, Chesterfield's student waiver policy, was partly closed, however, when the school board voted to restrict waivers on the basis of unanticipated growth and a desire for more uniformity. A recent countywide change to the policy that allowed families to enroll in schools outside their zones ended some exemptions, removing the possibility of leaving assigned schools because a sibling attended a different one or because childcare was more convenient

to an alternative location. Chesterfield still allows exceptions for children of employees who work in schools in other zones and special cases based on emotional, social, or family concerns, among other reasons. If awarded, families have to provide transportation to the out-of-zone school, a barrier for many. Waivers also can be denied on the basis of poor attendance, academic performance, or behavior. Cole testifies to the impact of the policy shift saying that "the waiver system has changed dramatically. I only approved 12 [waivers for families wanting to enroll from other zones] last year, mostly for staff reasons." He goes on to say that the waiver system highlights families' desire to enroll in Ecoff as "there are still people who try not to follow the rules, people who want to come in [from other zones] . . . [W]e take that as a point of flattery but we have to follow the rules."

38. Elizabeth Anderson, *The Imperative of Integration* (Princeton, NJ: Princeton University Press, 2010).

39. Virginia Department of Education, restricted use student-level data, 2016 analyzed by Ashlee Lester.

40. Green v. County School Board of New Kent County, U.S. 695 (1968). See also Wendy Parker, "Desegregating Teachers," *Washington University Law Review* 86 (2008): 1–52.

41. Scott Page, *The Diversity Bonus: How Great Teams Pay Off in the Knowledge Economy* (Princeton, NJ: Princeton University Press, 2017).

42. The American Institutes of Research, in reviewing the literature on SEL to date, suggests that all are key to reaping the benefits associated with the programming. Juliette Berg et al., "The Intersection of School Climate and Social and Emotional Development," American Institutes for Research (Washington, DC: Robert Wood Johnson Foundation, 2017).

43. Gordon W. Allport, *The Nature of Prejudice* (New York: Basic Books, 1954); Thomas Pettigrew and Linda Tropp, "A Meta-Analytic Test of Intergroup Contact Theory," *Journal of Personality and Social Psychology* 90, no. 5 (2006): 751–83.

44. Tamara Wilder, Rebecca Jacobsen, and Richard Rothstein, *Grading Education: Getting Accountability Right* (New York: Teachers College Press/EPI, 2008).

45. Edutopia, "Social and Emotional Learning: A Short History," George Lucas Educational Foundation, October 6, 2011, https://www.edutopia.org/social -emotional-learning-history; Daniel Goleman, *Emotional Intelligence: Why It Can Matter More Than IQ* (New York: Bantam Books, 2005).

46. Joseph Durlak et al., "The Impact of Enhancing Students' Social and Emotional Learning: A Meta-Analysis of School Based Universal Interventions," *Child Development* 82, no. 1 (2011): 405–32, doi:10.1111/j.1467-8624.2010.01564.x.

47. David Osher et al., "Advancing the Science and Practice of Social and Emotional Learning: Looking Back and Moving Forward," *Review of Research in Education* 40, no. 1 (2016); 644–81, doi:10.3102/0091732X16673595; James J. Heckman and Tim Kautz, "Hard Evidence on Soft Skills," *Labour Economics* 19, no. 4 (2012): 451–64, doi:10.3386/w18121; Megan McClelland et al.,

"Links Between Behavioral Regulation and Preschoolers' Literacy, Vocabulary, and Math Skills," *Developmental Psychology* 43, no. 4 (2007): 947–59, doi:10.1037/0012-1649.43.4.947.

48. Jeneen Interlandi, "The Brain's Empathy Gap," *New York Times*, March 19, 2015, https://www.nytimes.com/2015/03/22/magazine/the-brains-empathy-gap.html.

49. Prudence Carter and Kevin Welner, eds. *Closing the Opportunity Gap: What America Must Do to Give Every Child an Even Chance* (New York: Oxford University Press, 2013).

50. "Ecoff Elementary General School Information," Virginia Department of Education, http://schoolquality.virginia.gov/schools/ecoff-elementary#fndtn-desktopTabs-accountability; "School Accreditation Ratings," Virginia Department of Education, http://www.doe.virginia.gov/statistics_reports/accreditation_federal_reports/accreditation/index.shtml.

51. Joshua Cole, "A New Angle: Creating Equity in Education," *Diversity in Ed* (Spring 2017): 46–49.

52. Cole.

53. Alfredo Artiles et al., "Over-Identification of Students of Color in Special Education: A Critical Overview," *Multicultural Perspectives* 4, no. 1 (2002), doi: https://doi.org/10.1207/S15327892MCP0401_2.

54. Ecoff Elem: Chesterfield County Public Schools, Civil Rights Data Collection, 2015, https://ocrdata.ed.gov/Page?t=s&eid=275665&syk=8&pid=2275.

55. Vanessa Remmers, "Racial Barriers to Gifted Classes Are Widespread and Persistent. Chesterfield Schools Is Looking to Break Them Down," *Richmond Times Dispatch*, March 10, 2018, https://www.richmond.com/news/local/chesterfield/racial-barriers-to-gifted-classes-are-widespread-and-persistent-chesterfield/article_137dacbb-e6db-5e2f-a729-20df3b1ae692.html; John B. Gordon III and Tameshia V. Grimes, "Equity Committee Recommendations" (Presentation to the Chesterfield County School Board, Chesterfield, VA, December 12, 2017), http://mychesterfieldschools.com/wp-content/uploads/schoolboard/Equity_Committee_Recommendations_2017.pdf.

56. Jason Grissom and Christopher Redding, "Discretion and Disproportionality: Explaining the Under-representation of High-Achieving Students of Color in Gifted Programs," *AERA Open*, 2016, doi: https://doi.org/10.1177/2332858415622175.

57. Catherine P. Bradshaw, Mary M. Mitchell, and Phillip J. Leaf, "Examining the Effects of Schoolwide Positive Behavioral Interventions and Supports on Student Outcomes," *Journal of Positive Behavior Interventions* 12, no. 3 (2010): 133–48.

58. Cole, "A New Angle."

59. All out-of-school suspensions were short term. There were no in-school suspensions, referrals to law enforcement, or expulsions reported, earning Ecoff the distinction of being in the lowest 10% of the district across these

categories. ProPublica, "Ecoff Elementary," in *Miseducation*, https://projects
.propublica.org/miseducation/school/510084002177.

60. These are rooted in the acronym TEAM: T = Treat everyone with respect, E =
    Everyone follows directions, A = Accept responsibility, M = Make good choices.

61. Louise Derman-Sparks, Carol Tanaka Higa, and Bill Sparks, "Children, Race
    and Racism: How Race Awareness Develops," *Teaching For Change*, 1980,
    https://www.teachingforchange.org/wp-content/uploads/2012/08/ec_children
    raceracism_english.pdf.

62. Megan Gannon, "Race Is a Social Construct, Scientists Argue," *Scientific
    American*, February 5, 2016, https://www.scientificamerican.com/article
    /race-is-a-social-construct-scientists-argue/.

63. Dena Swanson et al., "Racial Identity Development During Childhood," in
    Handbook of African American Psychology, eds. Helen Neville, Brendesha Tynes,
    and Shawn Utsey (Los Angeles: Sage Publications, 2009), 269–81.

64. Malikkah K. Rollins, "Breaking It Down: Contributing Factors to Racial
    Identity Development in Elementary and Middle School Youth" (master's
    thesis, Smith College, 2010); Tissyana C. Camacho et al., "School Climate and
    Ethnic-Racial Identity in School: A Longitudinal Examination of Reciprocal
    Associations," *Journal of Community & Applied Social Psychology* 28, no. 1 (2017),
    doi:10.1002/casp.2338.

65. YWCA Minneapolis, "Development of Racial Identity by Age," https://www
    .equityalliancemn.org/uploads/7/4/4/0/74401303/ywca_development_of
    _racial_identity_by_age.pdf; Derman-Sparks et al., "Children, Race and Rac-
    ism"; Beverly Tatum, *Why Are All The Black Kids Sitting Together in the Cafeteria:
    And Other Conversations About Race* (New York: Basic Books, 1997); Mica Pol-
    lock, *Everyday AntiRacism: Getting Real About Race in School* (New York: The New
    Press, 2008).

66. Pamela Perry, *Shades of White: White Kids and Racial Identities in High School* (Dur-
    ham, NC: Duke University Press, 2002).

67. John Rogers et al., *Teaching and Learning in the Age of Trump: Increasing Stress and
    Hostility in America's High Schools* (Los Angeles: UCLA's Institute for Democracy,
    Education and Access, 2017), https://idea.gseis.ucla.edu/publications/teaching
    -and-learning-in-age-of-trump.

68. Vanessa Remmers, "State Superintendent of Public Instructions James Lane on
    His Legacy in Chesterfield and What Comes Next: 'I Tried to Create a Culture
    to Say, 'It's Okay to Try.''" *Richmond Times Dispatch*, June 14, 2018, https://
    www.richmond.com/news/local/education/state-superintendent-of-public
    -instruction-james-lane-on-his-legacy/article_ab076ce8-a82d-53a9-9512
    -4ff730668ebe.html.

69. Another one of my hats: in its first year, I served as co-chair of Chesterfield's
    equity committee with Dr. Grimes.

70. Vanessa Remmers, "Major Shifts Underway for Growing English Language
    Learners I Chesterfield Classrooms," May 23, 2017, https://www.richmond

.com/news/local/chesterfield/major-shifts-underway-for-growing-english
-language-learners-in-chesterfield/article_d6d2a4de-990f-55ea-b40a-4ae599
48720c.html; Gordon and Grimes, "Equity Committee Recommendations."

71. Cole would later lead the committee on culturally responsive teaching for the
school system's equity committee. In 2019, he accepted a position coordinating Virginia Commonwealth University's School of Education's efforts to
coordinate professional development with area school districts.

72. Allport, *The Nature of Prejudice*.

Chapter 4

1. Under the Obama administration, a federally funded program to improve low-
performing schools through the arts; as of 2018, a public-private partnership
run through the John F. Kennedy Center.

2. Lightly edited for brevity's sake.

3. "NCES Common Core of Data," NCES, https://nces.ed.gov/ccd/.

4. "School Quality Profiles: Binford Middle," VDOE, 2017, http://schoolquality
.virginia.gov/schools/binford-middle#fndtn-desktopTabs-enrollment. In 2017,
of the 417 students enrolled, 78% were black, 17% were white, and the remain-
der identified as Asian, Latinx or with two or more races.

5. Genevieve Siegel-Hawley et al., *Miles to Go: A Report on School Segregation in Virginia, 1989–2010* (Los Angeles: UCLA Civil Rights Project, 2013).

6. William Frey, "Will This Be the Decade of Big City Growth?" (Washington, DC:
Brookings Institution, June 2012).

7. Michael Petrilli, *Diverse Schools Dilemma: A Parent's Guide to Socioeconomically
Mixed Public Schools* (Washington, DC: Thomas B. Fordham Institute, 2012);
see, also, Emily Badger, Quoctrung Bui, and Robert Gebeloff, "The Neighborhood Is Mostly Black, the Home Buyers Are Mostly White," *New York Times*,
April 27, 2019, https://www.nytimes.com/interactive/2019/04/27/upshot
/diversity-housing-maps-raleigh-gentrification.html?smid=nytcore-ios-share.

8. According to the VDOE, between 2015 and 2017, about 750 more white students enrolled in RPS than in the past, translating to 12% of the city's overall
enrollment. The Latinx student population has grown far more rapidly, accounting for 15% of RPS's enrollment in 2017, and the share of black students
correspondingly declined to 70%.

9. Shelley Kimelberg and Chase Billingham, "Attitudes Toward Diversity and
the School Choice Process: Middle-Class Parents in a Segregated Urban Public
School District," *Urban Education* 48 no. 2 (2012): 198–201, doi:10.1177
/0042085912449629.

10. James Ryan, *Five Miles Away, A World Apart* (New York: Oxford University Press,
2010).

11. Richard Rothstein, *The Color of Law* (New York: Liveright Publishing Corpora-
tion, 2017); David Rusk, *Inside Game Outside Game: Winning Strategies for Saving
Urban America* (Washington, DC: Brookings Institution Press, 1999).

12. Jennifer Holme and Kara Finnigan, *Striving in Common: A Regional Equity Framework for Urban Schools* (Cambridge, MA: Harvard Education Press, 2018); Gary Orfield, "Metropolitan School Desegregation: Impacts on Metropolitan Society," in *In Pursuit of a Dream Deferred: Linking Housing and Education Policy*, eds. J. Powell and J. Kay (New York: Peter Lang, 2001).

13. Merhige wrote, "It is not within the Court's power to remedy either the poverty itself or the ancillary effects of such poverty." Bradley v. Baliles, 829 Fed. Rep. 2d 1308 (CA 1987).

14. Gary Orfield and Susan Eaton, *Dismantling Desegregation: The Quiet Reversal of Brown v. Board of Education* (New York: The New Press, 1996).

15. Erica Frankenberg and Genevieve Siegel-Hawley, "Reassessing the School Housing Segregation Link in the Post-Parents Involved Era," *Wake Forest Law Review* 48 (2013).

16. Erica Frankenberg, "Assessing Segregation Under a New Generation of Controlled Choice Policies," *American Educational Research Journal* 54, no. 1 (2017).

17. Daniel Duke, *The School That Refused to Die: Continuity and Change at Thomas Jefferson High School* (Albany: State University of New York Press, 1995).

18. Joshua Cole, "Richmond Public Schools: Post-Court Mandated School Desegregation (1986-2006)" (PhD diss., Virginia Commonwealth University, 2009).

19. Michael Paul Williams, "No Hope Without Change at Binford Middle School," *Richmond Times Dispatch*, November 26, 2014, https://www.richmond.com /news/local/williams-no-hope-without-change-at-binford-middle-school /article_ebd09807-5fbc-5832-88d0-424ea3199efd.html.

20. Duke, *The School That Refused to Die*; Genevieve Siegel-Hawley and Erica Frankenberg, "Designing Choice: Magnet School Structures and Racial Diversity," in *Educational Delusions?: Why Choice Can Deepen Inequality and How to Make Schools* Fair, eds. Gary Orfield et al. (Berkeley: University of California Press, 2013). Post-unitary status, efforts to implement a more typical magnet school concept fell far short of a systematic voluntary integration program. A task force researched the feasibility of establishing an array of magnet schools in city high schools, essentially expanding the model school idea to the secondary level, and RPS submitted a failed application for federal magnet funding. Materials related to magnets overtly denied that the programs were designed to draw in white students, stating instead that they would "allow for a distribution of students without regard to where they live."

21. Duke, *The School That Refused to Die*; Ellen Goldring and Clair Smrekar, "Magnet Schools and the Pursuit of Racial Balance," *Education and Urban Society* 33, no. 1 (2000): 17–35.

22. Though the white population in Byrd Park has increased markedly in the past eight years. Without controls on the market, white interest in city living, coupled with more readily available wealth and credit, has accelerated the pace of racial change in urban neighborhoods like Byrd Park. See Badger, Bui, and Gebeloff, "The Neighborhood Is Mostly Black, the Home Buyers Are Mostly White."

23. Amy Chozick, "You Know the Lorena Bobbitt Story. But Not All of It," *New York Times*, January 30, 2019, https://www.nytimes.com/2019/01/30/arts /television/lorena-bobbitt-documentary-jordan-peele.html.

24. According to Binford's former gifted instructor. This trend has been well documented in other cities like New York. See, e.g., Allison Roda, *Inequality in Gifted and Talented Programs: Parental Choices about Status, School Opportunity and Second-Generation Segregation* (New York: Palgrave McMillan, 2015); Christine Veiga, "To Integrate Specialized High Schools, Are Gifted Programs Part of the Problem or the Solution?," *Chalkbeat*, July 17, 2018, https://chalkbeat.org /posts/ny/2018/07/17/to-integrate-specialized-high-schools-are-gifted-programs -part-of-the-problem-or-the-solution/.

25. Amanda Lewis and John Diamond, *Despite the Best Intentions: How Racial Inequality Thrives in Good Schools* (New York: Oxford University Press, 2015).

26. Jeannie Oakes, *Keeping Track: How Schools Structure Inequality* (New Haven, CT: Yale University Press, 2005).

27. Roslyn Mickelson, "Thee Cumulative Disadvantages of First- and Second-Generation Segregation for Middle School Achievement," *American Educational Research Journal* 52, no. 4 (2015): 657–92, doi:10.3102/0002831215587933.

28. Kevin Welner and Carol Corbett Burris, "Alternative Approaches to the Politics of Detracking," *Theory into Practice* 45, no. 1 (2006): 90–99.

29. Sarah Garland, "Who Should Be in the Gifted Program?," *Slate*, March 12, 2013, http://www.slate.com/articles/health_and_science/science/2013/03/gifted_and _talented_education_cities_try_to_make_programs_more_inclusive.html.

30. John Hattie, *Visible Learning: A Synthesis of over 800 Meta-Analyses Relating to Achievement* (New York: Routledge, 2012).

31. "ElSi—Elementary/Secondary Information System," NCES, https://nces.ed.gov /ccd/elsi.

32. Williams, "No Hope Without Change at Binford Middle School."

33. Justin Mattingly, "Rezoning Again at Issue as Richmond School Leaders Consider Demolition of South Side Middle School," *Richmond Times Dispatch*, September 12, 2018, https://www.richmond.com/news/local/education/rezoning -again-at-issue-as-richmond-school-leaders-consider-demolition/article _0a87488b-bd40-5706-9341-c5871f6e25bc.html.

34. *Middle School Renaissance* (Richmond, VA: Richmond Public Schools, 2012), http://web.richmond.k12.va.us/Portals/0/assets/Partnerships/pdfs/mm renaissance2172012.pdf.

35. The push to develop themes got swamped by the urgent need to meet accountability mandates. During the same time frame, all of Richmond's schools earned accreditation. Andy Jenks, "Richmond schools Reach 100 Percent Accreditation," *NBC 12*, September 15, 2010, http://www.nbc12.com /story/13161381/richmond-schools-reach-100-percent-accreditation/.

36. Richmond Public Schools School Board, "Growing Binford Middle School," Richmond Public Schools, 2015, https://www.boarddocs.com/vsba/richmond

/Board.nsf/files/9TD35F6DBD36/$file/Binford%20enrollmentand
transportationoptions.pdf; Zachary Reid, "Details About New Program at
Binford Middle School," *Richmond Times Dispatch*, February 9, 2015, https://
www.richmond.com/news/local/city-of-richmond/details-about-new-program
-at-binford-middle-school/article_be617fe2-dcec-5d49-9eaa-689ae4ca8088
.html.

37. VCU and another local postsecondary institution, the University of Richmond,
agreed to partner with Binford to provide professional development and extracurricular arts integration.

38. "SpringBoard," College Board, https://springboard.collegeboard.org/.

39. Richmond Public Schools School Board, "Growing Binford Middle School."

40. She also speaks fluent Portuguese.

41. Wendy Parker, "Desegregating Teachers," *Washington University Law Review* 86
(2008): 1–52.

42. Jennifer Holme, "Buying Homes, Buying Schools: School Choice and the
Social Construction of School Quality," *Harvard Education Review* (2002), 72,
no. 2, 177–206; Annette Lareau and Kimberly Goyette, *Choosing Homes, Choosing
Schools: Residential Segregation and the Search for a Good School* (New York: Russell
Sage Foundation, 2014).

43. Amy Stuart Wells, "The Process of Racial Resegregation in Housing and
Schools: The Sociology of Reputation," in *Emerging Trends in the Social and
Behavioral Sciences,* eds. Robert Scott and Stephen Kosslyn (New York: John
Wiley & Sons, 2015), https://onlinelibrary.wiley.com/doi/full/10.1002
/9781118900772.etrds0457.

44. Jeffrey Henig et al., *The Color of School Reform: Race, Politics, and the Challenge of
Urban Education* (Princeton, NJ: Princeton University Press, 1999); Maia Cuc-
chiara, *Marketing Schools, Marketing Cities: Who Wins and Who Loses When Schools
Become Urban Amenities* (Chicago: The University of Chicago Press, 2013).

45. Basement bathrooms, which were the subject of a superintendent tweet, were
remodeled by the PTA and Fan association, a concrete example of the impact
a more highly resourced PTA and community can have on conditions within
a school. Rachel Levy, "The Intersection of Economic Disadvantage and Race
and the Expanded Role of Parent-Led School-Supporting Nonprofit Organizations in K–12 Public Schools in the Richmond, Virginia, Metropolitan Area:
A Mixed Methods Approach" (PhD diss., Virginia Commonwealth University,
2018).

46. Anette Lareau, *Unequal Childhoods: Class, Race, and Family Life* (Berkeley: Uni-
versity of California Press, 2011); Gill Crozier, "Interrogating Parent-School
Practices in a Market-Based System. The Professionalization of Parenting and
Intensification of Parental Involvement: Is This What Schools Want?," in *The
Wiley Handbook of Family, School, and Community: Relationships in Education,* eds.
Steven Sheldon and Tammy Turner-Vorbeck (Hoboken: John Wiley & Sons,
2019); Claire Miller, "The Relentlessness of Modern Parenting," *New York*

Times, December 25, 2018, https://www.nytimes.com/2018/12/25/upshot/the
-relentlessness-of-modern-parenting.html.

47. Linn Posey, "Middle- and Upper Middle-Class Parent Action for Urban Public
Schools: Promise or Paradox?," *Teachers College Record* 114 (2012): 1–43; Shelley
M. Kimelberg and Chase Billingham, "Attitudes toward Diversity and the
School Choice Process: Middle Class Parents in a Segregated Urban Public
School District," *Urban Education* 48, no. 2 (2013), doi: https://doi.org/10.1177
/0042085912449629; Lareau, *Unequal Childhoods*; Richard Reeves, *Dream
Hoarders: How the American Upper Middle Class Is Leaving Everyone Else in the Dust,
Why That Is a Problem, and What to Do About It* (Washington, DC: The Brookings
Institution, 2017); Nikole Hannah-Jones, "Choosing a School for My Daughter
in a Segregated City," *New York Times,* June 9, 2016, https://www.nytimes.com
/2016/06/12/magazine/choosing-a-school-for-my-daughter-in-a-segregated
-city.html.

48. Amy Stuart Wells, Jacquelyn Duran, and Terrenda White, "Southern Graduates of School Desegregation: A Double Consciousness of Resegregation Yet
Hope," in *Integrating Schools in a Changing Society: New Policies and Legal Options for
a Multiracial Generation*, eds. Erica Frankenberg and Elizabeth Debray (Chapel
Hill: The University of North Carolina Press, 2011).

49. Jack Schneider, *Beyond Test Scores: A Better Way to Measure School Quality* (Cambridge, MA: Harvard University Press, 2017).

50. *Middle School Renaissance* (Richmond, VA: Richmond Public Schools, 2012),
http://web.richmond.k12.va.us/Portals/0/assets/Partnerships/pdfs/mm
renaissance2172012.pdf; *Dreams 4 RPS: Richmond Public Schools 2018-23 Strategic
Plan* (Richmond, VA: Richmond Public Schools, 2018), https://www.rvaschools
.net/cms/lib/VA02208089/Centricity/Domain/4/Dreams%204%20RPS/Dreams
4RPS-English.pdf.

51. Daniel McFarland, "Resistance as Social Drama: A Study of Change-Oriented
Encounters," *American Journal of Sociology* 109, no. 6 (May 2004): 1249–1318.

52. All key conditions for positive intergroup contact. See Gordon Allport, *The
Nature of Prejudice* (New York: Addison-Wesley, 1954).

53. According to in-house data not yet publicly available.

54. Current RPS gifted identification revolves around a single test, usually administered in kindergarten or first grade. Of the 94 Binford students identified as
gifted in 2019, 37% were white, about double the overall white student enrollment in the school and about triple the overall white student enrollment in
the district. Internal data provided by Binford.

55. Virginia Department of Education, restricted-use student-level data, analyzed
by Ashlee Lester.

56. Lewis and Diamond, *Despite the Best Intentions*; Pamela Perry, *Shades of White: White
Kids and Racial Identities in High School* (Durham, NC: Duke University Press, 2002).

57. Full disclosure: I was involved with the group but am writing about it from the
perspective of other participants.

58. Charles Willie and Susan Greenblatt, *School Desegregation and the Management of Social Change* (New York: Longman, 1981).

59. Residents leave the program with a graduate degree in teaching or education and a teacher's license.

60. Katherine Phillips, "How Diversity Makes Us Smarter," *Scientific* American, October 1, 2014, https://www.scientificamerican.com/article/how-diversity -makes-us-smarter/.

61. Christopher Tienken and Yong Zhao, "How Common Standards and Standardized Testing Widen the Opportunity Gap," in *Closing the Opportunity Gap: What America Must Do to Give Every Child an Even Chance*, eds. Prudence Carter and Kevin Welner (New York: Oxford University Press, 2013), 111–22.

62. William Cross, *Shades of Black* (Philadelphia: Temple University Press, 1991).

63. Janet Helms, "Toward a Model of White Racial Identity Development," in *College Student Development and Academic Life*, eds. Karen Arnold and Ilda King (New York: Routledge, 2013).

64. "School Quality Profiles: Binford Middle."

65. Richard Rothstein, "For Public Schools, Segregation Then, Segregation Since," Economic Policy Institute, August 27, 2013, https://www.epi.org/publication /unfinished-march-public-school-segregation/; Robert Putnam, *Our Kids: The American Dream in Crisis* (New York: Simon and Schuster, 2015).

66. In 2016, the latest year for which I had access to student-level data by race and economic disadvantage.

67. Prudence Carter and Kevin Welner, *Closing the Opportunity Gap: What America Must Do to Give Every Child an Even Chance* (New York: Oxford University Press, 2013); National Center for Education Statistics, *School Composition and the Black-White Achievement Gap* (Washington, DC: Author, 2015), https://nces.ed.gov /nationsreportcard/subject/studies/pdf/school_composition_and_the_bw _achievement_gap_2015.pdf.

68. Leah Lessard, Kara Kogachi, and Jaana Juvonen, "Quality and Stability of Cross-Ethnic Friendships: Effects of Classroom Diversity and Out-of-School Contact," *Journal of Youth and Adolescence* 48, no. 3 (2019), https://link.springer .com/article/10.1007/s10964-018-0964-9.

69. Justin Mattingly, "Richmond Expands After-school Programs to Give Students Wider Experiences," *Richmond Times Dispatch*, December 23, 2018, https:// www.richmond.com/news/local/education/richmond-expands-after-school -programs-to-give-students-wider-experiences/article_717a8813-a140-5cd7 -a92e-a48348a3c495.html.

70. See *Communities in Schools*, https://www.communitiesinschools.org/.

71. Elizabeth Anderson, *The Imperative of Integration* (Princeton, NJ: Princeton University Press, 2010).

72. Justin Mattingly, "New Richmond Superintendent Jason Kamras Wants to Transform City Schools: 'I Will Be Undeterred,'" *Richmond Times Dispatch*, February 10, 2018, https://www.richmond.com/news/local/education/new

-richmond-superintendent-jason-kamras-wants-to-transform-city-schools /article_f5693c57-a594-5fd9-9d3e-8104107d2f07.html; Carol Wolf, "The New Guy," *Style Weekly*, May 8, 2018, https://www.styleweekly.com/richmond/the -new-guy/Content?oid=8749921.

73. Justin Mattingly, "Q&A: Richmond Schools Superintendent Jason Kamras on Turning over Rocks, Specialty Schools and Being a First-time Superintendent," *Richmond Times Dispatch*, August 28, 2018, https://www.richmond.com/news /local/education/q-a-richmond-schools-superintendent-jason-kamras-on -turning-over/article_e0df9f3e-d12a-555b-82fa-a4d824ae54f7.html.

74. See item 1.1. in Richmond Public Schools, "Dreams4RPS: Richmond Public Schools 2013-23 Strategic Plan," https://www.rvaschools.net/cms/lib /VA02208089/Centricity/Domain/4//Dreams%204%20RPS/Dreams4RPS -English.pdf; Mattingly, "Q&A."

75. These include groups like Build a Better RPS, StayRVA, and Support Our Schools.

Chapter 5

1. CodeRVA received two state grants, one related to high school innovation and the other related to year-round schooling. "Governor McAuliffe Announces High School Innovation Planning Grant," Virginia Department of Education, June 24, 2015, http://www.doe.virginia.gov/news/news_releases/2015/06_june24_gov .shtml; "Year-Round and Extended Year Schools," Virginia Department of Education, http://www.doe.virginia.gov/instruction/year-round/index.shtml.

2. William H. Frey, *Melting Pot Cities and Suburbs: Racial and Ethnic Change in Metro America in the 2000s* (Washington, DC: Brookings Institution, May 2011), Table 5, https://www.brookings.edu/wp-content/uploads/2016/06/0504_census _ethnicity_frey.pdf.

3. Exurban growth may include residents moving from Richmond area suburbs into exurbs as well as residents moving into the Richmond area from other communities entirely.

4. Charles T. Clotfelter, *After Brown: The Rise and Retreat of School Desegregation* (Princeton, NJ: Princeton University Press, 2004); Kori J. Stroub and Meredith R. Richards, "From Desegregation to Reintegration: Trends in the Racial/ Ethnic Segregation of Metropolitan Public Schools," *American Educational Research Journal* 50, no. 3 (2013): 497–531, doi:10.3102/0002831213478462.

5. Ann Owens, Sean Reardon, and Christopher Jencks, "Income Segregation Between Schools and School Districts," *American Educational Research Journal* 53, no. 4 (2016): 1159–97, doi:10.3102/0002831216652722; Ann Owens, "Racial Residential Segregation of School-Age Children and Adults and the Role of Schooling as a Segregating Force," *The Russell Sage Foundation Journal of the Social Sciences* 3, no. 2 (2017): 63–80.

6. For a discussion of "legal localism," see David Dante Troutt, *The Price of Paradise: The Costs of Inequality and a Vision for a More Equitable America* (New York: New York University Press, 2013); Milliken v. Bradley, 418 U.S. 717 (1974).

7. Genevieve Siegel-Hawley, Sarah Diem, and Erica Frankenberg, "The Disintegration of Memphis-Shelby County, Tennessee: School District Secession and Local Control in the 21st Century," *American Educational Research Journal* 55, no. 4 (2018): 651–92, doi:10.3102/002831217748880.

8. As a result of this funding system, a recent analysis from EdBuild showed nonwhite school districts received $23 billion less than white districts, though they served the same number of students. See "23 Billion," EdBuild, https://edbuild.org/content/23-billion.

9. Charles Tilly, *Durable Inequality* (Berkeley: University of California Press, 1999); Amanda Lewis and John Diamond, *Despite the Best Intentions: How Racial Inequality Thrives in Good Schools* (New York: Oxford University Press, 2015).

10. Erica Frankenberg and Gary Orfield, *The Resegregation of Suburban Schools* (Cambridge, MA: Harvard Education Press, 2012).

11. Janelle Scott and Amy Stuart Wells, "A More Perfect Union: Reconciling School Choice Policy with Equality of Opportunity Goals," in *Closing the Opportunity Gap: What American Must Do to Give Every Child a Chance*, eds. Prudence L. Carter and Kevin G. Welner (New York: Oxford University Press, 2013).

12. Scott and Wells. Numerous charter and private school options fragment student populations by race and socioeconomic status much the way numerous district boundary lines do. Jeremy Fiel, "Closing Ranks: Closure, Status Competition, and School Segregation," *American Journal of Sociology* 121, no. 1 (2015): 126–70, doi:10.1086/682027; Sean F. Reardon and John T. Yun, "Private School Racial Enrollment," in *Public School Choice vs. Private School Vouchers*, ed. R. D. Kahlenberg (New York: Century Foundation Press, 2003); Jongyeon Ee, Gary Orfield, and Jennifer Teitell, "Private Schools in American Education: A Small Sector Still Lagging in Diversity" (Los Angeles, UCLA Civil Rights Project, 2018); Megan Austin, Mark Berends, and R. Joseph Waddington, "Indiana's Choice Scholarship: Participation & Impact on Achievement" (Los Angeles, UCLA Civil Rights Project, 2018).

13. For a discussion of Connecticut's regional magnet schools, see Susan Eaton, *The Children in Room E4: American Education On Trial* (Chapel Hill, NC: Algonquin Books of Chapel Hill, 2009); for a discussion of regional charter schools, see Halley Potter and Kimberly Quick, *Diverse-by-Design Charter Schools,* (Washington, DC: The Century Foundation, 2018). See also Huriya Jabbar and Terri S. Wilson, "What Is Diverse Enough? How 'Intentionally Diverse' Charter Schools Recruit and Retain Students," *Education Policy Analysis Archives* 26, no. 165 (2018), doi:10.14507/epaa.26.3883 for important limitations related to diverse-by-design charters. For an example of a regional magnet school in Waco, TX, see Jennifer Ayscue et al., "Choices Worth Making: Creating, Sustaining, and Expanding Diverse Magnet Schools" (Los Angeles: UCLA Civil Rights Project, 2017), 25.

14. See, e.g., the Richmond Technical Center, the Richmond Math and Science Center, and local Governor's Schools.

15. These are often crucial stumbling blocks for successful regional efforts. See Jennifer Holme and Kara S. Finnigan, *Striving in Common: A Regional Equity Framework for Urban Schools* (Cambridge, MA: Harvard Education Press, 2018).

16. Though black students accounted for about 36% of the region's students and about 25% of applicants to Maggie Walker, they've consistently made up between 5% and 10% of the school's actual enrollment. Calculations by author based on data provided by Maggie Walker. These numbers reflect, in part, racial inequity in gifted and talented identification around the region.

17. See, for instance, the 2013 University of Richmond–Virginia Commonwealth University sponsored "Looking Back, Moving Forward" conference acknowledging the fortieth anniversary of the failed school district consolidation decision and charting a regional path for the future. See also the 2014 University of Richmond–Virginia Commonwealth University sponsored conference, "An Overlooked Choice? Regional Magnet Schools in Richmond."

18. "Leadership Metro Richmond," 2017, http://www.lmronline.org/.

19. I served on the advisory council in my capacity as university professor.

20. Other forms of choice like charter schools have been widely criticized on similar grounds. Diane Ravitch, *Reign of Error* (New York: Alfred A. Knopf, 2014).

21. Holme and Finnegan, *Striving in Common.*

22. Test-based admissions present numerous obstacles to equity. These include unequal opportunities to accumulate knowledge and/or prepare for tests (see, e.g., Joseph Fagan and Cynthia Holland, "Racial Equality in Intelligence: Predictions from a Theory of Intelligence as Processing," *Intelligence* 35, no. 4 (2007): 319–44, doi:10.1016/j.inell.2006.08.009) as well as the potential activation of anxiety related to confirming group stereotypes through underperformance, also known as stereotype threat. Claude Steele and Joshua Aronson, "Stereotype Threat and the Intellectual Test Performance of African Americans," *Journal of Personality and Social Psychology* 69, no. 5 (1995): 797–811; Claude Steele, "A Threat in the Air: How Stereotypes Shape Intellectual Identity and Performance," *American Psychologist* 52, no. 6 (1997): 613–29.

23. Ayscue et al., "Choices Worth Making"; Halley Potter, "Recruiting and Enrolling a Diverse Student Body in Public Choice Schools," in *Diverse Charter Schools* (Washington, DC: The Century Foundation, 2019).

24. Choice "Statistics," National Girls Collaborative Project, https://ngcproject.org/statistics.

25. Anthony P. Carnevale, Nicole Smith, and Michelle Melton, "STEM Executive Summary," Center on Education and the Workforce (Washingon, DC; Georgetown University, 2014).

26. "CodeRVA" (Washington, DC: Magnet Schools Assistance Program, 2016), https://innovation.ed.gov/files/2017/11/CodeRVARegionalHighSchoolNAR.pdf.

27. In compliance with the *Parents Involved* decision, race would be considered only if race-neutral methods were not effective in achieving the school's diversity goals.

28. Manya Walton et al., "Magnet Schools Assistance Program: Grantee Data Analysis Report" (Silver Spring, MD: Leed Management Consulting, Inc., 2014).
29. Walton et al.
30. See, for example, the 2017 lottery scandal in Washington, DC. Alejandra Motes, "Behind the D.C. School Lottery Scandal: A 'Crisis in Confidence,'" *Washington Post,* May 28, 2017, https://www.washingtonpost.com/local/education/behind-the-dc-school-lottery-scandal-a-crisis-in-confidence/2017/05/28/d8c3f010-409d-11e7-9869-bac8b446820a_story.html?utm_term=.a7de3fe3c03c.
31. If they need support, they can email a help desk, which has worked to lower its response time.
32. At a later stage of the process, applicants may receive additional points related to household income and the number of children in the home.
33. "CodeRVA."
34. There are, of course, significant drawbacks to the intensive marketing and outreach associated with schools of choice, despite the focus on equity and diversity. See Catherine Dimartino and Sarah Butler Jessen, *Selling School: The Marketing of Public Education* (New York: Teachers College Press, 2018).
35. Jack Dougherty, "School Information, Parental Decisions, and the Digital Divide: The SmartChoices Project in Hartford, Connecticut," in *Educational Delusions*, eds. Gary Orfield and Erica Frankenberg (Berkeley: University of California Press, 2013), 219–37.
36. Later, a partnership with Virginia Commonwealth University's school of advertising helped spread the CodeRVA word to female and Latinx applicants.
37. Amy Stuart Wells, *Seeing Past The 'Colorblind' Myth of Education Policy* (Boulder: National Education Policy Center, 2014).
38. Michael Bolling, "CodeRVA Executive Director's Report" (presented at CodeRVA Regional High School School Board Meeting, March 2018), https://docs.google.com/document/d/1vwCDUvHE2dAzjMe6ft_8tZyKBvdkmEAWfOgPpGPA9g0/edit.
39. Jack Buckley and Mark Schneider, *Charter Schools: Hope or Hype?* (Princeton, NJ: Princeton University Press 2009).
40. Significant corporate donations helped furnish the school.
41. Daniela Amador and R. Max Jenkins, *CodeRVA Regional High School Action Research: Expanding the Weighted Lottery and New Student Orientation* (Richmond, VA: University of Richmond Capstone, 2018).
42. Ongoing workshops with the Virginia Center for Inclusive Communities are planned, supported by the federal magnet school grant.
43. Amador and Jenkins, *CodeRVA Regional High School Action Research.*
44. For a review of the literature on long-term desegregation outcomes, including the effects of diverse social networks, see Amy Stuart Wells and Robert L. Crain, "Perpetuation Theory and the Long-Term Effects of School Desegregation," *Review of Educational Research* 64, no. 4 (1994): 531–55, doi:10.2307/1170586.

45. Sandra Graham, Anke Munniksma, and Janna Juvonen, "Psychosocial Benefits of Cross-Ethnic Friendships in Urban Middle Schools," *Child Development* 85, no. 2 (2014): 469–83, doi:10.1111/cdev.12159.

46. Amy Corning et al., "CodeRVA's First Year: Initial Formative Evaluation Report" (Richmond, VA: Metropolitan Educational Research Consortium, 2018).

47. Beverly Tatum, *Why Are All The Black Kids Sitting Together in the Cafeteria: And Other Conversations About Race* (New York: Basic Books, 1997).

48. Tatum.

49. Gordon W. Allport, *The Nature of Prejudice* (New York: Basic Books, 1954).

50. Corning et al., "CodeRVA's First Year: Initial Formative Evaluation Report."

51. Corning et al. Students also were more likely than a nationally representative sample of students to say there was at least one adult they would feel comfortable going to when they had a problem.

52. One white female, one white male, two black males, one Latinx female.

53. Ann Owens, Sean F. Reardon, and Christopher Jencks, "Income Segregation Between Schools and School Districts," *American Education Research Journal* 53, no. 4 (2016): 1159–97, doi:10.3102/00283126652722.

54. Erin Cech, "What Fosters Concern for Inequality Among American adolescents?," *Social Science Research* 61 (2017): 160–80.

55. Cech.

56. Bolling, "CodeRVA Executive Director's Report, March 2018."

57. The more flexible summer term provided additional time for students to catch up or get ahead in their coursework. Faculty also led regular community service expeditions to nearby nonprofits like the SPCA, college and career boosting opportunities that were built into school.

58. See, e.g., "Systemic Improvement Map" (Cambridge, MA: Harvard's Reimagining Integration: Diverse and Equitable Schools), https://rides.gse.harvard.edu/systemic-improvement-map. As further evidence of an emphasis on continual improvement around equity, CodeRVA also requested an equity audit, using MSAP funds, from its regional Equity Assistance Center, slated for the spring of 2019.

59. Bolling says that teachers can see him if they're having a problem with a student. Discipline issues are typically not severe at CodeRVA. There's been one fight since it opened almost two years ago.

60. Bolling, "CodeRVA Executive Director's Report, March 2018." Students have responded well to the positive motivation, sometimes joking about whether it is referral-worthy to pick up a fallen piece of paper (with the rationale that it aids the school community).

61. Dual-enrollment courses allow high school students to enroll in college-level courses and receive both high school and college credits.

62. CodeRVA provided remediation and enrichment for the test during the summer session.

63. See, e.g., "A School Where All Students Are Challenged and Supported" (Boulder: National Education Policy Center, 2019).

64. Carol Corbett Burris and Delia T. Garrity, *Detracking for Excellence and Equity* (Alexandria, VA: Association for Supervision and Curriculum Development, 2008).

65. "Bolling, "CodeRVA Executive Director's Report, March 2018."

66. Almost every CodeRVA faculty member has dual endorsements; it's a critical component of supporting diverse students in programs with a small staff.

Chapter 6

1. Emma Brown, "Trump's Education Department Nixes Obama-era Grant Program for School Diversity," *Washington Post*, March 26, 2017, https://www .washingtonpost.com/news/education/wp/2017/03/29/trumps-education -department-nixes-obama-era-grant-program-for-school-diversity/?utm_term =.4fedb6ade882.

2. Rachel Cohen, "A Lawsuit Threatens a Groundbreaking School Desegregation Case," *The Nation*, February 11, 2019, https://www.thenation.com/article /connecticut-segregation-schools-sheff/; Associated Press, "Affirmative Action Lawsuit Against Harvard in Judge's Hands," *NBC News*, February 14, 2019, https://www.nbcnews.com/news/asian-america/affirmative-action-lawsuit -against-harvard-judge-s-hands-n971776.

3. Blue Virginia, "Virginia Secretary of Education Atif Qarni on Institutional Racism, the Need for Increased Diversity in Leadership, *Blue Virginia*, February 3, 2019, https://bluevirginia.us/2019/02/virginia-secretary-of-education-atif -qarni-on-institutional-racism-the-need-for-increased-diversity-in-leadership\.

4. James Lane, "Resources to Support Student and Community Dialogues on Racism" (Superintendent's Memo #050-19, Virginia Department of Education, February 2019), http://www.doe.virginia.gov/administrators/superintendents _memos/2019/050-19.docx.

5. For a summary, see Roslyn Arlin Mickelson and Mokubung Nkomo, "Integrated Schooling, Life Course Outcomes, and Social Cohesion in Multiethnic Democratic Societies," *Review of Research in Education* 36, no. 1 (2012): 197–238, doi:10.3102/0091732X11422667; Amy Stuart Wells, Lauren Fox, and Diana Cordova-Cobo, *How Racially Diverse Schools and Classrooms Can Benefit All Students, K–12* (Washington, DC: The Century Foundation, 2016), https://tcf. org/content/report/how-racially-diverse-schools-and-classrooms -can-benefit-all-students/.

6. Parents Involved in Community Schools v. Seattle School District, No. 1, 551 US 701 (2007).

7. A useful example comes in the form of the National Education Policy Center's "Schools of Opportunity" recognition program. See http://schools ofopportunity.org/.

8. The Equity Assistance Centers, funded through the US Department of Education, are a good starting point; Equity Assistance Centers, "Contacts," US Department of Education, https://www2.ed.gov/programs/equitycenters /contacts.html. Erica Frankenberg and Elizabeth Debray, *Integrating Schools in a Changing Society* (Chapel Hill: University of North Carolina Press, 2011).

9. Christopher Tienken and Yong Zhao, "How Common Standards and Standardized Testing Widen the Opportunity Gap," in *Closing the Opportunity Gap: What American Must Do to Give Every Child a Chance*, eds. Prudence L. Carter and Kevin G. Welner (New York: Oxford University Press, 2013); Tamara Wilder, Rebecca Jacobsen, and Richard Rothstein, *Grading Education: Getting Accountability Right* (New York: Teachers College Press/Economic Policy Institute, 2008).

10. Ellen Goldring and Claire Smrekar, "Magnet Schools and the Pursuit of Racial Balance," *Education and Urban Society* 33, no. 1 (2000): 17–35, doi:10.1177 /0013124500331003.

11. "Phi Delta Kappan Poll," 2017, http://pdkpoll.org/.

12. Linda Tropp and Suchi Saxena, *Re-Weaving the Social Fabric of Integrated Schools: How Intergroup Contact Prepares Youth to Thrive in a Multiracial Society* (Washington, DC: The National Coalition on School Diversity, 2018).

13. Parents Involved in Community Schools v. Seattle School District.

14. Halley Potter, *What Other Districts Can Learn from New York City's School Diversity Plan, K–12* (Washington, DC: The Century Foundation, 2017), https://tcf.org /content/commentary/districts-can-learn-new-york-citys-school-diversity-plan/.

15. Erica Frankenberg, "Assessing Segregation Under a New Generation of Controlled Choice Policies," *American Educational Research Journal* 54, no. 1 (2017): 219S–250S, doi:10.3102/0002831216634462.

16. Halley Potter, *Recruiting and Enrolling a Diverse Student Body in Public Choice Schools, K–12* (Washington, DC: The Century Foundation, 2019), https://tcf .org/content/report/recruiting-enrolling-diverse-student-body-public-choice -schools/?agreed=1.

17. Erica Frankenberg, "The Promise of Choice: Berkeley's Innovative Integration Plan," in *Educational Delusions*, eds. Gary Orfield and Erica Frankenberg (Berkeley: University of California Press, 2013), 69–88.

18. Districts and schools employ various strategies to disseminate information about choice. These include designating personnel to oversee choice and designating space to centralize advising and information for families. In the Civil Rights Project's extensive research into federally funded magnet schools, we found that outreach coordinators often functioned as the former and family information centers as the latter. Jennifer Ayscue et al., "Choices Worth Making: Creating, Sustaining and Expanding Diverse Magnet Schools (Los Angeles: UCLA Civil Rights Project, 2016), https://www.civilrightsproject.ucla .edu/research/k-12-education/integration-and-diversity/choices-worth-making -creating-sustaining-and-expanding-diverse-magnet-schools.

19. Jack Dougherty et al., "School Information, Parental Decisions, and the Digital Divide: The SmartChoices Project in Hartford, Connecticut," in *Educational Delusions*, eds. Gary Orfield and Erica Frankenberg (Berkeley: University of California Press, 2013), 219–37.

20. Jack Schneider, *Beyond Test Scores: A Better Way to Measure School Quality* (Cambridge, MA: Harvard University Press, 2017).

21. Jennifer Holme, "Buying Homes, Buying Schools: School Choice and the Social Construction of School Quality," *Harvard Educational Review* 72, no. 2 (July 2002), https://doi.org/10.17763/haer.72.2.u6272x676823788r; Annette Lareau and Kimberly Goyette, eds., *Choosing Homes, Choosing Schools* (New York: Russell Sage Foundation, 2014).

22. Holme, "Buying Homes, Buying Schools."

23. "Stay RVA," https://stayrva.org/. A national network called Integrated Schools employs a similar tactic, asking families to commit to a school tour challenge of at least two schools. "Integrated Schools," https://integratedschools.org/.

24. In a different effort to build knowledge about school choices, education officials in Pasadena, California, realized that realtors were participating in a narrative that steered affluent families away from the local public system. They decided to bring realtors into district schools for tours and meetings with the principals, nurturing a reality-based understanding of the different options within the system and shifting the nature of information exchange accordingly. Jennifer Miyake-Trapp, "Changing the Perception of Pasadena United School District Through an Innovative Realtor Outreach Program" (Washington, DC: National Coalition on School Diversity, 2018), https://school-diversity.org/pdf/PasadenaRealtorFieldReport.pdf.

25. Tropp and Saxena, "Re-Weaving the Social Fabric of Integrated Schools."

26. Emily Douglas, "8 Promising Practices for Recruiting Diverse Educator Talent," *Education Week*, September 23, 2014, https://blogs.edweek.org/top schooljobs/k-12_talent_manager/2014/09/8_practices_recruiting_diverse _talent.html; Desiree Carver-Thomas, *Diversifying the Teaching Profession: How to Recruit and Retain Teachers of Color* (Washington, DC: The Learning Policy Institute 2018).

27. A 2016 report from The Century Foundation, for example, identified 100 districts experimenting with socioeconomic school integration; 40 of those districts reported shifting attendance boundaries as their primary strategy and 17 reported student transfer policies. Kimberly Quick, *How to Achieve Socioeconomic Integration in Schools* (Washington, DC: The Century Foundation, 2016), https://tcf.org/content/facts/achieve-socioeconomic-integration-schools/. A year later, Penn State's Center for Education and Civil Rights found 60 school systems engaging in voluntary school integration by considering race and/or SES, 20 of which relied on adjustments to attendance zone boundaries and 18 of which relied on transfers. Erica Frankenberg, Jeremy Anderson, and Kendra Taylor, *Voluntary Integration in U.S. School District, 2000–2015* (State College: Penn

State Center for Education and Civil Rights, 2017), https://cecr.ed.psu.edu /sites/default/files/Voluntary_Integration_Research_Brief_0.pdf. Earlier research out of Stanford, from 2011, uncovered 40 districts utilizing SES integration strategies; 28% used adjustments to attendance zones to further SES integration and 68% had some sort of transfer priority. Sean F. Reardon and Lori Rhodes, "The Effects of Socioeconomic School Integration Policies on Racial School Desegregation," in *Integrating Schools in a Changing Society*, eds. Erica Frankenberg and Elizabeth DeBray (Chapel Hill: University of North Carolina Press, 2011), 187–207.

28. Jeremey Anderson and Erica Frankenberg, "Voluntary Integration in Uncertain Times," *Phi Delta Kappan* 100, no. 5 (2019): 14–18; Quick, *How to Achieve Socioeconomic Integration*; Frankenberg et al., *Voluntary Integration in U.S. School Districts*; Reardon and Rhodes, "The Effects of Socioeconomic School Integration."

29. Student transfer policies that promote voluntary integration aren't considered as comprehensive as other methods like controlled choice or rezoning because they don't necessarily impact all, or even many, students. See, e.g., Anderson and Frankenberg, "Voluntary Integration in Uncertain Times."

30. New county planning document calls for more siting of affordable housing in low-income communities, a policy virtually guaranteed to exacerbate the east-west divide. For further exploration of these issues, see Erica Frankenberg and Gary Orfield, *The Resegregation of Suburban Schools: A Hidden American Crisis* (Cambridge, MA: Harvard Education Press, 2011).

31. Housing policy can become school policy if you design and build mixed-income neighborhoods near high-opportunity schools. In Montgomery County, Maryland, for instance, an early 1970s-era policy required developers to set aside 15% of stock for affordable housing in all new communities. As a result, a significant number of the county's low-income families have been able to access high-opportunity schools over the ensuing decades. See Heather Schwartz, "Housing Policy Is School Policy: Economically Integrative Housing Promotes Academic Success in Montgomery County, Maryland" (New York: The Century Foundation, 2010). At the federal level, during President Obama's second term, the Department of Housing and Urban Development (HUD) and the Department of Education sought to educate and incentivize local communities to target high-opportunity schools for families participating in affordable housing programs. See US Department of Housing and Urban Development, "Breaking Down Barriers: Housing, Neighborhoods, and Schools of Opportunity," *Insights into Housing and Community Development Policy* (2016). Around the same time period, a joint letter between ED, HUD, and the Department of Transportation directed state and local agencies to coordinate oversight and guidance around school construction and affordable housing, among other possibilities. This sort of interagency work, as common sense as it may seem, given the entangled relationship between school and housing segregation, has been sorely lacking.

32. Gary Orfield, *Must We Bus? Segregation and National Policy* (Washington, DC: Brookings Institution, 1978); transportation's centrality to school desegregation efforts made it a prime political target. As historian Matt Delmont's book, *Why Busing Failed*, reminds us, the politics of school desegregation quickly shifted from protecting the constitutional rights of black and brown students to protecting white families' rights to neighborhood schools. Matthew F. Delmont, *Why Busing Failed: Race, Media, and the National Resistance to School Desegregation* (Oakland: University of California Press, 2016).

33. Sarah A. Cordes and Amy Ellen Schwartz, "Does Public Transportation Close the School Quality Gap?" (Washington, DC: The Urban Institute, 2018), https://www.urban.org/research/publication/does-pupil-transportation-close-school-quality-gap.

34. Peter Irons, *Jim Crow's Children: the Broken Promise of the Brown Decision* (New York: The Penguin Group, 2002).

35. Robert L. Green and Thomas F. Pettigrew, "Urban Desegregation and White Flight: A Response to Coleman," *Phi Delta Kappan* 57, no. 6 (February 1976); US Department of Housing and Urban Development, "Breaking Down Barriers."

36. Amy Stuart Wells et al., *Boundary Crossing for Diversity, Equity and Achievement: Inter-district School Desegregation and Educational Opportunity* (Cambridge, MA: Charles Hamilton Houston Institute for Race and Justice, 2009).

37. Kara S. Finnigan, Jennifer Jellison Holme, and Myron Orfield, "Regional Educational Policy Analysis: Rochester, Omaha, and Minneapolis' Inter-District Arrangements," *Educational Policy* 29, no. 5 (2015), doi: https://doi.org/10.1177/0895904813518102.

38. Kara S. Finnigan and Jennifer Holme, "Regional Educational Equity Policies: Learning from Inter-district Integration Programs," The National Coalition on School Diversity 9 (2015), http://school-diversity.org/pdf/DiversityResearchBriefNo9.pdf.

39. Susan Eaton, *The Other Boston Busing Story: What's Won and Lost Across the Boundary Line* (New Haven, CT: Yale University Press, 2001); Carole Learned-Miller, *How to Support the Social-Emotional Well-Being of Students of Color: Research and Best Practices from Interdistrict Integration Programs*, (Washington, DC: The National Coalition on School Diversity, 2017).

40. Jennifer Holme and Kara Finnigan, *Striving in Common* (Cambridge, MA: Harvard Education Press, 2018).

41. Gary Orfield, "Metropolitan School Desegregation: Impacts on a Metropolitan Society," *Minnesota Law Review* 80 (1995); Myron Orfield, "Milliken and Meredith and Metropolitan Segregation," *UCLA Law Review* 62 (2015); Genevieve Siegel-Hawley, *When the Fences Come Down: Twenty-First Century Lessons from Metropolitan School Desegregation* (Chapel Hill: University of North Carolina Press, 2016).

42. Justin Mattingly, "1 in 4 Chesterfield Elementary Schools Would Be Affected By latest Round of Rezoning," *Richmond Times Dispatch*, October 10, 2018,

https://www.richmond.com/news/local/education/chesterfield/in-chesterfield
-elementary-schools-would-be-affected-by-latest-round/article_1df8ce36-35c8
-55e6-a0b4-e7236a79b598.html.

43. Keith Leithwood, Lawrence Leonard, and Lyn Sharratt, "Conditions Fostering Organizational Learning in Schools," *Educational Administration Quarterly* 34, no. 2 (April 1998): 243–76.

44. Gordon Allport, *The Nature of Prejudice* (Reading, MA: Addison-Wesley Publishing Company, 1954); Thomas Pettigrew and Linda Tropp, "A Meta-Analytic Test of Intergroup Contact Theory," *Journey of Personality and Social Psychology* 90, no. 5 (2006): 751–83, doi:10.1037/0022-3514.90.5.751.

45. Charles Willie and Susan L. Greenblatt, "School Desegregation: Racial Politics and Community Conflict Processes," in *Community Politics and Educational Change: Ten School Systems Under Court Order*, eds. Charles Willie and Susan Greenblatt (New York: Longman, 1981).

46. Scott Page, *The Diversity Bonus: How Great Teams Pay Off in the Knowledge Economy* (Princeton, NJ: Princeton University Press, 2017).

47. Many school systems allow principals to have at least partial control over the hiring process. "Bumping HR: Giving Principals More Say Over Staffing" (Washington, DC: National Counsel on Teacher Quality, 2017), https://www.nctq.org/dmsView/Bumping_HR_Giving_Principals_More_Say_Over_Staffing_NCTQ_Report.

48. Jason A. Grissom and Christopher Redding, "Discretion and Disproportionality: Explaining the Underrepresentation of High-Achieving Students of Color in Gifted Programs," *AERA Open* 2, no. 1 (2016): doi:10/1177/2332858415622175.

49. Anthony Bryck et al., *Organizing Schools for Improvement: Lessons from Chicago* (Chicago: University of Chicago Press, 2010); Barnett Berry, "Good Schools and Teachers for All Students: Dispelling Myths, Facing Evidence, and Pursuing the Right Strategies," in *Closing the Opportunity Gap*, eds. Prudence L. Carter and Kevin G. Welner (New York: Oxford University Press, 2013).

50. Cooperative grouping reduces competition, allowing student-generated knowledge to emerge and promoting teamwork toward a common goal. The Jigsaw classroom is one of the first and most notable examples of these cooperative techniques. It works like this. The instructor breaks up content into discrete pieces—say, paragraphs from a reading selection—and asks each child to be responsible for one. The work occurs first in groups where all of the children have been given the same content, and together they learn and make meaning of it. Then they move into heterogeneous groups, where the students take turns teaching one another the various components of the material they've mastered. The implicit message of this exercise is that all students contain knowledge related to an important piece of the puzzle—hence, the name and thereby the equal status and cooperation toward a shared goal of learning. Elliot Aronson, *The Jigsaw Classroom* (Beverly Hills: Sage Publications, 1978). We've long known that informal contact opportunities are critical. When the

Supreme Court finally ordered the "root and branch" elimination of school segregation, extracurricular activities were one of the six dimensions that communities had to consider (in the company of student and faculty composition) in developing desegregation plans (see Green v. New Kent). They remain a critical factor for courts deliberating over district requests for a judicial determination that they've eliminated dual systems of education. In our contemporary context, extracurriculars have also become a source and indication of widening inequality. See Robert Putnam, *Our Kids: The American Dream in Crisis* (New York: Simon and Schuster, 2015). A nationally representative sample of nearly 2,000 families additionally found wide disparities in child extracurricular participation among families earning less than $30,000/year and families earning more than $75,000. These disparities emerged early, with more affluent families far more likely than less affluent ones to begin extracurriculars before the age of five. Pew Research Center, *Parenting in America* (Washington, DC: Author, December 17, 2015), https://www.pewresearch.org/wp-content/uploads /sites/3/2015/12/2015-12-17_parenting-in-america_FINAL.pdf.

51. Samuel Gaertner and John Dovidio, "The Aversive Form of Racism," in *Prejudice, Discrimination, and Racism*, eds. Samuel Gaertner and John Dovidio (San Diego: Academic Press, 1986), 61–89.

52. Gloria Ladson-Billings, "Culturally Relevant Pedagogy 2.0: a.k.a the Remix," *Harvard Educational Review* 84, no. 1 (2014): 74–84.

53. Gloria Ladson-Billings, "Toward a Theory of Culturally Relevant Pedagogy," *American Education Research Journal* 32, no. 3 (1995): 465–91.

54. For an excellent summary of related research, see Hillary Parkhouse, Jesse Senechal, and Julie Gorlewski, *Contexts of Cultural Diversity Professional Development in Schools* (Richmond, VA: Metropolitan Educational Research Consortium, 2018), Table 1. See also T. Dee and E. Penner, "The Causal Effects of Cultural Relevance: Evidence from an Ethnic Studies Curriculum, *American Educational Research Journal* 54, no. 1, 127–66.

55. Robert Lount Jr. and Katherine W. Phillips, "Working Harder with the Out-group: The Impact of Social Category Diversity on Motivation Gains," *Organizational Behavior and Human Decision Processes* 103, no. 2 (2007): 214–24; Katherine W. Phillips and Denise Lewin Loyd, "When Surface and Deep-level Diversity Collide: The Effects on Dissenting Group Members, *Organizational Behavior and Human Decision Processes* 99, no. 2 (2006): 143–60; Katherine W. Phillips, Katie Liljenquist, and Margaret A. Neale, "Is the Pain Worth the Gain? The Advantages and Liabilities of Agreeing with Socially Distinct Newcomers," *Personality and Social Psychology Bulletin* 35, no. 3 (2009): 336–50.

56. Jeanne L. Reid, "Racial/Ethnic Diversity and Language Development in the Preschool Classroom," in *School Integration Matters*, eds. Megan Hopkins, Liliana M. Garces, and Erica Frankenberg (New York: Teachers College Press, 2016), 39–55.

57. Sonya Douglass Horsford, *Learning in a Burning House: Educational Inequality, Ideology, and (Dis)Integration* (New York: Teachers College Press, 2011).

58. In 1975, a case study of a carefully planned, desegregating magnet school found evidence of a norm forbidding mention of race among faculty. Janet Schofield, *Black and White in School: Trust, Tension, or Tolerance* (New York: Teachers College Press, 1989). The faculty taboo influenced and constrained student dialogue. It arose from an anxious sense that teachers wouldn't be able to manage discussions of race effectively, which itself arose from a lack of training. Teachers further worried that an explicit acknowledgment of race might suggest prejudice or racism. Better, they reasoned, to operate as though Dr. King's dream of a color-blind society was reality. Thirty years later, a nationally representative sample of over 1,000 US teachers found similar evidence of faculty color blindness. About 96% of teachers from all racial and ethnic backgrounds reported treating students the same. Erica Frankenberg with Genevieve Siegel-Hawley, *Are Teachers Prepared for America's Diverse Schools?* (Los Angeles: UCLA Civil Rights Project, 2008), https://civil rightsproject.ucla.edu /research/k-12-education/integration-and-diversity/are-teachers-prepared-for -racially-changing-schools.

59. Mica Pollock, ed., *Everyday AntiRacism: Getting Real About Race in School* (New York: The New Press, 2008).

60. Glenn E. Singleton and Cyndie Hays, "Beginning Courageous Conversations about Race," in *Everyday AntiRacism*.

61. Roslyn Arlin Mickelson, "Subverting Swann: First- and Second-Generation Segregation in the Charlotte-Mecklenburg Schools," *American Educational Research Journal* 38, no. 2 (2001): 215–52; Jeannie Oakes, *Keeping Track: How Schools Structure Inequality* (New Haven, CT: Yale University Press, 2005).

62. Claude M. Steele and Joshua Aronson, "Stereotype Threat and the Intellectual Test Performance of African-Americans," *Journal of Personality and Social Psychology* 69, no. 5 (1995): 797–811; Amanda Lewis and John Diamond, *Despite the Best Intentions* (New York: Oxford University Press); Grissom and Redding, "Discretion and Disproportionality."

63. Willis D. Hawley, "Designing Schools That Use Student Diversity to Enhance Learning of All Students," in *Lessons in Integration: Realizing the Promise of Racial Diversity in American Schools*, eds. Erica Frankenberg and Gary Orfield (Charlottesville: University of Virginia Press, 2007), 44.

64. *Why, How, and What of the RIDES Equity Improvement Cycle* (Cambridge, MA: Harvard's Reimagining Integration: Diverse and Equitable Schools, 2018). https://docs.google.com/document/d/1a_gQya9rimShcApt569JHI0WN3CV Z5vLtLHgCXJQ5Vg/edit.

65. In New York, the advanced diplomas are known as the Regents exam. A strong evidence base informs the recommendation of eliminating the lowest-level track. Jeannie Oakes and Amy Stuart Wells, "Detracking for High Student

Achievement," *Educational Leadership* 55, no. 6 (1998): 38–41; Susan Yonezawa, Amy Stewart Wells, and Irene Serna, "Choosing Tracks: 'Freedom of Choice' in Detracking Schools," *American Educational Research Journal* 39, no. 1 (2002): 37–67, doi:10.3102/00028312039001037.

66. Carol Corbett Burris and Kevin G. Welner, "Classroom Integration and Accelerated Learning Through Detracking," in *Lessons in Integration*, 207–27.

67. These included support classes with an average of 8 students.

68. Burris and Welner, "Classroom Integration."

69. Burris and Welner.

70. Jo Boaler, "'Opening Our Ideas': How a Detracked Mathematics Approach Promoted Respect, Responsibility, and High Achievement," *Theory into Practice* 45, no. 1 (2006).

71. Russell J. Skiba et al., "Parsing Disciplinary Disproportionality: Contributions of Infraction, Student, and School Characteristics to Out-of-School Suspension and Expulsion," *American Educational Research Journal* 51, no. 4 (2014): 640–70, doi:10.3102/0002831214541670.

72. For a summary, see Adai Tefera, Genevieve Siegel-Hawley, and Rachel Levy, *Why Do Racial Disparities in School Discipline Exist? The Role of Policies, Processes, People, and Places* (Richmond, VA: Metropolitan Educational Research Consortium, 2017).

73. Rebecca S. Bigler, John M. Rohrbach, and Kiara L. Sanchez, "Children's Intergroup Relations and Attitudes," *Advances in Child Development and Behavior* 51 (2016): 121–69, doi:10.1016/bs.acdb.2016.05.005. An intentionally diverse charter school in Brooklyn designs routine, carefully structured evening activities during which families share food with one another, work on art identity projects, or play basketball together. Brooklyn Prospect Charter School (presentation at the National Coalition on School Diversity's *A Struggle We Must Win: Advancing School Integration through Activism, Youth Voice and Policy Reform*, New York, October 18–19, 2018).

Research Notes

1. D. Waldorf and P. Biernacki, "Snowball Sampling: Problems and Techniques of Chain Referral Sampling," *Sociological Methods and Research* 10, no. 2 (1981), 141–63.

2. Important research regulations make it very difficult to interview younger children.

3. H. Bernard, *Research Methods in Cultural Anthropology* (Newbury Park, CA: Sage Publications, 1988).

4. Jennifer Ayscue et al., "Choices Worth Making: Creating, Sustaining and Expanding Diverse Magnet Schools" (Los Angeles: UCLA Civil Rights Project, 2017), https://www.google.com/search?q=choices+worth+making&rlz=1C1GC EU_enUS822US822&oq=choices+worth+making&aqs=chrome..69i57j69i60.2 013j1j4&sourceid=chrome&ie=UTF-8; Jennifer Ayscue and Genevieve Siegel-

Hawley, "Magnets and School Turnarounds: Revisiting Policies for Promoting Equitable, Diverse Schools," *Educational Policy Analysis Archives* (forthcoming).

5. Maia Bloomfield Cucchiara, *Marketing Schools, Marketing Cities* (Chicago: University of Chicago Press, 2013); Jennifer Burns Stillman, *Gentrification and Schools* (New York: Palgrave McMillan, 2012); Linn Posey-Maddox, *When Middle Class Parents Choose Urban Schools* (Chicago: University of Chicago Press, 2014).

6. M. Miles, A. Michael Huberman, and Johnny Saldana, *Qualitative Data Analysis*, 3rd ed. (Thousand Oaks: Sage Publishing, 2013). Copies of the interview protocols are available upon request from the author.

7. Miles, Huberman, and Saldana.

8. John Creswell, *Qualitative Inquiry and Research Design*, 2nd ed. (Thousand Oaks: Sage Publications, 2007).

About the Author

Genevieve Siegel-Hawley, PhD, is an associate professor in the School of Education at Virginia Commonwealth University. She examines the scope and dynamics of school segregation and resegregation in US metropolitan areas, along with policies for promoting more integrated schools and communities. Siegel-Hawley has published numerous articles dealing with these topics in journals like *Teachers College Record*, the *Harvard Educational Review*, *Educational Researcher*, and the *Urban Review*. She is also the author of *When the Fences Come Down: 21st Century Lessons from Metropolitan School Desegregation* (UNC Press, 2016), an analysis of school and housing segregation in four southern metropolitan areas. Siegel-Hawley received her doctorate in urban schooling from UCLA and her master's in educational policy and management from Harvard. She is a Richmond native and a proud graduate of and former teacher in Richmond Public Schools.

Index